PRAISE FOR **SLEEPERS**

"In his controversial memoir *Sleepers,* Carcaterra remembers harrowing months in the Wilkinson Home for Boys and the elaborate vengeance he and his friends exacted against the guards. He tells it all in spare, stylish prose . . . [with] relentless momentum and sheer drama. . . . *Sleepers* is a thriller, to be sure, but it is equally a wistful hymn to another age."
—*The Washington Post Book World*

"A terrifying account of brutality and retribution, searing in its emotional truth, peopled with murderers, sadists, and thugs, but biblical in its passion and scope." —*People*

"Compelling." —*USA Today*

"A riveting story delicious with revenge . . . Carcaterra mixes horror, laughter, and pathos to show that justice, like love, is in the eye of the beholder." —*Publishers Weekly* (starred review)

"A gut-wrenching piece of work . . . Carcaterra's graphic narrative grips like gunfire in a dark alley."
—*The Atlanta Journal-Constitution*

"A powerful book, hard to forget . . . Carcaterra is an excellent writer, changing pace here and there but never letting the reader go. . . . Sensitive, humorous, and harrowing, featuring dialogue with perfect pitch." —*The Denver Post*

BY LORENZO CARCATERRA

A SAFE PLACE:
A TRUE STORY OF A FATHER,
A SON, A MURDER

SLEEPERS

APACHES

GANGSTER

STREET BOYS

PARADISE CITY

CHASERS

MIDNIGHT ANGELS

THE WOLF

TIN BADGES

SHORT STORY

THE VULTURE'S GAME

SLEEPERS

SLEEPERS

LORENZO CARCATERRA

BALLANTINE BOOKS

NEW YORK

2019 Ballantine Books Trade Paperback Edition

Published in the United States by Ballantine Books,
an imprint of Random House,
a division of Penguin Random House LLC, New York.

BALLANTINE and the HOUSE colophon are
registered trademarks of Penguin Random House LLC.

Originally published in hardcover in the United States
by Ballantine Books, an imprint of Random House,
a division of Penguin Random House LLC, in 1995.

This book contains an excerpt from the forthcoming book
Tin Badges by Lorenzo Carcaterra. This excerpt has been set for
this edition only and may not reflect the final content
of the forthcoming edition.

ISBN 978-0-593-15815-9
Ebook ISBN 978-0-307-75665-7

Printed in the United States of America on acid-free paper

randomhousebooks.com

2 4 6 8 9 7 5 3 1

Book design by Barbara M. Bachman

For sleepers everywhere

Sleeper (colloq.): 1. Out-of-town hit man who spends the night after a local contract is completed. 2. A juvenile sentenced to serve any period longer than nine months in a state-managed facility.

"Let's go say a prayer for a boy
who couldn't run as fast as I could."

—PAT O'BRIEN to the DEAD END KIDS in
Angels with Dirty Faces

Prologue

I SAT ACROSS THE TABLE FROM THE MAN WHO HAD BAT-
tered and tortured and brutalized me nearly thirty years ago. I
had imagined him to be in his sixties—he had seemed so old
to me back then—but, in fact, he was in his late forties, less
than a decade older than me. His thinning hair was combed
straight back, and his right hand, trembling and ash white,
held a filter tip cigarette. His left clutched a glass of ice water.
He looked at me from behind a pair of black-rimmed glasses,
his brown eyes moist, his nose running, the skin at its base red
and flaky.

"I don't know what you want me to say," he said in a voice
devoid of the power it once held. "I don't know where to start."

In my memory he was tall and muscular, arrogant and
quick-tempered, eager to lash out at those under his command
at the juvenile home where I spent nine months when I was
thirteen years old. In reality, sitting now before me, he was frail
and timid, thin beads of cold sweat forming at the top of his
forehead.

"I need to keep my job," he said, his voice a whining plea. "I
can't lose this one. If any of my bosses find out, if *anybody* finds
out, I'm finished."

I wanted to stand up and grab him, reach past the coffee
and the smoke and beat him until he bled. Instead, I sat there

and remembered all that I had tried so hard, over so many years, to forget. Painful screams piercing silent nights. A leather belt against soft skin. Foul breath on the back of a neck. Loud laughter mixed with muffled tears.

I had waited so long for this meeting, spent so much time and money searching for the man who held the answers to so many of my questions. But now that he was here, I had nothing to say, nothing to ask. I half listened as he talked about two failed marriages and a bankrupt business, about how the evil he committed haunts him to this very day. The words seemed cowardly and empty and I felt no urge to address them.

He and the group he was a part of had stained the future of four boys, damaged them beyond repair. Once, the sound of this man's very walk caused all our movement to stop. His laugh, low and eerie, had signaled an onslaught of torment. Now, sitting across from him, watching his mouth move and his hands flutter, I wished I had not been as afraid of him back then, that I'd somehow had the nerve and the courage to fight back. So many lives might have turned out differently if I had.

"I didn't mean all those things," he whispered, leaning closer toward me. "None of us did."

"I don't need you to be sorry," I said. "It doesn't do me any good."

"I'm beggin' you," he said, his voice breaking. "Try to forgive me. Please. Try."

"Learn to live with it," I told him, getting up from the table.

"I can't," he said. "Not anymore."

"Then die with it," I said, looking at him hard. "Just like the rest of us."

The pained look of surrender in his eyes made my throat tighter, easing the darkness of decades.

If only my friends had been there to see it.

* * *

THIS IS A TRUE STORY ABOUT FRIENDSHIPS THAT RUN deeper than blood. In its telling, I have changed many of the names and altered most of the dates, locations, and identifying characteristics of people and institutions to protect the identities of those involved. For example, I have changed the location of the murder trial, which did not take place in Manhattan. I've also changed where people live and work—and made many of them a lot better looking than they really are. It is a story that has taken two years to write and parts of two decades to research, forcing awake in all the principals memories we would have preferred to forget. I have been helped in the re-creation of the events of this story by many friends and a few enemies, all of whom requested nothing more in return than anonymity. So while their deeds have been accurately documented, their names—heroes and villains—will remain unknown.

However hidden their identities, this is still my story and that of the only three friends in my life who have truly mattered.

Two of them were killers who never made it past the age of thirty-five. The other is a nonpracticing attorney living within the pain of his past, too afraid to let it go, finding reassurance instead in confronting its horror.

I am the only one who can speak for them, and for the children we were.

BOOK ONE

"This much I do know—
there's no such thing
as a bad boy."

—SPENCER TRACY AS
FATHER EDDIE FLANAGAN IN
Boys Town

1

SUMMER 1963

LABOR DAY WEEKEND ALWAYS SIGNALED THE ANNUAL go-cart race across the streets of Hell's Kitchen, the mid-Manhattan neighborhood where I was born in 1954 and lived until 1969.

Preparations for the race began during the last two weeks of August, when my three best friends and I would hide away inside our basement clubhouse, in a far corner of a run-down 49th Street tenement, constructing, painting, and naming our racer, which we put together from lifted lumber and stolen parts. A dozen carts and their teams were scheduled to assemble early on Labor Day morning at the corner of 50th Street and Tenth Avenue, each looking to collect the $15 first-prize money that would be presented to the winner by a local loan shark.

In keeping with Hell's Kitchen traditions, the race was run without rules.

It never lasted more than twenty minutes and covered four side streets and two avenues, coming to a finish on the 12th Avenue end of the West Side Highway. Each go-cart had a four-man team attached, one inside and three out. The three pushed for as long and as hard as they could, fighting off the hand swipes and blade swings of the opponents who came close. The pushing stopped at the top of the 50th Street hill, leaving the rest of the race to the driver. Winners and losers crossed the finish clothesline scraped and bloody, go-carts often in pieces, driver's hands burned by ropes. Few of us wore gloves or helmets, and there was never money for knee or elbow pads. We kept full plastic water bottles tied to the sides of our carts, the fastest way to cool off hot feet and burning wheels.

The runt of the litter among my team, I always drove.

* * *

JOHN REILLY AND TOMMY MARCANO WERE SPREADING BLACK paint onto thick slabs of dirty wood with color-by-number brushes.

John was eleven years old, a dark-haired, dark-eyed charmer with an Irishman's knack for the verbal hit-and-run. His clear baby face was marred by a six-inch scar above his right eye and a smaller, half-moon scar below the chin line, both the results of playground falls and homemade stitches. John always seemed to be on the verge of a smile and was the first among my friends to bring in the latest joke off the street. He was a poor student but an avid reader, a mediocre athlete with a penchant for remembering the batting and fielding statistics of even the most obscure ballplayers. He loved Marx Brothers and Abbott and Costello movies and went to any western that played the neighborhood circuit. If the mood hit him the right way, John would prowl the streets of Hell's Kitchen talking and walking as if he were Ralph Kramden from *The Honeymooners*, proclaiming "Hiya, pal," to all the neighborhood vendors. Sometimes, in return for his performance, we would each be given free pieces of fruit. He was born with a small hole in his heart that required regular doses of a medication his mother often could not afford to buy. The illness, coupled with a frail frame, left him with a palpable air of vulnerability.

Tommy Marcano, also eleven, was John's physical opposite. He had his Irish mother's carrot-colored hair and his father's ruddy, southern Italian complexion. Short and flabby around the waist and thighs, Tommy loved sports, action movies, Marvel comics, and adventure novels. Above all else, Tommy loved to eat—meatball heroes, buttered rolls, hard cherry candy barrels. He collected and traded baseball cards, storing each year's set in team order inside a half-dozen Kinney shoeboxes sealed with rubber bands. He had a natural aptitude for math and built model ships and planes out of raw wood with skill and patience. He had a sensitive nature and a feel for the underdog, always cheering on teams and athletes that were destined to lose. He was quick to laugh and needed prodding to loosen the grip on his temper. A botched surgical procedure when he was an infant forced him occasionally to wear a pad and brace around his right leg. On those days Tommy chose to wear a black eye patch and tie a red handkerchief around his head.

Michael Sullivan, at twelve the oldest of my friends, was quietly hammering nails into a sawed-down Dr. Brown's soda crate.

The best student among us, Michael was a smooth blend of book smarts and street savvy. His Black Irish eyes bore holes through their targets, but his manner was softened by a wide, expansive smile. He kept his thick, dark hair short on the sides and long on top. He was never without a piece of gum in his mouth and read all the tabloids of the day, the only one among us to move beyond the sports pages to the front page. He was also never without a book, usually a rumpled paperback shoved inside the rear pocket of his jeans. Where we still favored the tales of Alexandre Dumas, Jack London, and Robert Louis Stevenson, Michael had graduated to the darker domain of Edgar Allan Poe and the chivalry and romance of Sir Walter

Scott. He initiated most of our pranks and had a cutting sense of humor that was doused with a wise man's instinct for fair play. He was our unofficial leader, a position he valued but never flaunted and one that required him to care for and maintain our collection of *Classics Illustrated* comics.

I was busily applying biker's grease onto two stroller wheels taken off a baby carriage I'd found abandoned on 12th Avenue.

"We need a better name this year," I said. "Somethin' that sticks in people's heads."

"What was it last year?" Tommy asked. "I forget."

"*The Sea Hawk,*" I reminded him. "Like the movie."

"Sea*weed* woulda been more like it," Michael said. That was his subtle way of reminding us that we hadn't done so well in the previous race, finishing next to last.

"Let's name it after the Count of Monte Cristo," John said.

"Nah," I said, shaking my head. "Let's name it after one of the Musketeers."

"Which one?" Tommy asked.

"D'Artagnan," I said immediately.

"To start with, he's not a *made* Musketeer," Michael said. "He just hangs with them."

"And he's only cool 'cause he's got three other guys with him all the time," Tommy said to me. "Just like you. Alone, we're talkin' dead man. Just like you. Besides, we'll be the only ones with a French guy's name on the side of our cart."

"That oughta be good enough to get our ass kicked by somebody," Michael observed.

"Go with the Count," John said. "He's my hero."

"Wolf Larsen's *my* hero," Tommy said. "You don't see me bustin' balls about gettin' *his* name on the cart."

"Wolf Larsen from *The Sea Wolf*?" I asked. "That's your *hero*?"

"Yeah," Tommy said. "I think he's a real stand-up guy."

"The guy's a total scumbag." Michael was incredulous. "He treats people like shit."

"Come onnn, he ain't got a choice," Tommy insisted. "Look at who he deals with."

"Scumbag or not," Michael said. "Wolf's name *would* look better on the cart."

"They'll think we named the friggin' cart after our dog," John muttered.

"We don't *got* a dog," Tommy said.

"Okay, it's settled," I told everybody. "We name the cart *Wolf.* I think it'll bring us luck."

"We're gonna need more than luck to beat Russell's crew," John said.

"We may lose this race," Michael announced. "But we ain't gonna lose it to Russell."

"He's always there at the end, Mikey," I said.

"We always look to block him at the end," Michael said. "That's our mistake."

"He stays away till then," Tommy said. "He's no dope. He knows what to do."

"Maybe," Michael said. "But this time we go and get him outta the race early. With him out, nobody comes near beatin' us."

"How early?" I asked.

"Right after Tony Lungs drops the flag," Michael said. "Near the hill."

"How?"

"Don't worry," Michael said. "I got a plan."

"I *always* worry when you say that," I said.

"Relax," Tommy said, putting the final paint strokes on the wood. "What could happen?"

* * *

A DOZEN GO-CARTS WERE READY TO GO, FOUR TO A ROW. I was behind the unsteady wheels of *Wolf,* on the front line, next to Russell Topaz's cart, *Devil's Pain.* The crowd of onlookers, drawn out by the heavy September heat, was larger than most years, standing two deep behind rows of illegally parked cars. Thick-armed men in white T-shirts held kids atop their shoulders, wives and girlfriends at their sides, red coolers filled with beer and soda by their feet. Tenement windows were open wide, old women leaning out, stubby arms resting on folded bath towels, small electric fans blowing warm air behind them.

I looked over at Russell, nodded my head, and smiled in as friendly a way as I could manage.

"Hey, Russell," I said.

"Eat shit, greaseball," he said back.

Little was known about Russell or the three other boys who were always with him, each as sullen as their leader. We knew he went to St. Agnes on West 46th Street, which meant he wore knickers. That alone was enough to permanently ruin his mood. He lived with foster parents on West 52nd Street, in a building guarded by a German shepherd. There were two other foster children in the family, a younger boy and an older girl, and he was as mean to them as he was to everybody else.

He liked to read. Many times I would see him in the back room of the public library on West 50th Street, his head buried in a thick book about pirates loose on the high seas. He played basketball on the playgrounds for pocket money and was never without a lit cigarette. He had no girlfriend, always wore a brown leather vest, and hated baseball.

I couldn't help but stare at Russell's cart. It was made of fresh wood and was unpainted except for the name stenciled on both sides. The rear wheels were thick and new and the brakes were molded from real rubber, not the blackboard erasers we used on ours. His crate seat was padded and the sides were smooth. He had on black gloves and a Chicago Bears helmet. His three teammates were in sweatpants and sneakers, had handkerchiefs tied around their heads, and also wore gloves.

"You a Bears fan?" I asked him, waiting for the starting flag to drop.

"No, asswipe," Russell said. "I'm not."

Russell was chubby with a round face, soft, pudgy hands, and a practiced sneer. A small scar decorated his right brow, and he never smiled, even in victory.

"They got a great coach," I said. "My dad says he's the best football coach ever."

"Who gives a shit?" was Russell's always-pleasant response.

"What's goin' on?" Michael asked, leaning next to me.

"We were just wishing each other luck," I explained.

"Never mind that," Michael told me, lowering his voice. "You all straight on what you have to do?"

"No," I said.

"Just remember, at the hill, don't swing away," Michael said. "Go right at him. It'll knock him off balance."

"What if it doesn't?"

"Then you're on your own," Michael said.

* * *

TONY LUNGS, OUR LOCAL LOAN SHARK AND THE BENE-factor of this yearly event, stepped forward, facing the carts, wiping his brow with the starter's flag. Below his checkerboard shorts were black loafers, no socks, and he also wore no shirt. The folds of his belly hung over the beltless loops of the garish pants. He ran a hand over his bald head, scanning the crowd: "What say we get this thing started?"

Tony lifted his right arm, holding the starter's flag high enough for all to see. The crowd began to chant and applaud, eager for action. I moved the go-cart a couple of inches forward, leaving only elbow room between Russell and myself.

"Remember," Michael whispered. "At the hill, make your cut. The rest is pure race."

Tony Lungs moved his head from left to right, checking to make sure the carts were in proper position.

"Get ready!" he shouted. "Get set! And remember, any fuck runs over my toes gets their ass kicked. Now, go!"

I ran over the starter's flag as Tommy, Michael, and John pushed our cart up the street.

"How are the pedals workin'?" Tommy asked, his face red from the effort.

"Good," I said.

"Watch yourself," John said, looking at the other carts. "I seen three zip guns already, and you *know* Russell's got something in his cart."

"Don't worry," Michael said. "Just get to the hill."

* * *

THE CROWD NOISE GREW LOUDER AS THE CARTS MADE their way past Fat Mancho's candy store, where all the betting action took place. The people of Hell's Kitchen would lay bets on anything, and go-cart racing was no exception. To the working poor of the neighborhood, gambling was as time-honored a tradition as church on Sunday morning, boxing matches on Friday nights, and virgin weddings all year round.

Devil's Pain was listed on the large blackboard outside Fat Mancho's store as the 3-1 odds-on choice. *Wolf,* our cart, was down as second favorite at 5-1. Freddie Radman's cart, *Eagle's Anger,* was the long shot in the field, going off at 35-1. That was primarily because the three years Radman had bothered to enter the race, he always quit halfway through, abandoning his vehicle and walking away. "You gonna waste a whole lotta time bettin' on Radman," Fat Mancho said. "Might as well set fire to your money."

* * *

WE WERE COMING UP TO THE EDGE OF THE HILL, TOMMY, Michael, and John sweaty and breathless from the hard pushing. We were in the middle of the pack, Russell still on our left, a Puerto Rican crew from Chelsea driving a purple cart on our right.

"More speed," I told the guys. "We're not getting there fast enough."

"Relax," Michael said. "We're right where we're supposed to be."

"If I go any faster, I'll have a heart attack," John muttered between wheezes.

The brake pads by my feet flapped against the sides of the cart and one of the front wheels started to wobble.

"I don't know if these brakes are gonna hold," I said.

"Don't think brakes," Michael hissed. "Think speed."

"How do I stop?" I asked with a hint of panic.

"You'll hit somethin'," Michael said. "Don't worry."

"That's what I love, Mikey," I told him. "You just think of everything."

* * *

AT THE TOP OF THE HILL I WAS ON MY OWN, TWO FEET from Russell's cart. We quickly glanced at each other, the sneer still on his face. I locked my cart against his, the spin of my wheels chopping at his wood, trying to move him over to the hard side of the curb.

"Don't, man," Russell shouted. "You're gonna lose a wheel."

A cart driven by a pock-faced redhead in goggles was up

behind me, pushing me even closer into Russell. My hands were raw and my legs stiff. We came down fast, the carts bunched together, my hopes of knocking Russell from the race diminishing with each wobbly spin of my front wheel.

At the south end of 11th Avenue, a few feet from a Mobil gas station crowded with onlookers, the front wheel finally gave way and snapped off. The cart tilted down, breaking pace with Russell, small sparks shooting from the pavement.

"You're lookin' at a wheelchair," Russell yelled at me as he zoomed past, snarl locked in place, not even the slightest hint of pity in his voice.

I was heading straight for a street divider, the eraser brakes my feet were pumping now as useless to me as the rest of the cart. The remaining carts had gone straight down the street, toward 12th Avenue. The skin on my hands was split and streams of blood ran through my fingers. Holding the ropes as tight as I could, I used my weight to steer away from the divider.

The cart was starting to lose some speed, but still moved with enough force to do damage. My arms were tired and I couldn't hold the ropes any longer: The nylon ridges were cutting in too deep. I let go and braced myself against the sides of the Dr. Brown case. The cart veered wildly left and right, bounced across 11th Avenue, past a double-parked station wagon, jumped the curb, and slammed against the side of a corner mailbox.

I got out, kicked it angrily over onto its side, and sat down on the fender of a parked Chevy. I put my face up to the sun and my elbows on the trunk and waited for Michael, Thomas, and John to make their way down the hill toward me.

"YOU OKAY?" JOHN WANTED to know, pointing to my hands, which were bleeding badly.

"What happened?" Michael asked. "We saw you locked in with Russell, then we lost you in the crowd."

"Woulda taken a bulldozer to knock over Russell's cart," I said.

"Next year we gotta steal better wood," Tommy said. "And maybe get better sets of wheels."

"I'm sorry," I said. "I thought we'd do better."

"That's okay," Michael said. "Not your fault. You just suck as a driver."

"Mikey's right," John said. "You ain't exactly Andretti behind the wheel."

"I ain't got a wheel, first of all," I said. "And Andretti's got brakes."

"Little things," Michael said sadly. "You let little things get to you."

"I hate you guys," I said.

"Next year we'll get you a parachute." John patted me on the back. "Make your bailout a lot easier."

"And gloves too," Tommy said. "Black ones. Like the real race drivers wear."

"I *really* hate you guys."

We walked together back to Tenth Avenue and Fat Mancho's candy store to get some ice and clean rags for my bloody hands.

2

MY THREE FRIENDS AND I WERE INSEPARABLE, HAPPY and content to live within the closed world of Hell's Kitchen. The West Side streets of Manhattan were our private playground, a cement kingdom where we felt ourselves to be nothing less than absolute rulers. There were no curfews to contend with, no curbs placed on where we could go, no restrictions on what we could do. As long as we stayed within the confines of the neighborhood.

Hell's Kitchen was a place where everyone knew everything about everybody and everybody could be counted on. Secrets lived and died on the streets that began on West 35th and ended on West 56th, bordered on one side by the Hudson River and on the other by the Broadway theater district. It was an area populated by an uneasy blend of Irish, Italian, Puerto Rican, and Eastern European laborers, hard men living hard lives, often by their own design.

We lived in railroad apartments inside redbrick tenements. The average rent for the typical six rooms was $38 a month, gas and utilities not included, payment due in cash. Few mothers worked and all had trouble with the men they married. Domestic violence was a cottage industry in Hell's Kitchen. Yet there was no divorce and few separations, for Hell's Kitchen was a place where the will of the Church was as forceful as the demands of a husband. For a marriage to end, someone usually had to die.

We had no control over the daily violence that took place behind our apartment doors.

We watched our mothers being beaten and could do little more than tend to their wounds. We saw our fathers romance other women, sometimes dragging us along to serve as alibis. When their anger turned to us, our fathers were just as brutal. Many were the mornings when my friends and I would compare bruises, welts, and stitches, boasting of the beatings we had taken the previous night.

A lot of the men drank, stomachs full of liquor fueling their violent urges. Many of them gambled heavily, large portions of their union paychecks making their way into the pockets of bookies. This lack of table money also contributed to the charged atmosphere of our private lives.

Yet despite the harshness of the life, Hell's Kitchen offered the children growing up on its streets a safety net enjoyed by few other neighborhoods. Our daily escapades included an endless series of adventures and games, limited only by imagination and physical strength. There were no boundaries to what we could attempt, no barricades placed on the quest for fun and laughter. While many were the horrors we witnessed, our lives were also filled with joy. Enough joy to fend off the madness around us.

In the summer months my friends and I played games that ran the gamut of inner-city pastimes in the early 1960s: sewer-to-sewer stickball with sawed-down broom handles substituting for bats and parked cars used as foul lines; eighteen-box bottlecap tournaments, where a cap filled with melted candle wax was hit by hand into numbered chalk squares; Johnny-on-the-pony; stoop ball and dodge ball; knock hockey and corner pennies. In the evenings, wearing cutoff T-shirts and shorts, we washed off the day's heat with the cold spray of an open fire hydrant.

In the fall, roller hockey and ash can football took over the streets, while in the winter we would fashion sleds from cardboard boxes and wooden crates and ride them down the icy slopes of 11th and 12th Avenues.

Throughout the year we collected and hoarded baseball cards and comic books and, on Monday and Friday nights, walked the two long blocks to the old Madison Square Garden on Eighth Avenue to watch as many boxing and wrestling matches we could sneak our way into, innocently believing both sports to be on the same professional level: To us, Bruno Sammartino was Sonny Liston's peer.

We raced pigeons across rooftops and dove off the 12th Avenue piers into the waters of the Hudson River, using the rusty iron moorings as diving boards. We listened to Sam Cooke, Bobby Darin, and Frankie Valli and the Four Seasons on portable radios and imitated their sounds on street corners late into the night. We started to think and talk about girls, hormones fueled by the cheap skin magazines handed down to us by older boys. We went to the movies once a week and saw the second acts of any Wednesday Broadway matinee that caught our fancy, allowed in by the ticket matrons who worked the theaters and were our neighbors. Inside those ornate and darkened halls, standing in the back or sitting on the top steps of the balcony, we laughed at the early comedies of Neil Simon, were moved by the truth of *A View from the Bridge,* and admired the pure showmanship of *My Fair Lady.* The only show we avoided was *West Side Story,* insulted by its inaccurate depiction of what we thought of as our way of life.

There was also an active competition among the four of us to see who could come up with the best and boldest prank.

Tommy had his best moment when he set loose a small

shopping bag filled with mice during a Saturday afternoon mass honoring a retiring nun. The sight of the mice sent the nearly two dozen nuns in attendance running for the front doors of Sacred Heart Church.

Michael scored a bull's-eye when he got a number of older kids to help him switch the living room furniture in the apartments of two men who had a decade-long feud raging between them.

On one hot summer afternoon, John climbed three floors of fire escapes to reach the crammed clothesline of the meanest woman in the neighborhood, Mrs. Evelyn McWilliams. Hanging upside down and shirtless, his legs wrapped around thin iron bars, he took her laundry off the line, folded the clothes neatly as he could, put them in an empty wine box, and donated them to the Sisters of Sacred Heart Convent, to be distributed to the needy.

For the longest time my pranks never measured up to those my friends managed with such apparent ease. Then, two weeks into the 1963 school year, I found a nun's clacker in a school hallway and was ready for the big leagues.

* * *

THE GIRLS SAT ON THE LEFT-HAND SIDE OF THE CHURCH, the boys on the right, all of us listening to another in a series of inane lectures on the sacrament of confirmation. Three nuns, in white habit and cloth, sat behind the four rows of girls. One priest, Father Robert Carillo, sat behind the boys. It was early afternoon and the lights of the large church were still dark, votive candles casting shadows over the wall sculptures depicting Christ's final walk.

I was in the last row of boys, left arm resting on the edge of the pew, right hand in my jacket pocket, fingers wrapped around the found clacker. To a nun, a clacker was the equivalent of a starter's pistol or a police whistle. In church, it was used to alert the girls as to when they should stand, sit, kneel, and genuflect, all based on the number of times the clacker was pressed. In the hands of a nun, a clacker was a tool of discipline. In my pocket, it was cause for havoc.

I waited until the priest at the altar, white-haired and stoop-shouldered, folded his hands and bowed his head in silent prayer. I squeezed the clacker twice, the signal for the girls to stand. Sister Timothy Morris, an overweight nun with tar-stained fingers and a crooked smile, shot up in her seat as if hit by a bolt. She quickly clacked once, returning the confused girls to their seats. I clacked four times, getting them to genuflect. Sister Timothy clacked the girls back into position, shooting a pair of hateful eyes across the rows of pews filled with boys.

I gave the clacker three quick hits and watched the girls stand at attention. The priest at the altar cut short his prayer, casually watching the commotion before him, listening as the echoes of the dueling clackers bounced off the walls of the church. The boys kept their eyes rooted to the altar, holding their smiles and silencing their snickers. Sister Timothy clacked the girls back to their seats, her cheeks visibly red, her lips pursed.

Father Carillo slid into my row, one hand holding on to my left elbow.

"Let me have the clacker," he said without turning his head.

"What clacker?" I asked, doing the same.

"Now," Father Carillo said.

I took my hand out of my jacket pocket, moved the clacker across my knees, and palmed it over to Father Carillo. He took it from me without much body movement, each of us glancing over toward Sister Timothy, hoping she had not noticed the quick pass-off.

The priest spread his arms outward and asked all in attendance to rise. Sister Timothy snapped her clacker three times and watched as the girls rose in unison, nodding her head in approval at the two nuns to her left.

"Let us pray," said the priest.

Father Carillo, his back straight, his eyes focused on the altar, his face free of emotion, gave the clacker in his hand one soft squeeze.

The girls all sat back down. Sister Timothy fell into her pew. The priest at the altar lowered his eyes and shook his head. I looked over at Father Bobby, my mouth open, my eyes unable to hide their surprise.

"Nuns are such easy targets," Father Bobby whispered with a wink and a smile.

* * *

HELL'S KITCHEN WAS A NEIGHBORHOOD WITH A STRUC-tured code of behavior and an unwritten set of rules that could be physically enforced. There was a hierarchy that trickled down from the local members of both the Irish and Italian mobs to a loose-knit affiliation of Puerto Rican numbers brokers and loan sharks to small groups of organized gangs recruited to do a variety of jobs, from collections to picking up stolen goods. My friends and I were the last rung on the neighborhood ladder, free to roam its streets and play our games, required only to follow the rules. On occasion, we would be recruited for the simplest tasks, most of them involving money drop-offs or pickups.

Crimes against the people of the neighborhood were not permitted, and, on the rare occasions when they did occur, the punishments doled out were severe and, in some cases, final. The elderly were to be helped, not hurt. The neighborhood was to be supported, not stripped. Gangs were not allowed to recruit anyone who did not wish to join. Drug use was frowned upon and addicts were ostracized, pointed out as "on the nod" losers to be avoided.

Despite the often violent ways of its inhabitants, Hell's Kitchen was one of New York's safest neighborhoods. Outsiders walked its streets without fear, young couples strolled the West Side piers without apprehension, old men took grandchildren for walks in De Witt Clinton Park, never once looking over their shoulders.

It was a place of innocence ruled by corruption. There were no drive-by shootings or murders without reason. The men who carried guns in Hell's Kitchen were all too aware of their power. Crack cocaine had yet to hit, and there wasn't enough money around to support a cocaine habit. The drug of choice when I was a child was heroin, and the hard-core addicts numbered a handful, most of them young and docile, feeding their needs with cash handouts and petty thievery. They bought their drugs outside the neighborhood since dealers were not welcome in Hell's Kitchen. Those who ignored the verbal warnings, wrote them off as the ramblings of pudgy old men, paid with their lives.

One of the most graphic images I can recall from my childhood is of standing under a streetlight on a rainy night, holding my father's hand and looking up at the face of a dead man, hanging from a rope, his face swollen, his hands bound. He was a drug dealer from an uptown neighborhood who had moved heroin in Hell's Kitchen. A packet of it had killed the twelve-year-old son of a Puerto Rican numbers runner.

It was the last packet the dealer ever sold.

* * *

FRIENDSHIPS WERE AS IMPORTANT AS NEIGHBORHOOD loyalty. Your friends gave you an identity and a sense of belonging. They afforded you a group you could trust that extended beyond the bounds of family. The home lives of most of the children in Hell's Kitchen were unruly and filled with struggle. There was little time for bonding, little attention given to nurturing, and few moments set aside for childish pleasures. Those had to be found elsewhere, usually out on the street in the company of friends. With them, you could laugh, tell stupid jokes, trade insults and books, and talk about sports and movies. You could even share your secrets and sins, dare tell another person what you thought about important childhood issues such as holding a girl's hand.

Life in Hell's Kitchen was hard. Life without friends was harder. Most kids were lucky enough to find one friend they could count on. I found three. All of them older, probably wiser, and no doubt smarter. There is no memory of my early years that does not include them. They were a part of every happy moment I enjoyed.

I wasn't tough enough to be part of a gang, nor did I care for the gang members' penchant for constant confrontation. I was too talkative and outgoing to be a loner. I lived and survived in a grown-up world, but my concerns were that of a growing boy—I knew more about the Three Stooges, even Shemp, than I did about street gangs. I cared more about a trade the Yankees were about to make than about a shooting that happened three buildings down. I wondered why James Cagney had stopped making movies and if there was a better cop in the country than Jack Webb on *Dragnet*. In a neighborhood where there was no Little League, I worked on throwing a curveball like Whitey Ford. Surrounded by apartments devoid of books, I pored through the works of every adventure writer the local library stocked. Like most boys my age, I molded a world of my own and stocked it with the people I came across through books, sports, movies, and television, making it a place where fictional characters were as real to me as those I saw every day. It was a world with room for those who felt as I did, who hated Disney but loved Red Skelton, who would take a Good Humor bar over a Mister Softee cone, who went to the Ringling Brothers circus hoping that the annoying kid shot out of the cannon would *miss* the net, and who wondered why the cops in our neighborhood couldn't be more like Lee Marvin from *M Squad*.

It was a world made for my three friends.

* * *

WE BECAME FRIENDS OVER A LUNCH.

Word spread one afternoon that three pro wrestlers—Klondike Bill, Bo Bo Brazil, and Haystack Calhoun—were eating at a Holiday Inn on 51st Street. I rushed there and found Michael, John, and Thomas standing outside, looking through the glass window that fronted the restaurant, watching the large men devour thick sandwiches and slabs of pie. I knew the guys from the school yard and the neighborhood, but had been too intimidated to approach them. The sight of the wrestlers eliminated such concerns.

"They don't even stop to chew," John said in wonder.

"Guys that big don't have to chew," Tommy told him.

"Haystack eats four steaks a night at dinner," I said, nudging my way past Michael for a closer look. "*Every* night."

"Tell us somethin' we don't know," Michael muttered, eyes on the wrestlers.

"I'm gonna go and sit with them," I said casually. "You can come if you want."

"You know them?" John asked.

"Not yet," I said.

THE FOUR OF US walked through the restaurant doors and approached the wrestlers' table. The wrestlers were deep in conversation, empty plates and glasses the only remnants of their meal. They turned their heads when they saw us.

"You boys lost?" Haystack Calhoun asked. His hair and beard were shaggy and long and he was wearing bib overalls large enough to cover a banquet table. The wrestling magazine stories I had read about him put his weight at 620 pounds and I was amazed that anyone that big could slide into a booth.

"No," I said.

"Then what do you want?" Klondike Bill asked. His hair and beard were darker and thicker than Calhoun's and he was half his weight, which made him the second biggest man I'd ever seen.

"I've watched you guys wrestle a lot," I said. I pointed a finger to the three behind me. "We all have."

"You root for us to win?" Bo Bo Brazil asked. He was more muscular than his cohorts, and looked like sculpted stone leaning against the window, his shaved black head gleaming, his eyes clear and bright. Bo Bo's one noted move, the head-crushing co-co-butt, was said to be a weapon harsh enough to leave an opponent paralyzed.

"No," I said.

"Why not?" Calhoun demanded.

"You usually fight the good guys," I said, my palms starting to sweat.

Haystack Calhoun lifted one large hand from the table and placed it on my shoulder and around my neck. Its weight alone made my legs quiver. He was breathing through his mouth, air coming out in thick gulps. "Your friends feel the same way?"

"Yes," I said, not giving them a chance to respond. "We all root against you."

Haystack Calhoun let out a loud laugh, the fat of his body shaking in spasms, his free hand slapping at the tabletop. Klondike Bill and Bo Bo Brazil were quick to join in.

"Get some chairs, boys," Calhoun said, grabbing a glass of water to wash down his laugh. "Sit with us."

WE SPENT MORE THAN an hour in their company, crowded around the booth, treated to four pieces of cherry pie, four chocolate shakes, and tales of the wrestling world. We didn't get the impression that they made a lot of money and, judging by their scarred faces and cauliflower ears, we knew it wasn't an easy life. But the stories they told were filled with exuberance and the thrill of working the circuit in arenas around the country, where people paid money to jeer and cheer every night. To our young ears, being a wrestler sounded far better than running away to join the circus.

"You boys got tickets for tonight?" Haystack asked, signaling to a waitress.

"No, sir," John said, scraping up the last crumbs of his pie.

"Get yourself over to the box office at seven," Calhoun said, slowly squeezing out of his side of the booth. "You'll be sittin' ringside by seven-thirty."

We shook hands, each of ours disappearing into the expanse of theirs and thanked them, looking up in awe as they smiled and rubbed the top of our heads.

"Don't disappoint us now," Klondike Bill warned on his way out. "We wanna hear you boo loud and clear tonight."

"We won't let you down," Tommy said.

"We'll throw things if you want," John said.

We stood by the booth and watched as they walked out of the inn and onto Tenth Avenue, three large men taking small steps, heading toward Madison Square Garden and the white lights of a packed arena.

* * *

I WAS THE YOUNGEST OF MY FRIENDS BY THREE YEARS, and yet they treated me as an equal. We had so much else in common that once I was accepted, my age never became an issue. A sure sign of their acceptance was when, less than a week after we met, they gave me a nickname. They called me Shakespeare, because I was never without a book.

We were each the only child of a troubled marriage.

MY FATHER, MARIO, WORKED as a butcher, a trade he learned in prison while serving six years of a five-to-fifteen-year sentence for second-degree manslaughter. The victim was his first wife. The battles my father fought with my mother, Raffaela, a silent, angry woman who hid herself in prayer, were neighborhood legend. My father was a con man who gambled what little he earned and managed to spend what he never had. Yet he always had time and money to buy me and my friends ice cream cones or sodas whenever he saw us on the street. He was a man who seemed more comfortable in the company of children than in a world of adults. Growing up, for reasons I could never put into words, I was always afraid my father would disappear. That one day he would leave and not return. It was a fear fed by his separations from my mother, when I would not hear from him for weeks.

MICHAEL, TWELVE, WAS THE eldest of my friends. His father, construction worker Devlin Sullivan, had fought in Korea and, for his trouble, earned a steel plate in his head. Always angry, Mr. Sullivan had a foul mouth and great thirst. Tall and strapping, muscular from the work, he kept his wife at a distance, living for weeks with an assortment of mistresses who soaked his money and then sent him packing. Michael's mother, Anna, always took him back and forgave him all trespasses. Michael never spoke about his father, not in the way I always did about mine, and seemed uncomfortable the rare times I saw them together.

His parents' marriage fed in Michael a distrust about the strong neighborhood traditions of marriage, family, and religion. He was the realist among us, suspicious of others' intentions, never trusting the words of those he didn't know. It was Michael who kept us grounded.

His stern exterior, though, was balanced by a strong sense of honor. He would never do anything that would embarrass us and demanded the same in return. He never played practical jokes on those he perceived as weaker and he always rose to defend anyone he believed unable to defend himself. That rigid code was reflected in the books he read and the shows he watched. The only time I ever saw him on the verge of tears was near the end of a Broadway production of *Camelot,* affected by Lancelot's betrayal. His favorite of the Three Musketeers was the more troubled Aramis, and when we played games based on TV shows or movies, Michael always sought out the role of leader, whether it was Vic Morrow's character on *Combat* or Eliot Ness in *The Untouchables.*

It was harder to make Michael laugh than the others. He was big brother and as such had to maintain a degree of maturity. He was the first among us to have a steady girlfriend, Carol Martinez, a half-Irish, half–Puerto Rican girl from 49th Street, and the last in our crew to learn to ride a bike. He was called Spots when he was younger because of the dozens of freckles that dotted his face and hands, but not often since he hated the name and the freckles had begun to fade the closer he got to puberty.

It was Michael who kept the older, explosive boys of the neighborhood at bay, often with nothing more than a look or movement. That ability reinforced his position as our leader, a title he accepted but never acknowledged. It was simply his role, his place.

IN THE YEARS WE spent together as children, Tommy Marcano's father was away in Attica in upstate New York, serving a seven-year sentence for an armed robbery conviction. Billy Marcano was a career criminal who kept his wife, Marie, out of his business affairs. Like most of the neighborhood mothers, Marie was devoutly religious, spending her free time helping the parish priests and nuns. During the years her husband was in prison, she remained a devoted wife, working a steady job as a telephone receptionist for an illegal betting parlor.

Tommy missed his father, writing him a letter every night before he went to bed. He carried a crumpled picture of the two of them together in his back pocket and looked at it several times a day. If Michael was the brains behind the group, Tommy was its soul. His was a gentle goodness, and he would share anything he had, never jealous of another's gift or good fortune. His street name was Butter, because he spread it across everything he ate and he seemed happiest when he had a fresh roll in one hand and a hot cup of chocolate in the other. He was shy and shunned any chance for attention, yet he played the dozens, a street game where the key is to out-insult your opponent.

I can never think of Tommy without a smile on his face, his eyes eager to share in the laugh, even if it came at his expense. The only time I saw a hint of sadness to him was when I was with my father, so I made an effort to include him in whatever we were planning to do together. My father, who liked to eat as much as Tommy did, usually obliged. When that happened, the smile was quick to return.

While Michael seemed older than his years, Tommy seemed far younger than eleven. He had a little boy's affability and eagerness to please. He had a fast tongue, was swift with a comeback, and never forgot a joke. His pranks were tinged with innocence. Tommy would never want to be leader of the group, never would have been comfortable with the burden. It was more in keeping with his personality to go along, to watch, to listen, and, always, to laugh.

He also had a natural ability to build things, working away on a discarded piece of wood or an old length of pipe from which would emerge a wooden train or a makeshift flute. He never kept his creations and never took money for his work. Many of the pieces he made were mailed to his father in prison. He was never told if his father received them and he never asked.

JOHN REILLY WAS RAISED by his mother, an attractive woman with little time to devote to anything other than church, her work as a Broadway theater usher, and her boyfriends. John's father was a petty hood shot and killed in a foiled armored truck heist in New Jersey less than a week after his son was born. John knew nothing of the man. "There were no photos," he once told me. "No wedding picture, no shots of him in the navy. Nobody talked about him or mentioned his name. It was as if he never existed."

John earned his discipline from the hands of his mother's various suitors, an endless stream of men who knew only one way to handle a boy. He seldom spoke about the beatings, but we all knew they took place.

Even though he was only four months younger than Michael, John was the smallest of the group and was nicknamed the Count, due to his fascination with *The Count of Monte Cristo*, which was also my favorite book. John was brash and had the sharpest sense of humor of any of us. He loved comedy and would spend hours debating whether the Three Stooges were gifted comedians or just jerks who beat each other up.

He was our heart, an innocent surrounded by a violence he could not prevent. He was the most handsome among us and often used a smile and a wink to extricate himself from trouble. He loved to draw, sketching sailboats and cruise ships onto thin strips of fine paper with a dark pencil. He would spend afternoons down by the piers feeding pigeons, watching waves lap against the dock, and drawing colorful pictures of the ocean liners in port, filling their decks with the familiar faces of the neighborhood.

He was a born mimic, ordering slices of pizza as John Wayne, asking for a library book like James Cagney, and talking to a girl in the school yard sounding like Humphrey Bogart. Each situation brought about its intended smile, allowing John to walk away content, his mission accomplished. He concealed the ugliness of his home life behind a shield of jokes. He never set out to hurt, there was too much of that in his own everyday moments. John, more than any one of us, was always in need of someone else's smile.

TOGETHER, THE FOUR OF us found in one another the solace and security we could not find anywhere else. We trusted each other and knew there would never be an act of betrayal among us. We had nothing else—no money, no bikes, no summer camps, no vacations. Nothing, except one another.

To us, that was all that mattered.

3

THE CATHOLIC CHURCH PLAYED A LARGE PART IN OUR lives. Sacred Heart was the center of the neighborhood, serving as a neutral meeting ground, a peaceful sanctuary where problems could be discussed and emotions calmed. The priests and nuns of the area were a visible presence and commanded our attention, if not always our respect.

My friends and I attended Sacred Heart Grammar School on West 50th Street, a large redbrick building directly across from P.S. 111. Our parents paid a $2 a month tuition fee and sent us out each morning dressed in the mandatory uniform of maroon pants for boys and skirts for girls, white shirts, and clip-on red ties.

The school was rife with problems, lack of supplies being the least of them. Most of us were products of violent homes, and therefore prone to violence ourselves, making playground fights daily occurrences. The fights were often in response to a perceived slight or a violation of an unwritten code of conduct. All students were divided into cliques, most based on ethnic backgrounds, which only added tension to an already tight situation.

In addition to the volatile ethnic groupings, teachers were faced with the barriers of language and the difficulties of over-crowded classrooms. After third grade, students were divided by sex, with the nuns teaching the girls and priests and brothers working with the boys. Each teacher faced an average class size of thirty-two students, more than half of whom spoke no English at home. To help support their families, many of the children worked jobs after school, reducing the hours they were free to concentrate on homework.

Few of the teachers cared enough to work beyond the three o'clock bell. There were a handful, however, as there are in all schools, who did care and who took the time to tutor a student, to feed an interest, to set a goal beyond neighborhood boundaries.

Brother Nick Kappas spent hours after school patiently helping me learn the basic English I had not been taught at home, where both my parents spoke Italian. Another, Father Jerry Martin, a black priest from the Deep South, opened my eyes to the hate and prejudice that existed beyond Hell's Kitchen. Still another, Father Andrew Nealon, an elderly priest with a thick Boston accent, fueled my interest in American history. Then there was Father Robert Carillo, my cohort in the clacker escapade, and the only member of the clergy who had been born and raised in Hell's Kitchen.

Father Bobby, as the neighborhood kids called him, was in his mid-thirties, tall and muscular, with thick, dark, curly hair, an unlined face, and an athlete's body. He played the organ at Sunday mass, was in charge of the altar boys, taught fifth grade, and played basketball for two hours every day in the school playground. Most priests liked to preach from a pulpit; Father Bobby liked to talk during the bump and shove of a game of one-on-one. He was the only priest in the neighborhood who challenged us to do better, and who was always ready to help when a problem arose.

Father Bobby introduced me and my friends to such authors as Sir Arthur Conan Doyle, Victor Hugo, and Stephen Crane, further instilling in us a passion for written words. He chose stories and novels by authors he felt we could identify with, and who could, for a brief time, help us escape the wars waged nightly inside our apartments.

It was through him that we learned of such books as *Les Misérables, A Tree Grows in Brooklyn,* and *A Bell for Adano* and how they could provide a night-light to keep away the family terror. It was easy for him to do so, because he had been raised in the same manner, under the same circumstances. He knew what it meant to find sleep under the cover of fear.

Other clergy were not as caring. Many took their cue from parents, using violence to enforce their classroom rules. In the Catholic school system of the 1960s, corporal punishment was acceptable. The clergy were, for the most part, given parental approval to deal with us however they saw fit. The majority of priests and brothers kept thick leather straps in a top drawer of their desk. Nuns preferred rulers and paddles. A closed fist or a hard slap was not out of the question.

No one used that show of force more than Brother Gregory Reynolds, a bald, middle-aged man with a jowly face and a round beer belly. He always held the leather belt in his hand, walking up and down the classroom aisles, swinging it at the slightest provocation. A missed homework assignment called for four sharp blows to each hand. Lateness carried a penalty of two shots. A smile, a smirk, a glance in the wrong direction, could easily set fire to his wrath and bring the leather belt crashing across a hand or face.

Brother Reynolds was an angry man, his frustration fueled by drink and an answer to a call he was ill suited to handle. We all at one time felt the pain of his strap. My friends and I dealt with him in much the same way we dealt with all our other problems, through humor, pranks, and wisecracks. If we couldn't beat them, we decided, we might as well laugh at them. It can safely be said that Brother Reynolds had more water balloons dropped on his head, more pizzas delivered to his door, more scarves, gloves, and hats stolen from his office than any clergyman in the history of Hell's Kitchen. He always suspected me and my friends, but he lacked proof.

One day I handed him all the proof he would ever need.

I was bored, halfway through a math class that never seemed to end. To pass the time, I reached behind me and, scraping snow off the windowsill, made a wetball. I was sitting in the last row next to the clothes closet. I bet a pimple-faced Puerto Rican kid named Hector Mandano a sour pickle that I could make the snowball curve, throwing it from my seat in the back out an open left window in the front. Windows were always open in class, regardless of weather conditions, since the teachers felt fresh air kept the students alert. We never objected, especially in the colder months, when the heat in the building was enough to make the strongest student sink into a pool of sweat.

Brother Reynolds had his back to me as he wrote a series of math problems on the blackboard. He was a few feet to the right of the open window. Since I had the utmost faith in my ability to throw a curveball, and since I would do anything for a sour pickle, I tossed the packed piece of snow across the room, convinced it would find its way.

Whitey Ford would not have been pleased with my throw. The snowball not only *didn't* curve, it actually picked up speed, moving like a missile toward the back of Brother Reynolds's head. It landed with the kind of splat I'd heard only in cartoons. The entire class took in one collective breath. My only hope to survive was that the snowball had landed hard enough to cause a hemorrhage.

It didn't.

Brother Reynolds flew down the aisle like a runaway bull, leather belt held high, swinging it from all sides, hitting the innocent and heading straight toward me, the guilty. He attacked me with an accumulation of rage and embarrassment, landing blows to my hands, head, and body, flailing away until he fell to his knees, exhausted. But nothing he did could stem the tide of laughter around him, which had grown so loud that it more than outweighed any pain I felt.

The memory of Brother Gregory Reynolds shaking snow from the back of his neck, his face lit like a flame, his eyes bloated with fury, his body too angry to form words, will be one that will stay with me always, as will the laughter heard in that classroom on that dreary day.

Brother Reynolds died less than two years after the incident, victim of a bad heart and too much drink. At his wake, his open casket surrounded by an array of flowers and a stream of mourners, someone in the back of the room brought up the story of the snowball that never curved.

The laughter began all over again.

4

SACRED HEART CHURCH WAS QUIET, ITS OVERHEAD LIGHTS shining down across long rows of wooden pews. Seven women and three men sat in the rear, hands folded in prayer, waiting to talk to a priest.

My friends and I spent a lot of time inside that small, compact church with the large marble altar at its center. We each served as altar boys, working a regular schedule of Sunday and occasional weekday masses. We were also expected to handle funerals, spreading dark clouds of incense above the coffins of the neighborhood dead. Everyone wanted to work funeral masses, since the service included a three-dollar fee and a chance to pocket more if you looked sufficiently somber.

In addition, we went to mass once a week and sometimes more, especially if Father Bobby needed someone to escort the elderly of the parish to weeknight services. Other times, I would just stop inside the church and sit for hours, alone or with one of my friends. I liked the feel and smell of the empty church, surrounded by statues of saints and stained glass windows. I didn't go so much to pray, but to relax and pull away from outside events. John and I went more than the others. We were the only two of the group to give any thought to entering the priesthood, an idea we found appealing because of its guaranteed ticket out of the neighborhood. A Catholic version of the lottery. We were much too young to dissect the issue of celibacy and spent most of our time fretting over how we would look wearing a Roman collar.

John and I were intrigued by the powers a priest was given. The ability to serve mass, say last rites, baptize babies, perform weddings, and, best of all, sit in a dark booth and listen to others confess their sins. To us, the sacrament of confession was like being allowed inside a secret world of betrayal and deceit, where people openly admitted dark misdeeds and vile indiscretions. All of it covered by an umbrella of piety and privacy. Confession was better than any book we could get our hands on or any movie we could see because the sins were real, committed by people we actually *knew.* The temptation to be a part of that was too great to resist.

There were two confessional booths on either side of Sacred Heart, lining the walls closest to the back pews, each shrouded with heavy purple curtains. The thick wood door at the center of the confessional locked from the inside. Two small mesh screens, covered by sliding wood panels, allowed the priest, if he could stay awake, to sit and listen to the sins of his parish. Every Saturday afternoon, from three to five P.M. a handful of parishioners would head into those booths. There, every affair, every curse, every transgression they made during the week, would be revealed. On those days there was no better place to be in Hell's Kitchen.

John and I sat in that church every Saturday afternoon. We knew Father Tim McAndrew, old, weary, and hard of hearing, always worked the first hour in one of the booths closest to the altar. Father McAndrew had a penchant for handing out stiff penalties for the slightest trespass, whether he heard it confessed or only thought he did. He was especially rough on children and married women. Self-abuse was worth a dozen Hail Marys and a half-dozen Our Fathers.

On a few occasions and always at my urging, John and I

would sneak into the booth alongside McAndrew's, shut the door, and hear the sins we had only read about. We couldn't imagine what the penalty would be for getting caught, but whatever it was, it couldn't possibly surpass the joy of hearing about a neighbor's fall from grace.

I WAS INSIDE THE second booth, squeezed onto the small wooden bench, my back against the cool wall. The Count, John Reilly, sat next to me.

"Man, if we get caught, they'll burn us," he whispered.

"What if our mothers are out there?" I asked. "What if we end up hearing *their* confessions?"

"What if we hear somethin' worse?" John said.

"Like what?" I couldn't imagine anything worse.

"Like a murder," John said. "What if somebody cops to a murder?"

"Relax," I said as convincingly as I could. "All we gotta do is sit back, listen, and remember not to laugh."

AT TEN MINUTES PAST THREE, two women from the back pew stood and headed for the first confessional, ready to tell their sins to a man who couldn't hear them. They moved one to each side, parted the curtains, knelt down, and waited for the small wood doors to slide open.

Seconds later the sides of our booth came to life.

"Here we go," I said. "Get ready."

"God help us," John said, making the sign of the cross. "God help us."

We heard a man's low cough on our right as he shuffled his way to a kneeling position and leaned his elbow on the small ledge facing him. He chewed gum and sniffed in deep breaths as he waited for the door to open.

"We know him?" John asked.

"Quiet!"

There was a woman's sneeze from the other side of the booth as she searched through an open purse for a tissue. She blew her nose, straightened her dress, and waited.

"Which one?" John asked.

"The guy," I said, and moved the small door to my right. The man's thick lips, nose, and stubble faced us, separated only by the mesh screen, his heavy breath warming our side of the booth.

"Bless me, Father, for I have sinned," he said, his hands folded in prayer. "It has been two years since my last confession."

John grabbed on to my shoulder and I tried to keep my legs from shaking. Neither of us spoke.

"I done bad things, Father," the man said. "And I'm sorry for all of them. I gamble, lose all my rent money to the horses. Lie to my wife, hit her sometimes, the kids too. It's bad, Father. Gotta get myself outta this hole. What can I do?"

"Pray," I said in my deepest voice.

"I *been* prayin'," the man said. "Ain't helped. I owe money to loan sharks. A lot of it. Father, you gotta help me. This the place you go for help, right? I got nowhere else to go. This is it."

John and I held our breath and stayed silent.

"Father, you there?" the man said. "Yes," I said.

"So," the man said. "What's it gonna be?"

"Three Hail Marys," I said. "One Our Father. And may the Lord bless you."

"Three Hail Marys!" the man said. "What the hell's that gonna do?"

"It's for your soul," I said.

"Fuck my soul!" the man said in a loud voice. "And fuck you too, you freeloadin' bastard."

The man stood up, pulled aside the purple drapes hanging

to his right, and stormed out of the booth, his outburst catching the attention of those who waited their turn.

"That went well," I said to John, who finally loosened his grip on my shoulder.

"Don't do the woman," John said. "I'm beggin' you. Let's just get outta here."

"How?" I asked.

"Don't take any more," John said. "Let 'em all go over to the other booth. Have 'em think no one's in here."

"Let's do one more," I said.

"No," John said. "I'm too scared."

"Just one more," I pleaded.

"No."

"Only one more."

"One," John said. "Then we're outta here."

"You got it," I agreed.

"Swear on it?"

"You can't swear in church," I said.

* * *

THE WOMAN'S VOICE WAS SOFT AND LOW, BARELY ABOVE a whisper. The edge of a veil hung across her face, her hands curled against the darkness of the booth, the tips of her fingernails scraping the base of the wood.

"Bless me Father," she began. "It has been six weeks since my last confession."

We both knew who she was, had seen her more than once walking the streets of Hell's Kitchen, arm in arm with the latest man to catch her fancy. She was a woman our fathers smiled about and our mothers told us to ignore.

"I'm not happy about my life, Father," she said. "It's like I don't want to wake up in the morning anymore."

"Why?" I asked, my voice muffled by the back of John's shirt.

"It's wrong," she said. "Everything I do is wrong and I don't know how to stop."

"You must pray," I said.

"I do, Father," she said. "Believe me, I do. Every day. It's not doing any good."

"It will," I said.

"I sleep with married men," the woman said. "Men with families. In the morning I tell myself it's the last time. And it never is."

"One day it will be," I said, watching her hands curve around a set of rosary beads.

"It's gonna have to be soon," the woman said, holding back a rush of tears. "I'm pregnant."

John looked at me, both hands locked over his mouth.

"The father?" I asked.

"Take a number," the woman said. The sarcasm could not hide the sadness in her voice.

"What are you going to do?"

"I know what *you* want me to do," the woman said. "And I know what I *should* do. I just don't know what I'm gonna do."

"There's time," I said, sweat running down my neck.

"I got lotsa things," the woman said. "Time just isn't one of 'em."

The woman blessed herself, rolled up the rosary beads, and put them in the front pocket of her dress. She brushed her hair away from her eyes and picked up the purse resting by her knees.

"I gotta go," she said, and then, much to our shock, she added, "Thanks for listening, fellas. I appreciate it and I know you'll keep it to yourselves."

She knocked at the screen with two fingers, waved, and left the booth.

"She knew," John said.

"Yeah," I said. "She knew."

"Why she tell us all that?"

"I guess she had to tell somebody."

John stood up and brushed against the wall, accidentally sliding open the small door to the confessional. A man knelt on the other side, obscured by the screen.

"Bless me, Father, for I have sinned," the man said, his voice baritone-deep.

"So?" John said. "What's that make you? Special?"

John opened the main door and we both walked out of the booth, our heads bowed, our hands folded in prayer.

5

WE SPENT AS MUCH TIME AS POSSIBLE OUTSIDE OUR
apartments. John and Tommy—the Count and Butter—had
no televisions at home, Michael—Spots—wasn't allowed to
watch anything when he was alone, which was most of the
time, and my parents would often just sit and watch the Chan-
nel 9 *Million Dollar Movie*. The radios in our apartments were
usually tuned to stations that focused on news from the old
hometowns of Naples or Belfast. So the bulk of our daily entertainment came from what we read.

We pored through the *Daily News* every day, working our
way back from the sports pages, letting Dick Young and Gene
Ward take us through the baseball wars, then moving to the
crime stories up front, ignoring all else in between. We never
bought the *Post,* having been warned about its Communist
leanings by our fathers, and you couldn't even *find* a copy of *The
New York Times* in Hell's Kitchen. We read and we argued over
the stories, blaming the writer if he dared offer criticism of a
favorite player or gloat over the tale of a criminal we thought
was being given a bum's ride.

We saved our money and sent away for *Classics Illustrated*
comics and waited patiently for the package to arrive in the
mail. What comic books we couldn't buy we stole from candy
stores outside the neighborhood, the four of us keeping a com-

bined collection in our basement clubhouse where we stored them all—*The Flash, Aquaman, Batman, Superman, Sgt. Rock, The Green Lantern*—in large boxes, protected by strips of plastic, each carton carefully labeled.

We collected baseball cards in the summer and traded them the year round. The cards, too, were organized and labeled, kept in team order in rows of shoeboxes. The hard piece of bubble gum which came with each pack was set aside until needed for the summer bottle-cap competition. Then the chewed gum would be mixed with candle wax and poured inside an empty 7Up bottle cap for use in the popular street game.

None of us owned any books and neither did any of our parents. They were a luxury few in Hell's Kitchen could afford—or would want. The bulk of the men were literate only to the extent that they could follow the racing sheet of a newspaper; the women limited their reading to prayer books and scandal sheets. People thought reading to be a waste of time. If they saw you reading, they figured you had nothing better to do and wrote you off as lazy. For me and my best friends it was a damn good thing we had a library to visit.

The public library in Hell's Kitchen was a large concrete gray building sandwiched between a tenement and a candy store. It was divided into two sections. The children's reading room faced Tenth Avenue and was always crowded. The adult section was in the back and was empty and quiet enough to hide a body in. It was well manned and well stocked, the half-dozen librarians accustomed to the unruly habits of their guests. It was open every day except Sunday, its large black doors swinging wide at nine.

My friends and I read quite a few books inside that library, after school on winter afternoons. We also created our own share of havoc. We laughed when we should have been quiet. We brought in food when it wasn't allowed. Sometimes, we slept at our seats, especially if the previous night had been hard. The library was the only place besides church and home where thievery was not permitted. In my time there, I can remember no book ever being stolen.

We also went there for the quiet. There was so much shouting and screaming in our lives, if we didn't have some kind of sanctuary, we might have gone crazy. Plenty of people in our neighborhood *did* go crazy. But not us. We had the library. It was like home should have been but never was. And, since it was like a home, we didn't just read, of course. We also raised a little hell.

* * *

I WAS SITTING AT A LIGHT WOOD TABLE IN THE BACK room of the library, reading a hardbound copy of *The Count of Monte Cristo,* immersed in the mental battle waged by Edmond Dantes in his desolate prison cell.

"C'mon Shakes," John said, nudging me with his elbow. "Do it."

"Not today," I said, gently putting down the book, careful not to lose my place. "Tomorrow, *maybe.*"

"Why not today?" Tommy demanded from the other side of the table.

"I don't feel like it," I said. "I wanna read."

"You can *always* read," John said.

"I can *always* knock over a row of books."

"I bet you two *Flash* comic books you can't do it today," John said.

"I'll toss in two *Green Lanterns,*" Michael added, raising his head from a *National Geographic* spread across his knees.

"The new ones?" I asked.

"Just got 'em the other day."

I nodded my head toward Tommy. "What about you?"

"What about me?" he wanted to know.

"What do you got?"

"Nothin'," Tommy said. "I just wanna see you do it."

"So?" Michael said. "What's it gonna be?"

"Pick a book," I sighed.

Moments later, I reached the top level of the library fiction shelf, a copy of *Moby-Dick* in my hand. John and Tommy were stationed at opposite ends of the aisle, watching for passing librarians. Below me, Michael held the wooden ladder with both hands.

"Take your time," he said. "They must all be on a coffee break."

There were twenty-five books on the shelf, all arranged by author. I pressed the dozen on my left to one side, tipping their covers toward the center. I did the same to the books on the other end, arranging them so that each depended on the weight of the novel beside it. I dropped *Moby-Dick* in the middle of the shelf, making slight adjustments until it caught the weight from both sides. I scanned the row with satisfaction and then moved down the steps of the ladder.

"Think it'll work?" Michael asked.

"It's a can't-miss," I assured him.

"Who should we get?" Tommy said, coming up behind my right shoulder. "You know, to test it out?"

"How about Kalinsky?" John suggested, one foot resting on the base of the ladder. "Everybody hates her."

"Not everybody hates her," Michael said. "So, let's leave her outta this."

"Sorry, Mikey," John said. "Forgot about her and your dad."

"Just pick somebody else," Michael said.

"How about Miss Pippin?" I asked. "Anybody's father goin' out with her?"

* * *

TOMMY STOOD AT THE COUNTER IN THE MIDDLE OF THE large room, patiently waiting as Miss Pippin, a tall, worried-looking blonde, stacked a handful of children's books on top of a file cabinet.

"Hello," she said, turning to face Tommy. "Do you need help?"

"I can't find a book," Tommy said.

"Do you know the name of the book?" she asked, moving her glasses from the chain around her neck to her eyes. "Or who wrote it?"

"It's called *Moby-Dick,*" Tommy said shyly. "I think a guy named Herman wrote it."

"You're half right," Miss Pippin said. "It was written by Herman Melville. It shouldn't be all that hard to find."

"That's great." Tommy nodded his head and slapped the top of the counter with his palms. "Did you know there was a movie made about it?"

"No," Miss Pippin said. "No, I didn't. But the book is much better."

"How do you know?" Tommy said. "If you didn't see the movie."

"I *know,*" Miss Pippin said, stepping out from behind the counter. "Follow me and we'll get you your book."

"Right behind you," Tommy said.

* * *

MISS PIPPIN RESTED HER HANDS ON THE EDGES OF THE step-ladder, scanning the bookshelves left to right. We sat at a table at her back, only Michael facing her. John and I were across from each other, catching quick glimpses of Miss Pippin in profile. We were settled behind the pages of large picture books, our eyes visible, peeking over above the covers.

"Well, you couldn't have looked for it very long," Miss Pippin said to Tommy. "There it is. Right up there."

"Where?" Tommy said. "I don't see it."

"Right there," Miss Pippin said, one sharp-nailed finger pointing up. "On the top shelf."

"I'm sorry, Miss Pippin," Tommy said. "I can't see it. I left my glasses in school."

"Since when do you wear glasses?" Miss Pippin asked. "I've never seen them on you."

"Just got 'em," Tommy said.

"All right, all right, I'll get you the book," Miss Pippin said. "But next time, don't be so quick to give up your search. Take the time to look for what you want to read."

"I will," Tommy said. "I promise."

MISS PIPPIN STARTED UP the steps of the ladder, one hand keeping her long, pleated skirt in place. Tommy stared up, his eyes eager to catch a flash of thigh. Michael turned to me and winked. John held the book he pretended to read well above his face, making valiant attempts to suppress his giggles.

"Keep it down," I whispered.

"She's almost there," Michael said, his voice even lower. "Couple more steps."

"Don't look up," I said. "Until it happens."

Tommy turned his head away as soon as he saw Miss Pippin's fingers wrap themselves around the spine of *Moby-Dick*. She gave the book a slight tug, inching it from its wedged-in slot. It slipped easily into her hand, releasing the pressure on the other books on the shelf, causing them all to fall in her direction.

The first two landed on the side of Miss Pippin's head, undoing the red ribbon in her hair and slamming her eyeglasses to the ground. A flurry of other books collapsed around her, loosening her grip on the ladder. The flat pages of an open novel hit her square on the chin, her body lurching down, off the ladder, to the ground.

"Oh, shit," Tommy yelled. "She's gonna fall."

Miss Pippin landed on her back, her eyes closed and her legs spread apart at angles. She lay quiet, an occasional moan rising up from the back of her throat. The copy of *Moby-Dick* was still clutched in her right hand.

"You think she's dead?" John asked, standing away from the table, his mouth open, his eyes fixed on Miss Pippin. "She can't be dead."

"Let's get outta here," Tommy said, stepping away from the crowd forming around the motionless librarian. "Let's get out now."

"Not until we find out if she's okay," Michael said.

An old woman, her arms wrapped around Miss Pippin's head, shouted for smelling salts. Two other women ran by with small cups filled with water from a cooler. A maintenance man, standing in a corner, leaning on the arm of a mop, mumbled on about calling an ambulance.

We stood in a group, a good distance from the crowd, aware of the suspicious eyes cast in our direction. John was the most nervous, lines of concern etched across his face. Tommy was sweating through his T-shirt, his breath coming in rushes. Michael's arms were folded against his chest, staring back at those who looked his way, masking his fear with a defiant stance.

I STOOD NEXT TO him, aware that whatever harm had been caused to Miss Pippin was my fault. I had performed the crammed-book trick dozens of times, each time to gales of laughter. This was the first time something bad had happened, and I didn't like how that made me feel.

I watched with outward relief as the hands and arms of three coworkers helped Miss Pippin to her feet. She stood unsteadily, her back resting against the shelf where the damage had been done, dozens of books scattered about her.

"Looks like she's gonna be okay," Michael said to me.

"Let's go, then," I said.

"In a minute," Tommy said. "Something I gotta do first."

"Let it go," John said. "Then for sure they'll get wise."

Tommy ignored the plea and stepped through the small cluster gathered around Miss Pippin, searching among the fallen books until he found the copy of *Moby-Dick*. He scooped it up and turned to face a still-dazed Miss Pippin.

"Thanks for finding the book," he said to her. "Didn't mean for you to go to all that trouble."

"You're welcome," she said, watching as Tommy turned his back and walked out of the library, slapping *Moby-Dick* against his thigh.

*   *   *

I WAS STANDING IN THE DOORWAY OF THE BUILDING next to Mimi's Pizzeria, licking an Italian ice, trying not to let the melting liquid drip onto my new white T-shirt.

"You know what crap like that does to your body?" Father Bobby asked, coming up to my left, a cigarette dangling from his lips. "Have you any idea?"

"Beats smoking," I said. "Cheaper too."

"Maybe," he said, tossing the cigarette to the ground and twisting it out with the heel of his sneaker. "So, what do you hear? Anything?"

"Nothing," I said. "Quiet. Nothing to do except wait to go to school."

Father Bobby was wearing a Yankee T-shirt under a blue button windbreaker, gray sweats, white socks, and low-cut Flyers, fresh from a two-hour basketball game. His face was ruddy, his hair combed back and still wet with sweat. Since he had been raised in the neighborhood, he pretty much knew all the rules and how best to break them. Anything we had *thought* of doing, he had already done years before. He never preached to us, fully aware that long sermons were not the way to go with my group. But he knew we liked and respected him and cared what he thought. There were so many ways to fall on the streets of Hell's Kitchen. Father Bobby tried to be there to break those falls.

"What about what happened at the library the other day?" he said, stepping up into the doorway next to me. "That sounded exciting."

"You mean Miss Pippin?" I asked, finishing the last of the ice.

Father Bobby nodded.

"That was rough," I said. "All those books falling on her. It was scary."

"I heard you were there," he said. "The other guys too. Looking for something good to read, I suppose."

"Something like that," I said.

"Strange business," he said, leaning even closer. "You know, a whole shelf of books falling on top of somebody's head. How do you figure a thing like that happens?"

"Accident, I guess," I said.

"Must be it," he said. "What else could it be?"

I wiped my hands and mouth with the clean corner of a folded napkin and said nothing.

Father Bobby pulled his hands out of his pockets, a stick of Juicy Fruit between his right thumb and forefinger. He had a smile on his face.

"It's got a name," he said, offering me the gum.

"What?" I asked, declining with a shake of my head.

"The shelf trick you and your buddies pulled. It's called keepers. I played it when I was your age. Never could get the whole shelf down though. You must be pretty good at it."

"Father," I said. "I don't know what you're talking about."

"Maybe I'm wrong," he said, still smiling. "Maybe I got wind of the wrong information."

"Sounds like you did," I said, shifting my weight. "Well, I'd better get going."

"I'll see you later tonight," Father Bobby said, turning away and walking toward the corner.

"What's tonight?" I asked.

"Going to drop off some books and magazines around the neighborhood," he said. "You know, for the elderly and disabled. People who can't get out on their own. I checked with your mother. She said you'd love to help."

"I bet she did."

"She wants you to be a priest, you know," he said as he wedged the slice of Juicy Fruit into his mouth.

"Do you?" I asked.

"I just want you to stay outta trouble, Shakes," Father Bobby said. "That's my only wish. For you and your friends."

"Nothin' else?"

"Nothin' else," Father Bobby said. "I swear."

"Priests shouldn't swear," I said.

"And kids shouldn't dump a row of books on a librarian," he said, waving and turning the corner, heading for church.

6

SUMMER 1964

WE HAD FOUR BATH TOWELS SPREAD ACROSS THE HOT black tar of the roof. A cooler filled with chunks of ice and a six-pack of 7Up rested against a slate-gray chimney. A portable radio played Diana Ross, singing soft and low. Clotheslines, crisscrossing rooftops and bent under the weight of laundry, supplied the only shade.

"It can't get any hotter," John said, his eyes closed to the sun, his upper body lobster red.

"Let's go swimming," I suggested, sitting next to him, the sun baking my back.

"We just got here," Michael said, lying down on the towel closest to the edge, an ice cube melting on his chest.

"So?" I said.

"I'm with Shakes." Tommy left his towel for the cool of the clotheslines. "I feel like an egg up here. We could get us some buttered rolls, a few more sodas, and head down to the docks."

"I'm still on my burn," Michael said.

"And Mrs. Hudson hasn't come home from work yet," John said. "*Nobody* can leave without seeing her."

Mrs. Hudson was a part-time secretary for a midtown travel agent. She wore short dresses and high heels in the summer and no bras the year round. She was married to a Pepsi-Cola truck driver who had two large hawks tattooed across both shoulders. She had a brown cat named Ginger and a loud wing-clipped parakeet who sat perched near her living room window and tweaked at the street traffic three stories below.

She left work every day at three-fifteen and headed straight for her apartment. During the hottest months she would strip off her clothes and sit by an open window, trying to catch a breeze. When her mood was light, she would look up at the roof across the way, smile, and wave.

Mrs. Hudson was the first naked woman any of us had ever seen.

Most days, she crossed the bedroom to the bathroom and washed her hair in the sink. She then returned to the open window and brushed her dark brown hair in the warmth of the sun.

As she brushed, we focused on her breasts. They were prob-ably average size, but appeared massive to our youthful eyes. Whatever her motives, Mrs. Hudson seemed to enjoy this summer ritual as much as we did.

"Here she comes!" Tommy shouted. "Right on time."

Within seconds, the four of us were perched by the edge of the roof. Mrs. Hudson was making her way down 51st Street, dressed in a black halter top and a black skirt cut at the thighs. Her pumps were white, the heels adding several inches to her height.

"I can't believe her husband lets her outta the house lookin' like that," I said.

"I can't believe her husband lets her outta the house," John said.

"She fool around, you think?" Tommy asked.

"I hope so," Michael said. "And I hope someday she'll fool around with me."

"Like you would know what to do," I said.

"What's to know?" Michael demanded.

"It's like the old song," John said. A smile spread across his face and his eyes lasered down on Mrs. Hudson as he broke into a high-voiced melody. "My body lies over the ocean. My body lies over the sea. My father lied over my mother. And that's how I came to be."

"Shakes is just nervous because he ain't ever done anybody," Tommy said.

I was incredulous. "What? You have?"

"You know Katie Riggio?" Tommy asked.

"The one with the iron teeth?"

"Braces, moron," Tommy said. "Anyway, I kinda did her last month."

"Where?" I asked.

"Forget where," Michael said, turning away from Mrs. Hudson. "How?"

"We went to a movie." Tommy started blushing, sorry now he ever mentioned the night and the girl.

"What movie?"

"I forget," Tommy said. "Something with James Coburn."

"He's pretty cool," I said. "You ever see *The Magnificent Seven*?"

"Forget James Coburn," Michael said. "Get to the good stuff."

"After the movie we went for a walk." Tommy now lifted his face to the sun. "Then I bought her an ice cream cone."

"*Bought* her an ice cream cone," John said, his eyes wide. "You *must* be in love."

"It was nice, you know," Tommy said. "Just walkin' and holdin' her hand."

"When did she drop her pants?" Michael cut in.

"In the hall of her aunt's apartment."

"Standing up?" I said.

"Against the wall," Tommy said.

"What did you do?" I asked, watching Mrs. Hudson appear in her window, breasts flopping against her chest.

"Fingered her," Tommy said.

"How'd it feel?" John asked.

"Like I had my hand in a glazed doughnut."

"Lucky bastard," Michael said.

"Wonder what it would feel like having your fingers inside Mrs. Hudson?" I asked.

"Like being inside a glazed doughnut *factory*," John said.

Our loud laughter caught Mrs. Hudson's attention. She stood up, stretched, and smiled.

"Maybe someday we'll know," I said.

"Maybe someday we'll all know," Michael said.

"It's something to live for," Tommy said.

"Sure is," John said. "It sure is."

* * *

THERE ARE FEW SECRETS INSIDE THE THIN WALLS OF A tenement.

Many nights would be spent staring up at a white ceiling, listening to passionate moans coming from a back room or an apartment across the hall. Our parents conducted their sexual lives as openly as they pursued their violent fights. We lived in the midst of a peasant stronghold, bred on foreign soil and lacking in physical inhibitions. Our folks were not, as a rule, liberal-minded, so talk of sex made them uncomfortable. But they would always return a direct question with a direct response.

The apartments were so cramped that private moments were difficult. During the summer, every available window was opened wide, dozens of voices bouncing off the back alleys below. Inside the shabby buildings, the men stripped down to their socks and underwear and women paraded about in bras, slips, and house slippers, shame taking a backseat to comfort.

Winter brought the opposite.

The rooms would turn so bitterly cold, the lack of heat would be so numbing, there was little else to do but huddle together under however many blankets could be found. We slept sitting up, on chairs, in front of the gas stove which would be left on all night, our stocking feet resting on the open door. You were never alone.

Out on the street, sex was a hot topic. Older guys talked in graphic terms about girls they had seduced, winking as they spoke. Pictures of naked women, ripped from the pages of skin magazines, were regularly passed down the aisles at school.

MICHAEL WAS THE MOST sexually experienced of the group, which meant that he had kissed a girl on more than one occasion. Since he was the oldest, he was also the only one of us invited to parties where girls outnumbered the boys. Those parties inevitably led to slow walks up the stairs to what was commonly known as tar beach. There, across the rooftops of Hell's Kitchen, many a neighborhood boy lost his virginity in the arms of an older, somewhat wiser, young woman.

While we attended many such parties, we were still a few years away from any serious sexual activity. If an older woman—which meant anyone older than we were—smiled in our direction, we considered the evening a success. If, on top of that, a jealous boyfriend didn't throw a punch at us when he caught her smiling, we went home thinking we were as cool as Steve McQueen.

We sought our romantic escapades elsewhere, often in the company of Carol Martinez, twelve, who was as much our friend as she was Michael's steady. Carol was a Hell's Kitchen half-breed. She inherited her temper and dark good looks from her Puerto Rican father, while her sarcastic wit and sharp tongue came courtesy of a strong-willed Irish mother who died in childbirth. Carol read books, worked after school in a bakery, and, by and large, kept to herself.

She ignored the pleas of the girl gangs to join their ranks, never carried a weapon, loved westerns as well as sappy love stories, and went to church only when the nuns forced her to go. Except for her father, Carol wasn't close to any members of her family and always appeared saddest around the holidays. The mothers of the neighborhood were fond of her, the fathers looked out for her, and the boys kept their distance.

Except for us. She was always comfortable in our company. She stood up to Michael's quiet authority, was conscious of my youth and Tommy's sensitivity, and fretted like a nurse over John's various illnesses. John had asthma and was quick to panic when caught in closed quarters or in any place he felt at a disadvantage, such as swimming far from shore. He also had a digestive defect and could not eat dairy products. He would get severe headaches, strong enough at times to make him drowsy. While John never complained about his health problems, including his minor heart condition, we were very much aware of them and considered them whenever we planned a prank or an outing.

So, while the older kids of Hell's Kitchen discovered sex on rooftops or in parked cars by the piers or in movie theater balconies, we sought a sense of romance in more traditional places. The five of us would sneak rides on the backs of horse-drawn carriages in Central Park, each taking a turn holding Carol's hand as the driver made his way around office buildings and apartment houses. We drank hot chocolate and watched older couples skate under the Rockefeller Center Christmas tree. We would walk through De Witt Clinton Park late at night, our shadows lit by a full moon, eating ice cream and telling Carol stupid jokes, in the hopes of making her laugh. If she did, she had to pay the laugh back with a kiss. She was a tough room to work, except when John told one of his jokes. Then, Carol would always laugh.

We would go to the circus, staring down from high up in the cheap seats at the long legs and firm breasts of the women who rode on top of the elephants, wondering if they would feel as soft and sexy next to us as they looked at a distance. We ignored Carol when she said that up close the women would look older than our mothers and be about as attractive.

Then, there were the Ice Capades.

The show would come into Madison Square Garden once a year, with the female skaters using the dressing rooms whose windows faced the 51st Street side of the Garden. The windows were thick and difficult to see through, with a wire-mesh barrier locked over them to prevent anyone from entering. But we weren't interested in *going* in, we were interested in *looking* in.

Two nights before the show was scheduled to arrive, we would go up to the street-level windows and, using a ratchet screw Michael had taken from his father's tool chest, would bore small holes into one of the windows. While we worked, Carol reluctantly stood watch. Within minutes, we had four holes in the window, one for each of us to press an eye onto.

On opening night, while crowds of families lined the front of the Garden waiting to see the skaters perform, my friends and I stood outside, bent over the window, one eye in each hole we had made, our mouths open wide, our imaginations running at full throttle, watching two dozen beautiful women, almost naked, get into their skater's outfits.

"This," Tommy said with assurance, "is what heaven must be about."

"In heaven they let you in," Michael said.

"Or at least give you chairs," John said.

For the three weeks of the show's run, my friends and I never missed our chance to see the Ice Capades.

7

WE WERE WELL SCHOOLED IN REVENGE.

Hell's Kitchen offered graduate workshops in correcting wrongs. Any form of betrayal had to be confronted and settled. Our standing in the neighborhood depended on how quickly and in what manner the reprisals occurred. If there was no response, then the injured party earned a coward's label, its weight as great as that of any scarlet letter. Men, boys, women, girls, were shot, stabbed, even killed for a variety of motives, all having to do with the simple act of getting even.

THE NEIGHBORHOOD HAD A long and proud criminal history.

IT WAS THE BIRTHPLACE of some of the more notorious gangs in America—the Gophers, the Gorillas, and the Parlor Mob Boys among them. It was also the home of Battle Annie Walsh, a chain-smoking, quick-tempered woman in charge of a band of female leg breakers. Walsh and her ladies were hired by downtown landlords to collect their past-due rents. On other days they would roam the streets and beat up anybody who caught their perverse fancies. The tabloids referred to Annie's crew as the Battle Row Ladies' Social and Athletic Club. The people in the area weren't as kind.

Hell's Kitchen also gave birth to three of the more infamous men of the early twentieth century—Cotton Club owner Owney "Killer" Madden, baby-killer Vincent "Mad Dog" Coll, and Monk Eastman, a shooter who left our streets a wanted man and returned a decorated World War I hero.

Once upon a time, early in its history, Hell's Kitchen was one of the more peaceful areas of Manhattan, known for its scenic beauty, wide expanses of grassy fields, stately homes, and cobbled streets. Much of it was farmland. It was *the* place for the moneyed crowds of Greenwich Village to spend lazy summer days playing by the water, picnicking under the stars, watching ships sail across the Hudson. Back then, they called it anything but hell.

The tenements and slaughterhouses arrived after the Civil War. Gangs, bringing with them the twin demons of graft and corruption, followed at the turn of the century. As the years passed and gangs grew in number, the violence spread. Riots were routine. Apartment doors were sealed shut with fear, the rattle of the newly constructed passing el trains helping to drown out the sounds of even the loudest gunshots. The neighborhood for which John Jacob Astor once, in 1803, paid a purchase price of $25,000, had, by the 1860s, turned into a dank and disreputable place, to be avoided by all but the desperate.

Out of the rubble of each passing decade rose a leader with a past as colorful as his name.

There was Dutch Heinrich, bossman of the Hell's Kitchen gang and a forerunner of famed bank robber Willie Sutton. Dutch never used a weapon, oozed charm and sincerity, and stole only from places known to carry large sums of money and securities. He took the Union Trust Company for $99,000 in 1872, using his gifts of bluff and blarney.

"One Lung" Curran was considered the best brawler ever to

walk the streets of Hell's Kitchen, this despite the fact that he was a tubercular and couldn't go more than fifteen minutes without spitting up thick wads of blood. Dr. Thomas "Lookup" Evans was an ex-con turned abortionist who took care of any brothel hooker who found herself pregnant. He committed suicide, allegedly after one of his abortion attempts ended in a woman's death.

Martin "Bully" Morrison was the first self-anointed king of Hell's Kitchen. He and his two sons, Jock and Bull, preyed on neighborhood Catholics, stealing everything from their pocket money to the chalices in their churches, out of which they greedily drank down buckets of beer.

By the time Owney Madden arrived to lay claim to his criminal throne, a sturdier brand of order had been restored to the streets. During Madden's reign, which stretched across the 1920s and '30s, more than 300,000 people lived in the area, mostly newly arrived German and Irish immigrants. The majority found work along the suddenly expansive waterfront, loading and unloading cargo inside the bellies of an endless supply of ships that fed into the harbor. Others sought work in the slaughterhouses that still dotted the neighborhood, killing cattle, goats, and pigs for low wages and one two-pound package of take-home meat a week. Still others opened saloons and diners, which would serve as watering holes and haunts for the laborers and their families.

Proceeds from each business made their way into Madden's pockets, in return for which he introduced the rules that kept the neighborhood in line. He helped turn it into a place where families could live, a place that was safe to everyone except strangers.

Johnny "Cockeye" Dunn took over after Madden's time passed. Under his leadership, the underground economy of Hell's Kitchen thrived, fed by stolen goods from all areas of the city. Prime cuts of meat and fresh fish were available at bargain prices. Off-the-rack jackets and slacks, price tags still visible, hung seductively in open trunks parked in friendly warehouses. Henchmen like Big John Savona took orders for shoes and leather belts, shipments that were hand delivered on the last Thursday of every month.

THERE WAS ALWAYS WORK to be had in Hell's Kitchen and the age of the employee was never a serious consideration. The better-paying jobs were illegal. In a neighborhood where fathers were always late with the rent or behind on loan shark payments, kids went for the easy money, dropping off paper bags at the precinct house or picking up numbers at the end of the day.

PETTY LARCENY AMONG THE Hell's Kitchen young also had its historical roots. At the turn of the century, children were sent out by their parents to steal coal and wood from the nearby rail yards and docks. Lifting the wallets of sailors on shore leave was a practice passed down from one generation to the next. Walking across town to steal groceries from the better-stocked markets was a habit that persevered well into the 1950s.

Corruption was a way of life in Hell's Kitchen and no profession was left unblemished. There were three resident doctors who worked the neighborhood, each making house calls on a regular basis. The fees, $5 or $10 depending on the doctor, were paid in cash. The insurance claim that was then filled out and signed by both the doctor and one of our parents listed the fee as $30. When the check arrived from the insurance company, the doctor was given a cut of the action. Again, in cash. The same practice, only in different form, held true for the pharmacists and dentists who worked the area.

"I saw the doctor at least once a week," Tommy once told me. "When I was sick and when I wasn't. He'd come over, sit at the kitchen table, have a cup of coffee, a piece of cake, and figure out what was wrong with me. Half the time he didn't even check me out. It was a great system. My mother would buy groceries from her end of the insurance money and the doctor eventually bought a house with his. Makes you wonder why they ever gave up house calls."

From the youngest age, a Hell's Kitchen child was told it was wrong to steal from anyone who lived in the neighborhood. The church was also sacred ground. Street muggings were rare, and the price for attacking an elderly person was steep.

Rumor circulated about one tough guy who robbed an old lady. He didn't hit her, just took her purse and the eight dollars it held. Word got out and the mugger was found. He had both his arms and legs broken and two fingers of each hand were removed. After that, when kids saw old ladies in the street, they *gave* them money. There were rules on those streets. Serious rules.

When my friends and I were young, Hell's Kitchen was run by a man named King Benny.

In his youth, King Benny had been a hit man for Charles "Lucky" Luciano and was said to have been one of the shooters who machine-gunned "Mad Dog" Coll on West 23rd Street on the night of February 8, 1932. King Benny ran bootleg with "Dutch" Schultz, owned a couple of clubs with "Tough Tony" Anastasia, and owned a string of tenements on West 49th Street, all listed in his mother's name. He was tall, well over six feet, with thick dark hair and eyes that never seemed to move. He was married to a woman who lived outside the neighborhood and had no children of his own.

"He was fourteen when I first met him," my father told me one night. "Wasn't much of anything back then. Always getting the shit kicked out of him in street fights. Then, one day, for who knows what reason, an Irish guy, about twenty-five years old, takes him and throws him down a flight of stairs. King Benny breaks all his front teeth in the fall. He waits eight years to get that Irish guy. Walks in on him in a public bathhouse, guy soaking in a tub. King Benny looks in a mirror, takes out his front teeth, lays them on a sink. Looks down at the guy in the tub and says, 'When I look in a mirror, I see your face.' King Benny pulls out a gun and shoots the guy twice in each leg. Then says to him, 'Now when you take a bath, you see mine.' Nobody ever fucked with King Benny after that."

* * *

THE LARGE ROOM WAS WRAPPED IN DARKNESS. THREE men in black jackets and black sport shirts sat at a table by an open window, playing *sette bello* and smoking unfiltered ciga-rettes. Above them, a dim bulb dangled from a knotted cord. Behind them, a jukebox played Italian love songs. None of the men spoke.

At the far end of the room, a tall, thin man stood behind a half-moon bar, scanning the daily racing sheet. A large white cup filled with espresso was on his left, a Kenmore alarm clock ticked away on his right. He was dressed in black shirt, sweater, shoes, and slacks, with a large oval-shaped ring on the fourth finger of his left hand. His hair was slicked back and his face was clean shaven. He chewed a small piece of gum and had a thick wood toothpick in the corner of his mouth.

I turned the knob on the old wooden door that led into the room and swung it open, thin shafts of afternoon sunlight creeping in behind me. No one looked up as I walked toward King Benny, the heels of my shoes scraping against the floor.

"Can I talk to you for a minute?" I asked, standing across

from him, on the far side of the bar, my back to the three men playing cards.

King Benny looked up from his racing sheet and nodded. He reached out for his coffee, raised it to his lips, and took a slow sip, eyes still on me.

"I would like to work for you," I said. "Help you out, do whatever you need."

King Benny put the cup back on the bar and wiped his lower lip with two fingers. His eyes didn't move.

"I can be a lot of help to you," I said. "You can count on that."

One of the men playing cards slid his chair back, stood up, and walked toward me.

"You the butcher's kid, am I right?" he asked, his three-day-old beard growing in gray, the bottoms of his teeth brown and caked.

"Yeah," I said.

"Well, what kind of work you lookin' for?" he asked, leaning his head toward King Benny.

"Whatever," I said. "It doesn't matter."

"I don't think we got anything, kid," he said. "Somebody musta steered you some wrong info."

"Nobody steered me wrong," I said. "Everybody says this is the place to come to for jobs."

"Who's everybody?" the man said.

"People from the neighborhood," I said.

"Oh," the man said. "Them. Well, let me ask ya, what the fuck do they know?"

"They know you guys got jobs," I said, moving my eyes from the old man and back to King Benny.

"Smart ass," the old man said, turning away, heading back to his chair and his game.

King Benny and I looked at each other, the coffee by his side growing cold.

"Sorry I wasted your time," I told him, looking away and heading toward the door.

I pulled the knob and opened it, letting in some gusts of air, letting out wisps of smoke.

"Hold it a minute," King Benny finally said.

"Yeah?" I said, turning my head to face him.

"Come back tomorrow," King Benny said. "If you wanna work."

"What time tomorrow?"

"Anytime," King Benny said, his eyes back on the racing sheet, his hand reaching for the cold cup of coffee.

* * *

MY FIRST JOB FOR KING BENNY PAID $25 A WEEK AND ate up only forty minutes of my time. Twice a week, on Monday mornings before school and Friday afternoons after dismissal, I went to the large room on 12th Avenue, where King Benny conducted his business. There, one of the three men would hand me a crumpled paper bag and direct me to one of the two nearby police precincts for its delivery.

It was a perfect way to handle payouts. Even if we got caught with the drop money, there wasn't anything the law could do about it. Nobody was going to jail for simply handing somebody a paper bag. Especially a kid.

NOT LONG AFTER I began work for King Benny, I was walking across Tenth Avenue, a paper bag filled with money nestled under my right arm. The spring afternoon was warm and cloudless; a mild threat of rain had disappeared with the lunchtime traffic. I stopped at the corner of 48th Street, waiting while two trucks drove past, leaving dust and fumes in their noisy wake.

I didn't notice the two men standing behind me.

The shorter of the two, dressed in tan slacks and a brown windbreaker, leaned across and grabbed my elbow, pulling me closer to him. The second man, taller and stronger, locked one of his arms into mine.

"Keep walkin'," he said. "Make a sound, you die."

"Where are we going?" I asked, trying to disguise my panic.

"Shut up," the shorter man said.

We had shifted direction and were moving toward the waterfront, walking down 47th Street, past a car wash and an all-night gas station. The shorter man tightened his grip on my arm as we walked, his foul breath warm on my neck.

"Here we are," he said. "Get in there. C'mon. Stop stallin'."

"You guys gotta be nuts," I said. "You know who you're takin' off?"

"Yeah, we know," the tall man said. "And we're scared shit-less."

The tall man ripped the paper bag from under my arm and pushed me crashing through the front of a tenement doorway. The inside hallway was dark and narrow, bloodred walls cold to the touch. A forty-watt bulb cast the stairs and cement floor in shadow. Three garbage cans, lids on tight, were lined up along-side the super's first-floor apartment. Down the far end of the hall a wood door, leading to a cluttered backyard, creaked open.

I was on my knees, watching the two men count the money from the paper bag. They stopped when they saw me staring.

"This is a lot of money for a kid," the tall man said, smiling. "Don't know if I would trust a kid like you with this much money. What if you lose it?"

"It's only money," I said, looking behind me at the door that led out the back way.

"Whatta ya get outta this?" the short man asked me. "What's your cut?"

"Don't get a cut," I said.

"Then you ain't nowhere as smart as you think," the short man said.

"Lots of people tell me that," I said, getting to my feet, rubbing my hands against my pants legs.

The tall man rolled the money back up, rubber bands holding the two bundles in place, and put them in the paper bag. He crumpled the bag again and shoved it inside the front pocket of his jacket. The short man had turned his back to me, checking out the street traffic through the open doorway.

Then the super's door clicked open.

The super, an old man in a sleeveless T-shirt and brown corduroy pants, stood in his doorway, staring at the three strangers in his building.

"What you do?" he said in a husky Italian accent. "Answer me. What you do here?"

"Relax," the tall man said, his words tight, controlled. "We were just leavin'. Okay with you?"

"What you do to the boy?" the old man asked, stepping out of the doorway, his arms by his sides, walking closer to me.

"They took my money," I said to the old man. "They followed me and took my money."

"You take money?" the old man asked, his voice an angry challenge.

"Kid's talkin' trouble," the tall man said. "Don't listen to him."

"It's in the bag," I said. "The money they took is in the bag."

The super's eyes moved to the paper bag, stuffed inside the tall man's jacket.

"Lemme see the bag," the old man said.

"Fuck you," the tall man said.

The old man brought a hand to the small of his back, his manner calm, his eyes steady. The hand came back holding a cocked .38-caliber pistol, its shiny silver cylinder pointed at the tall man's chest.

"Lemme see the bag," the old man said again.

The tall man took the bag from his jacket pocket and handed it to the old man, careful not to make a sudden move. The old man tossed the bag to me.

"Get out," he said. "Use the back door."

"What about them?" I asked.

"You care?"

"No," I said.

"Then go."

I turned around, shoved the bag under my arm, and ran out the building. I jumped the short back fence, cut through a small alleyway, and came out on 11th Avenue.

I never looked back, not even when I heard the four shots that were fired.

* * *

"I NEED SOMEBODY WITH ME," I SAID TO KING BENNY. "What if that old guy hadn't showed?"

"But he did," a man to King Benny's left said. "And he took care of it."

"Maybe next time we don't walk into the wrong building," I said, sweat lining my face.

"There ain't no next time," the man said, lighting a cigar.

"Maybe you just ain't up for the work," another of King Benny's men said. "Ain't as easy as you was thinkin'."

"I'm up to it," I insisted.

"Then there's no problem," the man behind me said.

King Benny brushed a stream of cigar smoke away from his eyes. His look was cold and steady, his black jacket and slacks sleek and tailored, a large-faced Mickey Mouse watch strapped to his left wrist.

"Whatta ya need?" he asked me, his lips barely moving as he spoke.

"My friends," I said.

"Your friends?" the man behind me asked, a laugh to the question. "What do you think this is, *camp*?"

"It won't cost you extra," I said. "You can take the money out of my end."

"Who are these friends?" King Benny asked.

"From the neighborhood." I looked directly at him. "You know their families, just like you know mine."

The guy behind me threw his hands up in the air. "We can't trust no kids."

"These kids you can trust," I said.

King Benny brushed aside a fresh stream of cigar smoke, pushed his chair back, and stood.

"Get your friends," he said, then turned and walked toward the rear of the room. "And, Tony," King Benny continued without looking back, his shoulders straight, his walk slow, his damaged right leg sliding across the floor.

"Yeah, King?" the man with the cigar in his mouth asked.

"Never smoke in here again," King Benny said.

8

FAT MANCHO WAS THE MEANEST MAN IN HELL'S KITCHEN and we loved him for it. He owned a candy store sandwiched between two tenements in the middle of 50th Street. His wife, a dour woman with a thin scar across her right cheek, lived on the second floor of one building. His mistress, who looked to be older than his wife, lived on the third floor of the other. Each woman collected monthly social security checks based on false disability claims. Both checks were signed over to Fat Mancho.

In the back room of the candy store, Fat Mancho ran a numbers operation, keeping for himself a quarter of every dollar that was bet. The store was owned, on paper, by Fat Mancho's mother, who allegedly lived in Puerto Rico and was never seen by anyone in Hell's Kitchen. Fat Mancho, who collected monthly welfare checks, also owned a piece of an open-air parking lot on West 54th Street, near the theater district. Fat Mancho was only in his mid-thirties, but because of his large bulk and unshaven face looked at least ten years older. He cursed at anyone he saw, had trust in only a handful, and made it his business to know everything that went on in the streets around him. Fat Mancho lived the American dream without ever having to do a day's work.

In Hell's Kitchen, the fast way was the preferred way.

———

WE WERE STANDING IN front of Fat Mancho's candy store, waiting to turn on the johnny pump. I had the heavy wrench hidden halfway down the back of my pants; my T-shirt hung out, covering what the jeans could not. John was next to me, an empty can of Chock Full o' Nuts coffee in his hand, both ends cut out. Behind us, two Puerto Rican rummies were giving Fat Mancho heat over the price of a can of Colt .45 malt liquor.

While it could safely be said that Fat Mancho hated most everyone he met, for some reason he tolerated us. To him, we were harmless street rats out for nothing more than a good time. He liked to joke with us, poke fun at everything we did, and insult us whenever he felt the urge. We had known him all our lives and felt that he trusted us. We would never steal from him or try to deceive him in any way. We never asked for money and never caused trouble in front of his store. He liked our company, liked it when we gave back as good as we got from him, his eyes gleaming on the rare occasions we bested his taunts. We always felt that Fat Mancho had a good heart and that he liked kids. He just never wanted anybody to know that.

"What is that shit anyway?" John wanted to know, pointing to the Colt .45s.

"Beer mixed with piss," Tommy told him, one foot resting on the fire hydrant in front of the store.

"Then the drunks are right," John said. "Mancho *is* chargin' them too much."

"When you gonna open up the pump?" Tommy asked.

"Cops are due for one more pass around," Michael said, standing behind him. "After that."

"Hey, Mancho," John yelled into the back of the store.

"What?" Fat Man said.

Can I use your bathroom?" John asked.

"Fuck you, punk," Fat Mancho said, laughing. This was his idea of major fun. "Wet your pants."

"That a no?" John asked me.

"I think so." I shrugged.

"Hey, Mancho," Tommy said. "Give the guy a break. He's really got to go."

"Blow me," Fat Mancho said, having a great time.

"That's it," Tommy said. "We're never gonna buy from your store again."

"Kill yourself," Fat Mancho said.

"C'mon," I said to John. "You can go at my place. I gotta pick something up anyway."

"You sure?"

"It's either there or the back of Fat Mancho's car," I said.

"Where's he parked?" John said.

"Let's go," I said.

* * *

APARTMENT DOORS IN HELL'S KITCHEN WERE NEVER locked during the day and ours was no exception. John and I took the two flights at full throttle, chasing Mrs. Aletti's black alley cat up the stairs ahead of us. We scooted past the large potted plant outside Mrs. Blake's and rushed to my door. I turned the handle and walked into the kitchen, John right behind me. The bathroom was on the left, next to the kitchen table, a Padre Pio calendar tacked to the wooden door which, for reasons known only to the previous tenant, locked from the outside. I could hear my mother whistling an Italian pop song from one of the back rooms. A fresh pot of espresso was on the stove, and two cups and a sugar bowl were on the table.

"Didn't think I was gonna make it," John said, reaching for the bathroom door.

"Hurry," I said. "Before you pee on the floor."

The door swung open and both John and I stood as still as ice sculptures.

There, on the bowl, in full white habit, sat Sister Carolyn Saunders, my second-grade teacher and one of my mother's best friends. She stared back, as motionless as we were.

She had a wad of toilet paper bunched up in one hand.

"Holy shit!" John said.

"Oh my God!" said Sister Carolyn.

We were back on the street in seconds, John nearly tripping down the final steps in his rush to get out of the building. Michael and Tommy were pitching pennies against a brick wall.

"That was quick," Michael said. "What'd you do, start in the hallway?"

"I'm dead," I said. "Dead and buried."

Tommy looked confused. "Because John took a piss in your house?"

"We saw a nun." John was bent over, hands to knees, trying to catch his breath.

"Where?" Michael asked. "In the hall?"

"On the bowl!" John said. "She was sittin' on Shakes's toilet! Takin' a piss!"

"No shit," Tommy said. "You never think of nuns doin' stuff like that."

"Which nun?" Michael asked.

"Sister Carolyn," I said, still shaking from the memory.

"Good choice," Tommy said. "She's really cute."

"Did you see her snatch?" Michael asked.

"A nun's snatch!" John said. "We're gonna burn like twigs for this, Shakes!"

"Relax," Michael said. "Nothin's gonna happen."

"What makes you so sure?" I asked.

"She's a nun, right? So she's not gonna tell. If people find out, it's more trouble for her than it is for you."

"Maybe," John wailed. "But we still shouldn't've seen what we saw."

"Are you kidding me?" Tommy said. "It don't get better than nun snatch."

"I only saw skin," John said. "I swear it. White clothes and white skin. Nothin' else."

"She say anything?" Tommy asked.

"Ask her yourself," Michael said, looking over John's shoulder. "She's coming this way."

"My heart just stopped," John said, his face pale, his voice cracking.

"She's coming for us," I said, turning my head in Sister Carolyn's direction, watching her walk down the steps of my apartment building, check for traffic, and make her way to where we were standing.

"What the fuck's that nun want?" Fat Mancho said, slurping a Yoo-Hoo and scratching at his three-day growth.

"Stay quiet, Fat Man," Michael said.

"Eat my pole," Fat Mancho said, walking back behind the bodega counter.

"Hello, boys," Sister Carolyn said, her manner calm, her voice soft.

She was young, her face clear and unlined. She was Boston big-city bred and had spent three years in Latin America working with the poor before a transfer brought her to Sacred Heart. Sister Carolyn was popular with her students and respected by their parents and, unlike some of the other nuns of the parish, seemed at ease among the people of Hell's Kitchen. Though she spoke no Italian and my mother hardly a word of English, they had formed a solid friendship, with Sister Carolyn visiting her an average of three times a week. She knew the type of marriage my mother was in and was always quick to check in on her after my father had administered yet another beating.

"Hey, Sister," Michael said casually. "What's goin' on?"

Sister Carolyn smiled and put one hand on top of John's shoulder. Nothing but fear was keeping John in his place.

"The bathroom's free now if you still need to use it," she said to him softly.

"Thank you," John mumbled.

"We're very sorry," I said.

"I know," she said. "Forget it happened. I already have."

"Thank you, Sister," I said.

"I'll see all you boys in church," she said, turning to leave.

"Bet on it," Tommy said.

"What a peach," John said, watching her as she walked up the street back to the convent on 51st, her long white skirt swaying at her feet.

"And not a bad-lookin' ass either," Michael said, winking at me.

"Fuck do any o' you know about ass," Fat Mancho said from behind his counter.

"I'm gonna go pee," John said, running back across the street. "Can't hold it in anymore."

"Watch now," Tommy said to me. "This time he walks in on your mother coppin' a squat."

"That happens," Michael said. "He might as well just throw himself out a window."

"He should throw himself out a window anyway," Fat Mancho said. "Useless fuck."

"Go wash your mouth out with shit, Fat Man," Tommy said.

"Set yourself on fire," Fat Mancho said. "All of you. Burn till you die."

We all looked over at Fat Mancho and laughed, walking away from his store, toward the fire hydrant and a dose of wet relief from the heat of the day.

9

FATHER ROBERT CARILLO WAS A LONGSHOREMAN'S SON who was as comfortable sitting on a barstool in a back-alley saloon as he was standing at the altar during high mass. Raised in Hell's Kitchen, he toyed with a life of petty crime before finding his religious calling. Carillo left for a midwestern seminary three weeks before his sixteenth birthday. When he returned ten years later, he asked to be assigned to the Sacred Heart parish.

As far as we were concerned, he wasn't like a priest at all. He would spring for pizza after an afternoon pickup game or twist a few neighborhood arms and raise money for new sports equipment for the gym. He was a friend. A friend who just happened to be a priest.

Like us, Father Bobby had an extensive comic book and baseball card collection, was an avid boxing fan, and favored James Cagney over any other actor. He had a small office near the back of the church, lined with books and old blues albums. At its center was a huge framed picture of Jack London standing on a snowbank. If I was ever tempted to steal something from Father Bobby's office, it was that picture.

Despite the criminal bent of the neighborhood, the church exerted considerable influence and its leaders were visible members of the community. Priests openly recruited boys for the priesthood, presenting the clerical life as a way out of Hell's Kitchen. Nuns often took girls aside to talk to them in frank terms about sex and violence.

The priests, nuns, and brothers of the neighborhood knew they served a violent clientele and they were there to tend to our physical and psychological wounds. They listened to battered wives who came to them for solace and gave words of comfort to frightened children. They helped when and where they could, careful not to stray outside the established framework of the neighborhood and always aware that there were a number of situations over which they held no control.

The clergy knew the rules of Hell's Kitchen. They knew some people had to break the law in order to feed their families. They knew the clothes many of us wore were bootlegged and the meat most of us ate came from stolen trucks. And they knew not to butt heads with someone like King Benny. But in the ways they could, they helped us. If nothing else, they offered a quiet room, some hot coffee, and a place to talk when you needed it. Few people in the neighborhood would have asked more from any religion.

Father Bobby cared for us in a significant way, and as much as we were capable of loving an outsider, we loved him for that care.

He knew the problems my mother and father were having, of the beatings she was handed and the debts he incurred. He tried to balance that by talking to me about books and baseball and verbally guiding me away from the fast money and easy times offered by King Benny and his crew.

He understood Michael's instinctive resistance to any outsider, even one from the neighborhood. He saw in Michael a boy who was given very little reason to trust. He sensed the loneliness behind his tough talk and the fear hidden by his swagger. Father Bobby knew that Michael was a boy who merely longed for a father who did more than lash out at his only son. He gave Michael distance, leaving a book he would like at his desk rather than handing it to him after school. He fed his streak of independence instead of fighting it.

He joked with John, keying in on a sense of humor built around insults and fast comebacks. He traded comic books with him, giving up valued *Flash* editions for mediocre *Fantastic Four* exploits, ignoring the sucker snickers after the deals were completed. On John's tenth birthday, he gave him a *Classics Illustrated* edition of *The Count of Monte Cristo*, a gift that moved John to tears.

He encouraged John's quiet desires to be an artist, sneaking him an endless supply of pencils and paper. In return, John would give Father Bobby original illustrations from a comic book series he was working on. John was also his favorite altar boy and Father Bobby made it a point to work as many masses with him as possible, even if it meant pulling him out of an early class.

"John would have made a good priest," Father Bobby told me years later. "He was filled with goodness. He cared about people. But he had a knack, like all you boys did, of being in the wrong place at the worst possible time. A lot of people have that knack and seem to survive. John couldn't."

BUT OF ALL OF US, Father Bobby was closest to Tommy.

BUTTER NEVER ADJUSTED TO having a father away in prison and, while he never talked about it, we knew it gnawed at his otherwise happy nature. Father Bobby tried to fill the paternal void, playing one-on-one basketball with him on spring evenings, taking him to James Bond movies on winter nights, helping him manage the pigeon coop Tommy kept on the roof of his building. He made sure Tommy was never alone on Father's Day.

Father Bobby had the soul of a priest but the instincts of a first-grade detective. He was a vigilant neighborhood presence, the first to take our class on outings and the first to question our outside involvements. He knew my friends and I did work for King Benny and was not pleased by that fact. But he understood the need for table money. In his time, Father Bobby had helped augment his own family's income by running errands for "Lucky" Jack and the Anastasia family.

He wasn't worried about the pocket money. He worried about the next step. The one where they ask you to pick up a gun. He didn't want that to happen to us. He wanted to get to the damage before it got started. Before we saw too many things we shouldn't be seeing. Unfortunately, there were things even Father Bobby couldn't prevent.

* * *

THE SCHOOL AUDITORIUM WAS FILLED TO OVERFLOW WITH balloons, poker tables topped with pitchers of beer and bowls of pretzels. Paper banners wishing the bride and groom luck lined the walls. A bald disc jockey in a wrinkled tux stood on a small stage, focused on a large stereo, four speakers, and three piles of records.

It was a neighborhood wedding reception, open to all.

The bride, a tall, dark-haired girl from 52nd Street, was five months pregnant and spent most of her time locked inside a bathroom off the main stairwell. The groom, a Mobil mechanic with bad teeth and a black beard, drank boilermakers and munched peanuts from a paper bag, well aware of the talk that said the child his wife carried belonged to someone else.

Outside, the night was rainy. Inside, large corner fans did nothing to still the heat.

"You know either one of 'em?" Tommy asked, chafing at the starched collar and tight tie around his neck.

"The guy," I said, drinking from a bottle of Pepsi. "You know him too. From the gas station. Lets us drink from his water hose."

"You're not used to seeing him without grease on his face," Michael said, filling the pockets of his blue blazer with salt pretzels.

"You think it's his kid?" Tommy asked.

"Could be anybody's kid," Michael said. "She's not exactly shy."

"Why's he marrying her?" I said. "I mean, if *you* know all about her, how come he doesn't?"

"Maybe it *is* his kid," Tommy said. "Maybe she told him it was. You don't know."

"That's right, Tommy," Carol Martinez said. "You *don't* know."

She was wearing a blue ruffled dress with a small white flower pinned at the waist. She had on ankle socks and her Buster Browns were shiny and new. Her hair was in a ponytail.

"Everybody's here," John said when he saw her.

"I'm a friend of Connie's," Carol said.

"Who's Connie?" John said.

"The bride, asswipe," Michael said, and led Carol by the arm off to dance.

*   *   *

THE THREE MEN CAME IN JUST AS THE BRIDE AND GROOM started slicing the three-tiered wedding cake. They stood off to the side, their backs to the front door, their hands nursing long-necked bottles of Budweiser. One of them had a lit cigarette hanging from the corner of his mouth.

We were standing in the shadows next to the disc jockey,

Michael and Carol holding hands, Tommy and John sneaking beers. I held a Sam Cooke 45, "Twistin' the Night Away," which was next on the play list.

"You know 'em?" Michael asked, putting his arm around Carol's shoulders.

"The one with the cigarette," I said. "I've seen him in King Benny's place a few times."

"What's he do for him?"

"He always passed himself off as a shooter," I said. "I don't know. Could be nothing more than talk."

"Why's he here?" Tommy asked.

"Maybe he likes weddings," John said.

THE THREE MEN WALKED toward the center of the room, their eyes on the groom, who was eating cake and sipping champagne from the back of his wife's spike-heeled shoe. They stopped directly across the table from the couple and rested their beers on a stack of paper plates.

"What do you want?" the groom asked, wiping his lips with the back of his hand.

"We come to offer our best," the man in the middle said. "To you and to the girl."

"You just done that," the groom said. "Now maybe you should leave."

"No cake?" the man in the middle said.

The crowd around the table had grown silent.

"C'mon, guys," a middle-aged man said, his speech slurred, the front of his white shirt wet from beer. "A wedding's no place for problems."

The man stared him back into silence.

"Maybe your friend's right," the man said. "Maybe a wedding's no place for what we have to do. Let's take it outside."

"I don't wanna go outside," the groom said.

"You got the money?"

"No," the groom said. "I ain't got that kind of money. I told you that already. It's gonna take a while."

"If you don't have the money," the man said, nodding toward the bride, "you know the deal."

She had not moved since the men approached, paper plate full of cake in one hand, empty champagne glass in the other, heavily made up face flushed red.

"I ain't gonna give her up," the groom said in a firm voice. "I ain't ever gonna give her up."

The man in the middle was quiet for a moment. Then he nodded and said, "Enjoy the rest of your night."

The three men turned away from the bride and groom and disappeared into the crowd, making their way toward the back door and the dark street.

* * *

WE SAT BRACED AGAINST THE THIN BARS OF THE FIRST floor fire escape, staring at the alley below. Four garbage cans and an empty refrigerator carton stood against one wall; the shadows of a forty-watt bulb filtered across the auditorium's back door. The rain had picked up, a steady Hudson River breeze blowing newly laundered sheets across the dirt and empty cans of the alley.

Michael had positioned us there. He was positive something was going to happen and he'd picked the most strategic place to observe the action.

We watched as the bride and groom stood in the narrow doorway, arms wrapped around each other, both drunk, kissing and hugging. The harsh light from the auditorium forced us to move back toward the window ledge.

The groom took his wife by the hand and stepped into the alley, moving toward 51st Street, holding a half-empty bottle of Piels in his free hand. They stopped to wave at a handful of friends crowding across a doorway, the men drunk, the women shivering in the face of the rain.

"Don't leave any beer behind," the groom shouted. "It's paid for."

"Count on that," one of the drunks shouted back.

"Good-bye," the bride said, still waving. "Thank you for everything."

"Let's go," the groom now said to his new wife. "It's our wedding night." With that, a grin stretched across his face.

The first bullet came out of the darkness and hit the groom just above his brown belt buckle, sinking him to his knees, a stunned look on his face. The bride gave out a loud scream, hands held across her chest, eyes wide, her husband bleeding just inches away.

The group by the door stood motionless, frozen.

The second shot, coming from the rear of the alley, hit the groom in the throat, dropping him face first onto the pavement.

"Help!" the bride screamed. "Jesus, God, please help! He's gonna die! Please help, *please!*"

No one moved. No one spoke. The faces in the doorway had inched deeper into the shadows, more concerned with avoiding the shooter's scope than with rushing to the side of a fallen friend.

SIRENS BLARED IN THE DISTANCE.

The bride was on her knees, blood staining the front of her gown, crying over the body of her dying husband. A priest ran into the alley, toward the couple. An elderly woman came out of the auditorium holding a large white towel packed with ice, water flowing down the sides of her dress. Two young men, sobered by the shooting, moved out of the doorway to stare down at the puddles of blood.

"Let's get outta here," John said quietly.

"So much for getting married," I said just as quietly.

Michael, Tommy, and Carol said nothing. But I knew what they were all thinking. It was what we were all thinking.

The street had won. The street would always win.

10

Fall 1965

MY FRIENDS AND I WERE UNITED IN TRUST.

There was never a question about our loyalty. We fed off each other, talked our way into and out of problems and served as buffers against the violence we encountered daily. Our friendship was a tactic of survival.

We each wanted a better life, but were unsure how to get it. We knew enough, though, to anchor our hopes in simple goals. In our idle moments, we never imagined running large companies or finding cures for diseases or holding elected office. Those dreams belonged to other places, other boys.

Our fantasies were shaped by the books we read and reread and the movies we watched over and over until even the dullest dialogue was committed to memory. Stories of romance and adventure, of great escapes and greater tastes of freedom. Stories that brought victory and cheers to the poor, allowing them to bask in the afterglow of revenge.

We never needed to leave the cocoon of Hell's Kitchen to glimpse those dreams.

We lived inside every book we read, every movie we saw. We were Cagney in *Angels with Dirty Faces* and Gable in *The*

Call of the Wild. We were *Ivanhoe* on our own city streets and the Knights of the Round Table in our clubhouse.

It was during those uninhibited moments of pretend play that we were allowed the luxury of childhood. Faced by outsiders, we had to be tough, acting older than our years. In our homes we had to be wary, never knowing when the next violent moment would come. But when we were alone we could be who we really were—kids.

We never pictured ourselves, as adults, living far from Hell's Kitchen. Our lives were plotted out at birth. We would try to finish high school, fall in love with a local girl, get a working-man's job, and move into a railroad apartment at a reasonable rent. We didn't see it as confining, but rather as a dramatic step in the right direction. Our fathers were men with sinful pasts and criminal records. We would not be.

I loved my parents. I respected King Benny. But my friends meant more to me than any adult. They were my lifeblood and my strength. Our simple dreams were nourished by a common soil.

We thought we would know each other forever.

* * *

"IT'S SIMPLE," MICHAEL SAID.

"You always say it's simple," Tommy said. "Then we get there and it ain't so simple."

"It's a new store," Michael explained. "Nobody knows us. We walk in, take what we need, and walk out."

"What do they have?" John demanded to know.

"At least fifty different titles," Michael said. *"Flash, Green Lantern, Aquaman,* you name it. Just waiting for us."

"How many work the store?" I asked.

"Two, usually," Michael said. "Never more than three."

"When?"

"Afternoon's the best time."

"You sure?"

"Follow the plan," Michael said, looking at us. "It'll work if we just follow the plan."

* * *

MY FRIENDS AND I WERE THIEVES WHO STOLE MORE FOR fun than profit. We took what we felt we needed but could not afford to buy. We never went to our parents for money, never borrowed from anyone, and never walked into a situation armed.

We hit candy stores for their comic books, toy stores for games, supermarkets for gum. And we were good at it. The few times we were caught, we either talked, fought, or cried our way out of trouble. We knew that *nobody* was going to send a kid to jail for rounding out a *Classics Illustrated* collection.

We kept our escapades from our parents. Though most of them were involved in small-time scams of their own, none would have been pleased to know their children were chasing fast on their heels. Still, Thou shalt not steal carried little weight in Hell's Kitchen. The neighborhood was a training ground for young criminals and had been throughout most of its history.

At the turn of the century, child thieves were called street sparrows. Many were orphaned, all were desperate. Bands of pickpockets roamed the streets, looking for a *hook* carrying a week's pay in his wallet. A few of the children were even brazen enough to hire themselves out as assassins, willing to kill for fees as low as three dollars. If captured, no matter how large or small their crimes, punishment was severe. The New York State prison system had little patience for street hoodlums of any age, and often sentenced them to long stretches in upstate hell-holes. The children of the streets accepted the sentences, powerless to do otherwise. If they survived their time behind bars, they came out deadlier than when they entered, schooled by older lawbreakers. If one happened to die while in custody, he became just another name on a crowded blotter.

The Russell Sage Foundation was formed in the early 1900s to study the living conditions of the children of Hell's Kitchen and determine if those conditions led to crime. After months surrounded by squalor and rampant despair, the social workers walked away with a hardened view. In one report, cited in Richard O'Connor's excellent 1958 history of the neighborhood, the plight of a Hell's Kitchen child was summed up in this manner: "The district is a spider's web. Of those who come to it, few ever leave. Now and then a boy is taken to the country or a family moves to the Bronx. Usually those who live here find they cannot get out. . . . The philosophy of the West Side youngster is practical and not speculative. Otherwise he could not fail to notice that the world in general, from the mother who bundles him out of an overcrowded tenement, to the grown-ups in the street playground where most of his time is spent, seem to think him very much in the way. . . . Everything he does seems to be against the law. If he plays ball he is endangering property. If he plays marbles or pitches pennies he is obstructing the sidewalk. Street fighting is assault and a boy guilty of none of these things may be loitering. In other words, he finds that property or its representatives are great obstacles between him and his pleasures in the street."

HELL'S KITCHEN HAD CHANGED physically in the decades since the Russell Sage Commission issued its report. Gone were the elevated trains, the boxcars filled with cattle heading for the Midwest that rumbled past tenement windows. The cows were still shipped by rail to slaughter, only now they traveled on flat rails. The streets were no longer strewn with garbage, but, considering the poverty of the area, clean and well kept. Graffiti was nonexistent and the storefronts and stoops of the apartment buildings were washed down regularly by the building superintendents.

The apartments were painted, by law, every three years, each room the same shade of white. It was not only the cheapest color; many thought the thick, oil-based mixture killed roach eggs and helped drive out rodents. For new occupants, the first three months in an apartment were free, an incentive offered by landlords to attract tenants to unattractive dwellings. It was not an unusual occurrence, therefore, for families to move as often as four times in a single year, sometimes on the same street, in order to live without ever paying rent.

Few could afford phones in their apartments, and so they lined up outside candy stores and bars. If someone did have a phone, the odds were he was either a bookie or a loan shark. No one else had that kind of money or needed to use the phone that often.

There was an order to life in Hell's Kitchen, one that remained undisturbed by the crime, murder, and madness. A sense of safety existed on those streets and in our apartments despite a diet of gang battles, contract killings, and domestic strife. There was a comfort zone to the violence, an acceptance of it as part of daily life, a lethal legacy passed from one generation to the next.

Money was tight, but there were certain barriers we wouldn't cross. "We followed the neighborhood rules," Tommy said one late night. "We stayed away from drugs, didn't touch booze, and carried no guns. We weren't interested in that stuff anyway. We didn't need a gun to get a comic book or pinch a meal in a restaurant. We were smarter than guys who pulled stickups. Maybe we didn't have the kind of pocket money they did, but we didn't have to duck into a hallway whenever a cop car passed by, either."

But we were thieves nonetheless, and working for King Benny emboldened our thievery.

Time spent in the company of made men, their allegiance sworn to a life of crime, led to a desire to flex our own criminal muscles. Where once we were content to walk out of a store with a handful of *Green Hornets,* we now felt the need to empty entire racks, from *Sgt. Rock* to the *Fantastic Four.*

In the neighborhood, the gaze on us intensified with each small job we pulled. The old-line hoods would glance our way, an acknowledged nod toward a new generation, as active in their recruiting methods as any Ivy League headhunter. We were the promise, the raw rookies who could one day hold the neighborhood together, score the deals, and keep the illegal traffic moving.

There were many roads a young man could travel on the streets of Hell's Kitchen. None promised great rewards. The majority turned into dead ends.

Career criminal was simply one such option.

* * *

MICHAEL WAS THE FIRST ONE IN THE CANDY STORE.

I followed soon after. Tommy and John—Butter and the Count—waited outside, close to the front door. The entry was curved and narrow, a hardwood candy stand running down the length of the counter. Two men worked the place, both middle-aged, both smoking. A small electric fan, pennant strips attached to the rim, whirred in a side corner.

Michael walked to the comic book racks, reached for a *Batman,* and handed it to me.

"Read that one yet?" he asked.

"No," I said, looking over my shoulder at the two men cutting open candy cartons. "It's new."

"Want it?"

"Not today," I said.

"What is it, Shakes?" Michael asked, racking back the *Batman.*

"Let's not do this," I said, lowering my voice to a whisper.

"Why not?"

"It just doesn't feel right."

"We're here *now,*" Michael said.

"And we can leave *now.*"

"Don't crap on me now, Shakes. We can do this. You and me."

"It feels different this time," I said.

"It feels different every time," Michael said.

"You sure?" I asked.

"I'm sure," Michael said.

I hesitated, then I nodded my compliance. "Make your move," I said.

Michael pulled three comic books from a top rack, well aware that the two men were staring in his direction. I took four *Sgt. Rock* comics from a lower shelf, put them under my right arm, and followed Michael farther down the aisle. Behind me, one of the men lifted the countertop and began to walk toward us. He was tall and thin, thick dark hair sitting in clumps on the sides of his head and a large, circular scar resting below his left eye. He had a small iron pipe in one hand.

Tommy and John came into the store, pushing and shoving as per the plan. The man behind the counter stared at them between puffs on a fresh cigarette.

"No trouble. No trouble in here," he said, his voice thick with a foreign accent, his cigarette filter clenched between stained teeth.

"I don't want trouble," John said to him, pushing Tommy against the newspaper trays. "I want candy."

"That's the last time you push me," Tommy said, picking up a paper and throwing it at John.

"Stop it!" the man behind the counter shouted. "Outside. You like a fight? Go outside."

The thin man facing us turned and walked away, moving toward Tommy and John and the front of the store. He walked slowly, slapping the base of the pipe against the palm of his hand.

"Get out, punks," the man said, giving John's shoulder a shove. "Get out!"

John turned and faced the store owner. Angrily, he put both hands on the man's shirtfront and pushed him back.

"Don't touch me," he said, watching the man tumble backward, the pipe falling on top of discarded editions of the *New York Post*.

Things immediately got out of hand. The man jumped to his feet, his face red with embarrassment, and rushed John, catching him around the chest and dropping him to the ground. He straddled John's upper body and gripped his face with one hand while the other formed a fist.

Tommy ran up from behind. He threw one arm around the man's throat and shoved a knee into the base of his spine.

Michael and I made our way to the front of the store, the sides of our jackets filled with dozens of comic books. We kept our eyes on the man behind the counter, watching for him to make a move. He never looked our way, frozen by the sight of his partner in a scrap with two boys.

John now freed one arm and landed two short blows to the man's stomach. Tommy scored with a steady torrent on the side of the man's head, causing his ear and temple to flush. The man fell to one side, tumbling off John, the bulk of his weight resting against the candy counter. One arm was dangling, free, inches from the iron pipe he had moments earlier dropped.

"We ain't *ever* comin' here again," John said, back on his feet, shouting at the man behind the counter. He reached over, picked up a copy of the *Daily News,* and threw it down on the head of his fallen enemy.

Michael and I moved past Tommy, John, and the two men and walked out of the store, our stolen gains snug in their place.

John turned and followed us out. That left Tommy alone with the two men.

And before any of us knew what was happening, the man on the ground grabbed the iron pipe and came to his feet swinging, mouth twisted in rage.

"I kill you, punk!" he shouted. "I kill you!"

The blows landed in rapid succession.

The first blow glanced off Tommy's shoulder. The second found a spot above his right eye, drawing blood. The third landed on the hard edge of Tommy's left wrist, the bone immediately giving way.

Tommy, his knees buckling from the pain, inched his way out of the store. A fourth shot caught him on the back of the neck, sending him crashing against the door and out to the street. Tommy fell to the cement, his eyes lifeless, his body limp.

John was the first to reach his side. "I think he killed him," he said, staring up at me and Michael.

"Then he's gonna have to kill us too," Michael said.

"I no fight you," the man with the pipe said, his anger receding, his arms by his sides. "No problem with you. No problem!"

"Yeah you do," Michael said as he nudged his way forward. "Your *only* problem is with me."

Michael opened the front of his blue denim jacket and reached a hand into one of the inside sleeves. He pulled out four folded, stolen comic books and dropped them to the ground. Then he yanked four more books from his other sleeve. When he reached both hands into the back of his jeans and took out three more, dropping them all at his feet, the man moved toward him, stepping over Tommy's body.

"I kill all of you," he said with teeth clenched.

"You're gonna have to," Michael said, balling his hands into fists, an arm's length from the pipe.

"This is bad," I remember saying. "This is so bad."

The man left his feet and swung the pipe, missing Michael's head by inches.

My eye caught John, his arms around Tommy, sweat streaking down his forehead, concern etched on his face. As a crowd collected, I looked at the faces surrounding me, the men focused on the action, most of them smoking, a few offering Michael free advice.

No one ever broke up a fight on the streets of Hell's Kitchen, no matter who the combatants were, regardless of the weapons used. A street fight was a respected ritual and no one dared step in.

Fights took place for any number of reasons, from unpaid debts to three-way love affairs gone sour, but the overwhelming majority occurred because they were the fastest and easiest way to settle a dispute.

Great street fights were talked about in the same nostalgic manner in which old boxers were recalled. The more street fights somebody had, the higher the esteem in which he was held.

Short of murder, nothing proved manhood more.

Michael swung a sharp right and missed, grunting loudly as the punch sailed over the man's head. A fast follow-up left also failed. Large sweat circles formed on the back of his jacket and under both arms. As the crowd drew closer, the man moved to narrow the gap between the two. He took three steps forward, flashing the pipe, holding it low, squinting against the overhead sun, staring at Michael's face.

He swung the pipe, short, fast, and hard, landing one across Michael's hip. A second blow caught him on the side of the face. Another quick swing, this one grazing Michael's jaw, sent him backward, hands reaching for the ground, his head just missing the side of a fire hydrant.

The man walked to where Michael lay and raised the pipe over his head.

"You no steal from me again," he said in a voice meant for everyone to hear. "*Nobody* steal from me again."

Michael's arms hugged the hydrant, his eyes cloudy, thin streams of blood streaking down his lips. John stood next to Tommy, his face emptied of all emotion other than fear. Butter still had his back to the candy store wall. There were tears running down his face.

I couldn't move. I stood there, shivering in the afternoon sun, my legs heavy and numb, my stomach queasy, looking down at the beaten body of my best friend.

The crowd sensed a finish and closed the circle even tighter, breaking off any chance of a quick escape.

The street wanted someone to die.

"Drop the pipe!"

The voice came out of the shadows.

It was confident and webbed with the threat of violence. The man with the iron pipe took two steps back when he heard it, panic invading his macho veneer. I turned my head and saw King Benny standing there, a cup of espresso in one hand, a copy of *Il Progresso* in the other. He was flanked by two men, dressed in black, arms at their sides.

"Didn't hear me?" King Benny asked.

"Yes," the man said, his voice breaking. "I hear."

"Then do it," King Benny said.

The pipe fell to the ground, loud enough to echo.

"You wanna finish this?" King Benny asked, looking down at Michael.

"Yeah," Michael said, pulling himself up against the side of the hydrant. "I do."

"Then hurry," King Benny said. "It's gettin' late."

Michael was up on shaky legs. He turned and faced his opponent.

"Fight me," Michael said to him.

"No," the man said, his eyes on King Benny.

Michael charged the man, both of them falling to the ground, arms and legs in full swing. He landed two hard punches against the side of the man's head and then threw a crushing elbow to the base of his nose.

The man swung once and missed, a steamless punch thrown more in frustration than anger. Michael answered with two more closed blows to the face, the second drawing blood. The men in the crowd whistled and applauded each landed punch.

"Kid's got him now," a fat man in an oil-stained work shirt said. "Couple more, the bastard'll be done for good."

"Too bad he ain't got a knife," a short man lighting a pipe said. "He could cut him for sure."

Michael landed three more punches, all flush to the man's face. He jumped to his knees, slamming an ankle against the man's throat. Two more punches to the neck and a quick kick to the chest brought it to an end.

Michael stepped over the man, ignored the pleas of the crowd to finish his foe, and walked to the comic books strewn on the ground. He bent down, picked each up, and went back to where he had left the man. He stood over him, staring for a minute, and then dropped the comic books across his face and chest.

"You can keep your comic books," Michael said. "I don't want 'em anymore."

11

As we grew older, the violence around us intensified. The moment a boy's age hit double digits, he was no longer a mere nuisance to the older neighborhood kids; he was a potential threat. The most minor infractions could easily escalate into major street brawls.

We had now also reached an age where we were targeted by outsiders looking for quick scores.

Puerto Ricans coming down from San Juan Hill in upper Manhattan would jump a kid, lift his money, and head back home. Blacks from Inwood, near the Heights, would cross the designated racial divide of Ninth Avenue. Traveling in packs of a half-dozen or more, they would swarm, attack, and leave before any retaliation could be mounted.

A number of the local street gangs attempted to recruit us, without success. The idea of being a gang member never held much appeal and neither did the idea that we had to kick back portions of earnings to the leader of the pack we joined.

We also weren't keen on the initiation process most gangs required: rubbing hot pieces of iron on your arm until all the skin came off; scarring you with strange, permanent tattoos; forcing you to pick a fight with the toughest guy from a rival gang, and *if* you beat him you were in. If you lost, you were a forgotten man. It wasn't for us. We stayed with who we trusted and we covered each other's backs. Just like in the western movies we admired.

* * *

THE WORST BEATING I EVER GOT IN HELL'S KITCHEN CAME not from my father or any other man or boy. It was at the hands of Janet Rivera, street leader of the Tornadoes.

GIRL GANGS HAD, THROUGHOUT Hell's Kitchen history, been in many ways the most vicious. Unlike their male counterparts, the girls often attacked without warning or reason. They were also the more aggressive criminals, wantonly stalking passersby for street muggings and casing buildings for doorway robberies. They did not belong to any organized crime faction, but worked as independent operators, hired out for the best price.

IN THE '60S, THESE GANGS could already trace their lineage back to the Lady Gophers, who terrorized the Manhattan waterfront at the turn of the century. The Lady Gophers had a special calling card: They left the amputated hands and fingers of their victims behind. A few years later, Sadie the Cat and her crew beat and mugged at will. Gallus Meg was a match for any man she came across, boasting till death of never having lost a fistfight. Hellcat Maggie was said to have once beaten four of the toughest members of the Pug Uglies Gang into submission on a Tenth Avenue street corner, then taken a fifth one home to her boardinghouse bed.

A number of the female gang leaders who lived long enough

to survive their street battles opened saloons in their later years. Not surprisingly, many served as bouncers in their own watering holes.

"They *demanded* respect, those women," one of King Benny's back-room men once told me. "They didn't take any shit, they were always ready for a fight. Knew how to run a business, too, turned a profit on most things they touched. They were tough and mean and everything they did, they made sure they did better than a man. They fought dirty, drank till they were drunk, and slept with whoever they wanted. For a time there, they ran the Kitchen and they ran it well."

The prevailing image of the mid-twentieth-century Hell's Kitchen street gang comes from the musical *West Side Story*. While Leonard Bernstein's masterpiece contains traces of truth—the racial tensions, a sense of place, the fear of falling in love on forbidden turf, the inability to move beyond social labels—such elements weren't enough for neighborhood cynics.

West Side Story was the most hated film in Hell's Kitchen.

"That movie sucked," Fat Mancho complained. "Guys dancin' around like jerks, girls hangin' on to their boys for life, cops dumb as flies. All bullshit. Made the gangs look soft. Made *everybody* look soft. In real life, soft didn't last long. They *buried* soft in Hell's Kitchen."

* * *

JANET RIVERA STOOD IN FRONT OF THE MONUMENT AT the entrance to De Witt Clinton Park and popped the lid of a can of Rheingold. She was with three friends, all members of her street gang. One of them, Vickie Gonzalez, had a straight razor in the back pocket of her Levi's. Janet swigged the beer and watched me walk into the park with John, both of us bouncing spauldeens against the ground.

"Hey!" she yelled. "Get your asses over where I can see them."

"Now what," John muttered.

"They're just breakin' balls," I said. "We got no beef with them."

"We got no time for this," John said.

"Let's see what they want," I said.

"C'mon," Rivera said. "Don't be draggin' ass on me."

"She is one ugly girl," John said as we made our way toward the monument. "Her family must take ugly pills."

"You pricks walk through the park like you own it," Rivera said, pointing at us with the hand holding the beer. "Where the fuck you think you're goin'?"

"We're gonna play some ball," I said. "I don't think there's a problem with that."

"You're wrong," Rivera said. "There is a major fuckin' problem."

"Fill us in, gorgeous," John said.

We knew what the problem was. Two weeks earlier, Michael, rushing to Tommy's defense, got into a street brawl with a Puerto Rican kid named Rapo from the West 60s. He won the fight and forced Rapo to walk out of Hell's Kitchen buck naked. Unfortunately, Rapo was Janet Rivera's cousin, and she was looking to us for a payback.

Vickie Gonzalez put a hand in the pocket that held the razor. The other two girls wrapped sets of brass knuckles around their hands. Janet Rivera tossed her beer can into a clump of grass behind her. None of them looked happy. What *would* make them happy would be to leave me and John the way Michael had left Rivera's cousin—beaten, bruised, and naked. Neither one of us was eager to see that happen, and it left us with only one choice, one that any tough, street-savvy Hell's Kitchen hard case would have made. We decided to run.

"Through the fence!" I yelled to John as we started. "Head for the candy store."

"They catch us, we're dead," John said. "That ugly one wants to kill me. I can tell."

"They're *all* ugly," I said, looking over my shoulder. "And what's worse is they're *all* fast."

We ran through a circular hole in a fence on the 11th Avenue side of the fields, across the red clay pitcher's mound and out the other side, past the Parkies' way station and the sprinkler pool. We were crisscrossing around the black pool bars when I slipped on a sandhill and landed on my side against a cement edge.

John stopped when he saw me fall.

"Get up, Shakes," he urged. "They're right on us."

"I can't," I said.

"You better," John said.

The pain in my side was intense, jolts sharp and sudden.

"You keep running," I said. "Go for Butter and Mikey. Get them here."

"I can't leave you," John said.

"You'll be back in five minutes," I said a lot more bravely than I felt. "What can they do to me in five minutes?"

I stayed on the ground, clutching my side, watching John run down the hills of De Witt Clinton Park.

It was not the fear of getting a beating that held me. It was the fear of catching that beating from a girl gang. As I lay there, watching Rivera and her crew close in, I imagined the taunts and ridicule that would come, from friends and strangers alike. A lot of boys in Hell's Kitchen took home cuts and bruises handed out by Rivera and her Tornadoes. Not one of them ever admitted to it, at least publicly, and I was not about to be the first.

Janet Rivera stood over me and smiled, exposing a thin row

of cracked teeth. "I knew a little fucker like you couldn't out-run us."

"You didn't outrun me," I said. "I took a break and waited for you to catch up."

Rivera walked over toward Gonzalez, putting one hand around her shoulder.

"I *hate* clowns," she said. "They're not funny, you know? They only *think* they're funny."

"What they did to Rapo, that ain't funny neither," Gonzalez said, brushing the heel of her sneaker against my leg. "But I bet they laughed."

"Gimme your belt," Rivera said. "We're gonna teach this clown to be serious."

The park was empty except for an old rummy sleeping under a pile of newspapers on a bench. My face and arms were glazed with sweat and my right leg twitched from tension. One of my shoelaces had come undone and I couldn't breathe free of pain.

Gonzalez stood over me and opened her straight razor. She leaned down and grabbed the top of my white shirt and cut it in half, stopping just above my pants.

"This is for Rapo," Rivera said, swinging the belt above her shoulder.

"Hurt him," Gonzalez said. "Make him hurt."

Rivera's lashes landed across my face and neck, the pain causing my eyes to well with tears. She then lowered the gate of her swing, my chest and stomach now taking the force of the blows. My chest was soon red, the sting as hard as anything I'd felt, a steady torrent of belt against flesh.

Rivera landed one last blow and stopped.

"You wanna piece?" she said to Gonzalez.

"He ain't man enough for me to whip," Gonzalez said, look-ing at me with a smile.

"Thank you," I mumbled.

The first rock landed next to Rivera's feet. The second hit her above the thigh. Gonzalez turned her head and caught one on the arm. The two girls who were holding me down let go and moved away.

"We're goin'," one of them said. "No more of this."

I looked past Gonzalez, at the fence behind the sprinklers and saw Michael and John climbing over. Tommy stood facing the fence, tossing rocks over the side.

Gonzalez looked down at me, her eyes filled with hate. She took a deep breath, bent closer to me, and spit her bubble gum above my right eye. She took two steps back and let out two kicks to my groin, the hard rubber of her sneakers finding a mark both times.

"So long, fucker," she said. "Be seein' you again."

When they got to me, Michael and John lifted me up, hands wrapped under my shoulders.

I was slow stepping my way out of the park, toward the bar on 52nd Street. The inside of my chest felt as seared as the outside. But more than anything, I was humiliated.

"I don't want anybody to know," I said.

"Might be in the papers tomorrow," John smirked. "Not every day one of King Benny's boys gets his ass bopped by some girls."

"It would've been better if they killed me," I said.

"You're right," Tommy said. "Much easier to explain."

"This only proves what we always knew," Michael said.

"What?"

"You can't fight for shit."

"I hear they make guys have sex with 'em," John said. "You know, force 'em."

"Now I'm sorry we came along," Michael said. "You might have finally gotten laid."

"I think I'm gonna faint," I said.

"Ugly sex is better than no sex," John said.

"Anybody asks, tell 'em a gang from Inwood came down and kicked my ass," I said.

"Which gang?" Tommy asked.

"The Cougars," I said. "They're pretty tough."

"How about the gang from the School for the Blind?" John said. "You could say they bumped into you on the street. You had no choice. You hadda fight 'em."

"There was eight of them and only one of you," Tommy said. "The deck was stacked."

"And they had dogs too," John said. "You didn't have a chance."

"All I know is the Count of Monte Cristo never got his ass kicked by a girl," Michael said.

"He was lucky," I sighed. "He didn't know Janet Rivera."

12

SUMMER 1966

MY FRIENDS AND I WERE AS CONSUMED BY SPORTS AS we were by books and movies. We followed every pro sport with religious fervor and adolescent passion, except for golf, which was too silly to be considered, and tennis, which we thought was played only in England.

We were rabid New York Rangers fans. Our favorite player was Earl Ingerfield, a hard-skating journeyman who often made it a point to talk to us outside the team doorway. He gave us new hockey sticks every season, which we used in the street games we played on the cement grounds of Printing High School. A crushed can or a roll of black tape was our puck; we wore sneakers in place of skates and our net was a wall.

We loved boxing, finding grace and a certain degree of solace in the savagery of the sport. Middleweight contender Joey Archer was the local hero, winning most of the bouts he fought inside Madison Square Garden. But we found his style dull and plodding compared to the inside power and speed of Dick Tiger, a brave warrior from Nigeria who would eventually wear both the middleweight and light-heavyweight crowns. In later years, Tiger died much before his time, an impoverished man who had seen his country turn into war-ravaged Biafra, and whose new leaders stole his fortune.

We went to the six-day bike races in the fall and listened to Italian and Irish soccer matches on portable radios. We cared little for Knicks basketball and barely tolerated Giants football, though we played both sports with frenzy. We followed horse racing more out of habit than interest. In Hell's Kitchen, the track was sacred ground and the bulk of the betting was on the nine daily races coming out of whichever local track was in session.

But the sport we loved the most was baseball.

On summer afternoons we flipped baseball cards against other kids, looking to walk away with a bundle of new and valuable additions. We memorized statistics of current and former players and were able to cite the most mundane. We followed the daily exploits of our favorite New York Yankees as if they were members of our own families. We winced if Tom Tresh had a bad day at the plate, Clete Boyer committed a rare error at third base, or Al Downing gave up another long home run. The Yankee teams of those years weren't really very good, but they were still the Yankees. *Our* Yankees. They were losers but they *acted* like winners. Just like us. Which is why we all loved them so much.

* * *

WE WERE SITTING ON THE FRONT STOOP OF MY APARTment building, shoeboxes filled with baseball cards by our feet. It was the last week of August 1966 and the New York Yankees were, for the first time in our lives, a last-place team.

"Tough loss," Tommy said, reading the box scores in the *Daily News*. "Now even the *Indians* are beatin' us."

"There's always the Mets," John said.

"Retards root for the Mets," Tommy said.

"What'd Mantle do yesterday?" Michael asked.

"Didn't play," Tommy told him.

"He's hurt," I said. "Again."

"Who they play tonight?" Michael asked.

"The Orioles," Tommy said. "Stottlemyre's pitching."

"Wanna go?" Michael asked.

"What's the point," I sulked.

"We'd get good seats," Michael said.

"Maybe they'll go on a tear," Tommy said. "Win about twenty-five in a row. Get back in the race."

"Maybe you'll wake up good-lookin'," John said.

"Nobody even wants to trade for 'em this year," I said, holding a handful of Yankee baseball cards.

"I got three Frank Robinsons and two Boog Powells," John said, looking through a shoebox. "Who you got?"

"Who you want?" Tommy asked.

"Tommy Davis," John said. "Powell for Davis straight up."

"I got Davis," I said.

"Trade?" John asked.

"I don't know about straight up," I said. "Davis is good."

"What?" John said. "Powell's a cripple?"

"Make the trade," Michael said.

"Straight up?" I said.

"Seems like a good deal," Michael said.

"How about you throw in a pitcher?" I asked John. "Any pitcher. I don't care who."

"Why?" John asked.

"Gives the deal weight," I said.

"Forget it," John said. "Powell for Davis. That's all."

"I got a Boog Powell," Tommy chimed in. "Only it's from last year."

"Doesn't matter," I said.

"You're gonna trade with *him* now?" John asked.

"Only if he gives me what I want," I said. "Powell and a pitcher for Davis."

"Diego Segui," John said. "I'll give you Diego Segui and Boog Powell for Tommy Davis."

"That's your best offer?" I asked.

"That's my *only* offer," John said.

"Deal," I said, exchanging cards with John.

"Fucked again," Michael said to Tommy.

"No, I wasn't," Tommy snickered. "I don't even *have* a Boog Powell."

"You *lied*?" John said.

"I *bluffed*," Tommy said.

"Why?" I asked.

"Get the deal movin', that's all," Tommy explained. "Or else you two woulda been yappin' here all day."

"You know, Butter, you're not as dumb as you look," Michael said.

"No," John said. "But he *is* as ugly as he looks. It's like hangin' out with that guy with the bells."

"What guy with the bells?" Tommy asked.

"The Hunchback of Notre Dame," I interpreted.

John nodded. "That's him."

"C'mon," Michael said. "Ditch the cards and let's go swimmin'."

"Where?" I asked. "The sprinklers?"

"No," Michael said. "The river. We can catch a bunch of eels if we're lucky."

"Why is that *lucky*?" Tommy asked.

"Because Mr. Mangnone'll give you three bucks for every eel you bring him at the store," I said. "Dead or alive."

"What's he do with 'em?" John asked.

"He eats 'em," I said.

"You're pullin' my prick."

"I wouldn't touch your prick," I said.

"Serious?" John said.

"Boils 'em first. Gets all that shit outta 'em. Then he cooks 'em in vinegar and oil. Lots of spices thrown in. It's pretty good."

"You ate eel?" John asked, his face twisted in disgust. "On your own? I mean, without nobody havin' a gun on you?"

"That's nothin'," Michael said. "Tell 'em what you have the day before Easter."

"Lamb's head," I said.

"I don't believe it," Tommy said.

"The *whole* head?" John asked.

"Except for the eyes," I said. "We give those to my grandmother."

"Oh, Jesus," John said. "Why?"

"She mixes 'em with oil and water," I said. "My mother says it cures headaches."

"Like aspirin?" Tommy said.

"Sort of," I said.

"You're like a freakin' cave man, Shakes," John said.

"What's that flower you like to eat?" Tommy asked.

"What flower?"

"The one your mother made that one time," Tommy said. "With all the leaves."

"Artichoke?"

"Yeah, that's the one," Tommy said.

"That's not a flower, moron," I said.

"Looked like one to me," Tommy said.

"Lamb's head and flowers," John said. "A feast."

"The Irish know nothin' about food," I said.

"I give you that," Tommy said.

"I give you *this*," John said, grabbing his crotch.

"What does an Irishman call a seven-course meal?" I asked.

"What?"

"A six-pack and a boiled potato," I said, initiating the Hell's

Kitchen game known as the dozens, where ethnic insults flew with abandon.

"How can you spot the bride at an Italian wedding?" John asked.

"How?"

"She's the one with the braided armpits," John said.

"What's Irish foreplay?" Tommy asked, standing up and moving from the stoop.

"What?"

"Brace yourself, Bridget," Tommy said.

"How many Irishmen does it take to change a light bulb?" I asked.

"How many?"

"Four," I said. "One to hold the bulb and three to turn the ladder."

"I'm goin' swimmin'," Michael said.

"We'll go with you," I said, following him toward the 12th Avenue piers.

"What do you call the captain of an Italian submarine?" John asked, in step behind us.

"Chicken of the sea," I answered.

"How many of these are there?" Michael asked.

"About a hundred," I said.

"You know them all, I bet," Michael said to me.

"Just about."

"And you're gonna let me hear 'em all today?"

"That's the plan," I said.

"I don't even know why I hang out with you guys," Michael said.

"You're lonely," I said.

"You're ugly," John said.

"You have no other friends," Tommy said.

"Must be it," Michael said.

"You think the water's too cold to swim in?" Tommy asked.

"That water's always cold," John said. "It's like swimmin' in chunks of ice."

"It's not the cold that bothers me," I said. "It's that other stuff."

"All that shit floatin' around the edges," John said. "You ever think whose toilet that was flushed out of?"

"No," Michael said. "I don't."

"And the rats," Tommy said. "I went under once and this huge, ugly bastard was doin' a *Sea Hunt* right alongside me."

"Makes you wanna puke," I said.

"Good place for it," John said.

"What wimps," Michael said, dismissing the three of us with a wave of his hand.

"Oh, sorry, I forgot," John said. "*Tarzan* here loves it. Makes him feel like a man."

"I don't *love* it," Michael said. "But it's all the water we got and bitchin' isn't gonna send the rats to Jersey."

"Mikey's right," I said. "Where else can you go and catch all the eels you want?"

"And get some asshole to buy 'em," John said.

"Dead or alive," Tommy said.

"Whatta we gonna do with the money we make?" John asked.

"How about Ho-Ho's and a movie?" Michael said.

"At the Beacon?" Tommy asked.

"Nothin' good's there," I said.

"What?" Michael said.

"Don't remember," I said. "Somethin' French."

"What's at the Loew's?" Tommy asked.

"*Von Ryan's Express,*" I said. "Greatest war movie ever."

"We've seen it four times," John moaned.

"We're talkin' a lotta eels," I said. "If we're gonna do a movie and Chinese."

"What's wrong with you, Shakes?" Michael said. "We don't need money for a movie."

"I'm gonna pass," John said.

"Why?" I asked.

"Gotta get home," John said.

"Trouble?" Michael said.

"Not yet." John shrugged. "But there will be. My mother's got herself a new boyfriend and he's lookin' to keep me in line."

"Need us?" Tommy asked.

"If I needed you guys, I'd be in *real* trouble," John said.

"That's no joke," Michael said, suddenly somber and quiet. "You can't trust anybody but us."

"I know," John said. "But I can handle this guy."

"Let's swim, then," I said. "After that, we walk John home."

"Okay with you?" Michael asked John.

"Okay with me," John said.

Tommy and John moved on ahead, reading the statistics on the backs of baseball cards as they walked. I stayed by Michael's side, our pace slower.

"You really serious about all that?" I asked. "That we can only trust each other."

"What do you think?" Michael asked.

"I think you are," I said.

"Then why'd you ask?"

"Wanted to make sure."

"Well, now you're sure."

"What about Johnny and Butter?"

"What about 'em?"

"You think they feel the same way?"

"I think we all do," Michael said.

"Think it'll always be like that?"

"It's like that now," Michael said.

"I want it to last longer than just now," I said.

"Maybe it will," Michael said. "Unless you start thinkin' like King Benny."

"*Nobody* thinks like King Benny," I said.

"Friends are like loans," Michael imitated a King Benny monotone. "Bad ideas."

"That's only because all his friends tried to kill him," I said.

"He'll go down one day," Michael said. "And it won't be a friend that does it."

"That's where you're wrong," I said. "Guys like King Benny never go down."

"Why's that?"

"They let others go down for 'em," I said. "They walk away clean."

"Yeah, but we're not like King Benny," Michael said. "We're not always gonna walk away clean. One of us might go down. That's why we have to stick together."

"Hey, do eels bite?" John asked, approaching the edge of Pier 82, gazing down at the murky water, its greasy waves lapping the sides of the dock.

"They suck," I told him.

"Like your mother," Tommy said.

"Except eels do it for free," John added.

Michael stripped off his shirt and stepped out of his sneakers. "Let's get wet."

"Last one in carries the eels," I shouted, taking a running jump into the water.

"First one in kills 'em," John shouted after me, stripping down to his underwear.

Butter stood atop one of the rusty moorings, naked, his body facing the sun. "Should I pee here or wait till I get in?" he said to Michael.

"Share it with the fish," Michael said. He ran up behind Butter and shoulder-blocked him into the water.

"Let's go, Mikey," I said. "We only got about an hour till the tide picks up."

Michael dove in backward and stayed under for as long as he could hold his breath, emerging twenty feet to our left.

"There's tons of 'em down there," he said. "We could make a lotta money today."

"Or we could get eaten alive by river rats," Tommy said.

"It's still better than goin' to the Yankee game," John said.

I remember that as a perfect afternoon. We spent the rest of the day in the water, chasing after small schools of eels, avoiding the rush of the rats, the sound of our screams and laughter bouncing off the iron shadows of the abandoned pier.

* * *

OUR FAMILY LIVES WERE KEPT SEPARATE FROM OUR street lives.

We each knew the problems that existed behind our doors, but we also understood ours to be situations that couldn't be improved by discussion. We never needed to organize play-dates or sleepovers. Our parents never socialized or made attempts at forming friendships.

"Our apartments were war zones," Michael described them. "But it was a war we were better off fighting on our own. We knew what was going on, we saw the cuts, the bruises. We heard the talk. We just chose to keep it to ourselves. Home was the one place where we couldn't help each other. Nothing we could do would change a thing. So we ignored it, didn't dwell on it, except for an occasional joke or comment. In a way, our problems just made our circle tighter."

There were no Boy Scout troops in Hell's Kitchen, but there was a Police Athletic League center on Tenth Avenue, which we were allowed to use free of charge. There, my friends and I boxed and hit the various bags and watched older boys spar and jump rope in preparation for the three-round bouts in the *Daily News*–sponsored Golden Gloves tournament.

We bowled at the lanes on Eighth Avenue and 54th Street, our weekly games paid for by the Sacred Heart parish, and we played in knock-hockey tournaments run by the De Witt Clinton Park Association. We shot dice in front of Fat Mancho's store for a dime a roll and pitched pennies against all comers. All of these activities were done with the knowledge and consent of our parents. In fact, we were given a parental green light on most things we wanted to do. All that was required was staying out of trouble and keeping our parents' participation to a minimum.

There were no curfews to worry about, but neither was there a danger of being snatched off a Hell's Kitchen sidewalk by a stranger or shot at random by a drive-by gunman. Our parents knew that as long as we stayed within the confines of Hell's Kitchen, we would be safe from any harm beyond street fights and sports injuries.

There were eyes everywhere. Hell's Kitchen was Mayberry with a temper. The neighborhood was like having one giant baby-sitter. One giant, very mean baby-sitter.

What little socializing did exist between adults and children would take place in the saloons and diners that dotted the area. The Eastern Europeans and their families flocked to the diners, while the Irish were more likely to frequent the saloons. The Italians and Puerto Ricans would bounce from one to the other.

Early in Hell's Kitchen history, diners and luncheonettes lined 11th and 12th Avenues, their booths filled with longshoremen fresh from four-day shifts, sailors on shore leave, couples on first dates, mothers with loud children. One such diner, called the Kitchen and owned by a German family named Heil, is credited with giving name to the neighborhood.

The saloons at first belonged to the gangs and were deemed unfit by most families.

As the gangs faded, the saloons turned into what they had been for many in their old country—a place to meet, swap stories, forget the mounting debts, share some laughs, and, above all else, drink. It was not an uncommon sight to walk into a Hell's Kitchen saloon on a Saturday afternoon and see it crammed with families, drinking, laughing, singing old songs, and remembering friends and relatives on distant shores.

It was a drinking culture broken along ethnic lines: strong whiskey for the Irish, homemade wine for the Italians, cold beer for the Puerto Ricans.

Drugs were not yet part of our world.

As much as our parents embraced drink, they had no patience for drugs and they put their trust in King Benny, the biggest eyes and ears in Hell's Kitchen, to keep them out.

King Benny used diplomacy when called for, force when necessary. He earned his money from old-fashioned mob enterprises—policy running, loan sharking, truck hijacking, swag sales, and prostitution. These crimes were quietly condoned by a police department warmed by weekly payoffs and supported by a neighborhood addicted to illegal action. King Benny ruled with a tight fist and lashed out with deadly purpose against any threat to his domain. A lot of people tried taking over his business during his reign and a lot of people ended up dead.

He would do favors for those he liked and ignored the financial requests of those he considered liabilities. He would listen to people with problems and offer opinions on how those problems could be solved. He was a father confessor without a conscience. His decisions were never rash and were always final. His words were, in Hell's Kitchen, respected as the law.

It was the only law not ever broken.

* * *

KING BENNY SHUFFLED THE CARDS, LARGE ESPRESSO CUP to his left, drawn window blind shielding his face from the sun. I sat across from him, chest near the edge of a small round table, hands folded, 7Up bottle at my side, waiting for the game to begin. I was eleven years old.

"Sure you wanna play me?" King Benny asked.

"Why not?"

"I cheat."

"Me too," I said.

"Good," he said, and opened the deal.

The game was *sette bello,* Italian blackjack, and the stakes were low, a penny a win, nickel on a two-card hit. We were in the middle of King Benny's club, three empty tables around us, the door behind us locked. White dust particles, heavy enough to hold, curled their way up toward the hanging overhead lights. A jukebox played Sinatra and "High Hopes."

"Hungry?" King Benny asked, tossing me two cards.

"No," I said. "Thanks."

"Sure?"

"I'm sure," I said.

"What's it gonna be?" he said, nodding toward my cards.

"Give a hit."

King Benny flipped a card from the top of the deck, his eyes on me.

"You're over," he said. "You're into me for a penny."

"Double or nothing," I told him.

"A sucker bet," he said, dealing out a fresh set of cards and sipping from his coffee.

I lost the first ten hands we played, King Benny picking up the pennies and piling them next to his cup. He kept the deck of cards in his right hand, dealing with one finger, his eyes always on me, never on the table. He shuffled the cards every other deal and ignored the phone when it rang.

"You always end up with a six," I said. "How is that?"

"Lucky," he said.

"Got any pretzels?" I asked.

"Behind the bar," he said. "Help yourself."

"Want anything?"

"What time is it?" he asked.

"Quarter to five," I said, looking at my Timex watch, a swag present he had given me.

"Too early," he said.

King Benny never ate before seven and slept only two hours a night. He always carried a thousand dollars in twenties and singles in his pants pocket, never wore a gun, and was said to have a brother in jail, doing natural life on a double murder charge.

I sat back down, picking at a bag of salt pretzels. He sipped his coffee, shuffled the cards, and leaned back in his chair.

"I hear you got trouble at home," he said, putting the cup back by his side.

"It's nothing."

"If it was nothing," he said, "I wouldn't have heard about it."

"My father owes money," I admitted.

"Who this time?"

"The Greek," I said. "He's six months late on the payments."

"How much?"

"Three thousand," I said. "As of yesterday. Goes up every day."

"Yeah," King Benny said. "It does."

"The Greek sent a coupla guys over late last night," I said. "Scare him a little."

"It work?"

"Scared or not," I said, "he doesn't have the money and can't get it from anybody else."

"No," King Benny said. "He can't."

"He's hiding out," I said. "Until it blows over or he makes a big score."

"Guys like your father never make big scores," King Benny said. "They just keep guys like me in business."

"Will they kill him?"

"No," he said. "He'll just wish they did."

"I got sixty bucks put aside," I told him. "My mother can come up with another forty. That should be good for something."

"Forget it," King Benny said.

"I can't forget it," I said. "He's my father."

King Benny shook his head. "The loan's been squared."

"Who squared it?"

"You did. This morning. The Greek picked up an envelope with three grand and a note from you. Him and your father are even."

I didn't show any real emotion. That wasn't allowed. All I said was "I can't pay you back right away."

"You don't have to pay me back at all," I was told.

"Why'd you do it?" I wanted to know. "You never liked my father."

"Still don't," King Benny said. "He lives or dies, don't mean a thing to me."

I took a drink of the 7Up.

"Thanks," I said. "Thanks a lot."

"Always watch out for men like your father," King Benny said. "They go down bad streets. And they never go down alone."

"He tries," I said. "He just gets caught up."

"There are other ways," he said. "Better ways. You should walk away from the table knowing that."

"He wants to make money," I said. "Same as everybody around here."

"Looking for easy money," King Benny said. "Every one of them. And guess what?"

"What?"

"Ain't no such thing," he said.

"Does my father know?" I asked. "About the payment."

"Not yet."

"Can I tell him?"

"Soon as you see him," he said.

The room was turning dark, the sun's shadows giving way to early evening. King Benny's coffee cup was empty and my soda was warm. The jukebox had abandoned Sinatra and settled now on "Don't Be That Way" by Benny Goodman. In a corner, an old steam radiator sizzled, despite the outside heat.

"He's down in a basement apartment on 47th Street," King Benny said. "Near Ninth Avenue."

"I know."

"He's not alone," he said.

"I know that too," I said.

"You want some dinner before you go?" he asked.

"What's it gonna be?"

"Pasta and snails," King Benny said.

"Maybe not," I said.

"It's good for you," King Benny said.

"I should go."

"One thing," King Benny said. "Before you go."

"What?"

"The business with the Greek," King Benny said. "It stays between you and me."

"He's gonna ask where I got the money."

"Lie," King Benny said.

"Can't," I said.

"He lies to *you*." King Benny pushed his chair back and stood up, cup clasped in both hands. "All the time."

"That's different."

"How?" Now King Benny walked to the bar, his face free of emotion.

"He's my father," I said.

"Think he cares?"

"Doesn't matter," I said. "*I* care."

King Benny nodded and turned, walking behind the bar, his right leg dragging across the floor.

"See you tomorrow," he said, his voice even.

"Only if I get to deal," I said.

"We'll cut for it," he said, washing his cup in the sink under the counter.

"You'll win the cut," I said. "You always do."

"Can't trust a thief," he said, drying off his hands. "Or a liar."

"Which are you?"

"Both," King Benny said.

He folded a hand towel in half and laid it on the bar. Then he walked over to the small wooden door at the end of the hall, turned the knob, and went into the kitchen, closing it softly behind him.

13

WINTER 1966

THE PIZZERIA WAS EMPTY EXCEPT FOR THE FOUR OF US at a back table and Joey Retard at the counter, shaking black pepper on a hot slice. Mimi was working the ovens and the register, his white shirt and work pants stained red with sauce.

"I'm gettin' another slice," I said, wiping my mouth with a napkin.

"Me too," John said.

"Get me a soda," Tommy said. "Orange. Lots of ice."

"You lose your legs in the war?" I said.

"I got no money either," Tommy said.

"Want anything?" I asked Michael.

"Half of Tommy's soda," he said.

John and I walked to the counter and stood next to Joey Retard. Joey was fourteen, with an honest face and a ready smile. He was always well dressed and was friendly with everyone in the neighborhood. He spoke slowly, stuttering his way through difficult phrases, his manner gentle, his eyes dark as olives.

Joey was adopted, taken out of a West Side orphanage by a childless Irish couple. He went to a special school on Ninth

Avenue and earned pocket money washing cars for King Benny. He was shy around girls, loved pizza with extra cheese, cheap horror movies, and sewer-to-sewer stickball. Every Halloween he walked the streets dressed as Stooge Villa from *Dick Tracy.*

"What's doin', Joe?" John asked him.

"Good," Joey said. "I'm good."

"You want anything?" I asked. "John's buyin'."

"Where'd you hear that?" John said.

"No," Joey said. "Thanks."

John ordered and I asked Joey how school was.

"I like it," Joey said.

"Am I really payin' for this?" John asked me, watching Mimi take the pizza out of the oven.

"You got money?"

"I'll take the Fifth," John said.

"I'll buy tomorrow," I said, grabbing a paper plate with a slice.

"Swear," John said, reaching a hand into his jeans pocket and pulling out two crumpled bills.

"Swear," I said, taking my pizza and soda back to the table.

"Grab the change for me," John said, patting Joey on the shoulder, reaching for the second slice.

"Can I keep it?" Joey asked.

"Knock yourself out," John said.

Joey was on his second slice when the burly man walked through the door.

He stood at the counter, hands in his pockets, ordered a large Coke, and watched Joey dust his pizza with black pepper.

"That's not too smart," the man said, taking a sip from his soda. "It's gonna taste like shit."

"I like pepper," Joey said, shaking some more on the crust. "I like pepper a lot."

"There's enough on it," the man said, reaching for the pepper shaker.

"No!" Joey said, pulling back, still holding the pepper in his hand. "My pizza."

"Lemme have the pepper, you fuckin' retard," the man said, grabbing Joey's hand until the shaker came loose.

"My pizza!" Joey said, his voice breaking from the strain, his eyes blinking like shutters. "My pizza!"

"There's your fuckin' pizza," the man said, pointing to the counter. "Nobody touched it."

"I want pepper!" Joey said, his words coming in short bursts, his hands by his sides. "I want pepper!"

The burly man smiled.

He looked over at Mimi, frozen in place behind the counter, and winked. He unscrewed the top off the pepper shaker.

"You want pepper, retard?" the man said.

Joey stared at the burly man, his body quivering, his eyes filled with tears.

"Here," the man said, pouring the bottle of pepper out over Joey's pizza. "Here's your fuckin' pepper."

Joey started to cry, full sobs rising from his chest, his hands slapping his sides.

"What's your problem now, retard?" the man asked.

Joey didn't answer. Tears ran down his cheeks and over his lips, snot ran out of his nose.

"Go on," the burly man said. "You fuckin' retards turn my stomach."

Joey didn't move.

"Go," the man said. "Before I slap the shit outta ya and really make you cry."

Michael walked past Joey and stepped to the counter, next to the burly man. He reached for the salt shaker, loosened the top, and poured the contents into the man's soda.

"You can leave now," Michael said to him, stirring the drink with his finger. "You and Joe are even."

"A tough little punk," the man said. "Is that what I'm lookin' at?"

"A dick with lips," Michael said. "Is that what I'm lookin' at?"

Tommy put an arm around Joey and moved him from the counter. John stood behind the burly man, hands in his pockets. I was across from the burly man, arms folded, waiting for his move.

"Four tough little punks," the burly man said. "And a cryin' retard."

"That's us," Michael said.

The burly man lifted a hand and slapped Michael across the face. The blow left red finger marks on Michael's cheeks and an echo loud enough to chill.

Michael stared at the man and smiled.

"The first shot should always be your best," Michael said. "And your best sucks."

"I'll show you my best, punk," the burly man said, moving off his feet and taking a full swing at Michael. "Your fuckin' teeth are gonna be all over the floor."

Michael ducked the punch, throwing his body against the burly man's stomach. Tommy and John jumped on the man from behind, pulling at his hair and neck. I grabbed the pizza slice with all the pepper on it and rubbed it into his eyes.

"Take it outside!" Mimi screamed.

John chewed on the man's ear, his bite hard enough to draw blood. Tommy started pounding at his kidneys. I took a red pepper shaker and rammed it against his face.

"My eyes!" the burly man said, trying to shake us off. "My fuckin' eyes."

Michael picked up a counter stool and started ramming it against the front of his legs. John had grabbed his thick hair and was knocking his head on the edge of the front door. I kept hitting him with the red pepper shaker until it broke above the bridge of his nose. Shards of glass mixed with blood ran down the front of his face.

The pain brought the man to his knees, one hand reaching for the counter.

"Never come in here again," Michael said, kicking at his crumpled body. "Hear me? *Never.*"

Mimi ran from behind the counter and grabbed Michael around the waist, pulling him away.

"You no wanna kill him," he said.

"Don't be too sure," Michael said.

* * *

OUR LIVES WERE ABOUT PROTECTING OURSELVES AND OUR turf. The insulated circle that was life in Hell's Kitchen closed tighter as we grew older. Strangers, never welcome, were now viewed as outsiders bent on trouble. My friends and I could no longer afford to let others do the fighting.

It was our turn to step up, and we were led, as always, by Michael.

Outside events meant little. In a society changing radically by the hour, we focused on the constants in our own small, controlled space.

It was the '60s, and we watched the images scattered nightly across TV screens with skepticism, never trusting the players, always suspecting a scam. It was the way we were taught to look at the world. Life, we had been told, was about looking out for number one, and number one didn't waste time outside the neighborhood.

On television, the young protesters we saw spoke about how they were going to change our lives and fix the world. But we knew they didn't care about people like us. While they shouted their slogans, my friends and I went to funeral services for the young men of Hell's Kitchen who came back from Vietnam in body bags. That war never touched those angry young faces we saw on TV, faces protected by money and upper-middle-class standing. They were on the outside yelling about a war they would never fight. To me and my friends, they were working the oldest con in the world and they worked it to perfection.

Civil rights had become the battle of the day, but on our streets it was a meaningless issue. There, gangs of different ethnic backgrounds and skin colors still waged weekly skirmishes. A growing army of feminists marched across the country, demanding equality, yet our mothers still cooked and cared for men who abused them mentally and physically.

Students would be killed on the campus of Kent State University in Ohio. Martin Luther King, Jr., and Senator Robert F. Kennedy would be shot dead. Governor George Wallace would take one in the spine.

Whole sections of American cities were about to burn to the ground.

The summer of love was set to bloom.

Drugs would go beyond the junkie.

The country was on a fast-ticking timer, ready to explode.

For me and for my friends, these developments carried no weight. They might as well have occurred in another country, in another century. The mating call of a new generation, one whose foundation was to be built on peace, love, and harmony, simply floated past us.

Our attention was elsewhere.

The week the students at Kent State were shot down, Tommy's father was stabbed in the chest in Attica prison and was put on a respirator for three months.

Michael's mother died of cancer during that summer and Carol Martinez had an uncle who was shot dead in front of an 11th Avenue bar.

While thousands of angry war protesters filtered into Washington, D.C., we sat with Father Bobby in a third-floor hospital ward, praying for John to recover from a punctured lung, a gift from one of his mother's over-zealous boyfriends. The man had had too much to drink and John said more than he should have about it and was given a severe beating as a result. He also suffered an asthma attack and was lucky to escape the night with his life.

One of the earliest lessons learned in Hell's Kitchen was that death was the only thing in life that came easy.

* * *

WE WERE DOWN 7-5 IN THE LAST INNING OF A LATE winter afternoon game of sewer-to-sewer stickball against Hector Garcia and three of his friends.

Tommy was at the plate, shaved-down broom handle in his hands, facing a thin, scar-faced Puerto Rican with a nasty spin to his spauldeen. We were in the middle of 50th Street, looking down at the piers, foul lines shaped by a yellow U-Haul on our left and a rummy sorting through a stolen A&P cart on our right.

I stood a few feet behind Tommy, legs straddling a sewer, eating a Ring-Ding and backing up the Puerto Rican's pitches. Michael and John were sitting on the hood of Fat Mancho's black Chevrolet, waiting their turn at bat.

"We need a hit," I told Tommy.

"Thank you, Casey Stengel," Tommy said, spitting across the sewer.

"Look at how that ball of his curves," John said, watching a pitch fly past Tommy for a swinging strike. "He's great."

"Maybe we just suck," Michael observed.

"He ain't *that* good," I said loud enough for the pitcher to hear. "We're makin' him look like Sandy Koufax."

"You asswipes make *everybody* look like Sandy Koufax," the Puerto Rican said with a big smile, holding the ball, wiping his face with his upper arm.

"Another fan," John said, winking at the pitcher. "We got 'em everywhere."

Tommy swung at the third pitch and lofted a high fly straight down the middle of the street. Hector, playing so deep he had to dodge street traffic, took two steps back and made a basket catch. Tommy tossed the broom handle back to me and walked over to Fat Mancho's car, head down, arms across his chest.

"Couple inches more and that ball woulda been there," Tommy said.

"Couple inches more and Hector woulda been laid out by a van," Michael said.

"You shitheads wanna quit now, you can," the pitcher said, smile still on his face.

"How do you say 'blow me' in Spanish?" John asked him.

"C'mon, Shakes," Michael said as I stepped in to take my swings. "Shove it down his throat."

"Swing that stick, loser," the pitcher said to me. "I can use the breeze."

"Chew my big one, you skinny prick," Fat Mancho shouted, his back against his storefront window, holding a sixteen-ounce can of Rheingold wrapped in a paper bag. "No way a little woman like you beats my boys."

"You the cheerleader?" the pitcher said. "Ain't you got no pom-poms?"

"You gonna be pullin' 'em outta your ass," Fat Mancho said. "Unless you throw that fuckin' ball."

I swung and missed the first pitch, the ball bouncing to the right, down and away.

"Wait him out, Shakes," Michael said. "You can hit him. Just wait him out."

I looked at the next two pitches, broom handle never off my shoulder.

"You gonna swing at anything, chump?" the pitcher asked. "Or you just like to watch me throw the ball?"

"Take it slow, Shakes," Michael said. "Swing at what you want."

I let another pitch go by, rested the broomstick against my legs, and wiped both hands on the front of my jeans. A circle of old men stood in front of Fat Mancho's store, a case of beer by their feet, lit cigarettes on their lips, jackets zipped against the wind.

"Next one's the one, Shakes," Michael said.

"How do you know?" I said.

"He's not gonna waste more throws," Michael said. "Look how pissed he's gettin'. He's gonna put down a fat one, let you hit it. Figures somebody'll catch the ball."

"He might be right," I said.

But he wasn't. I hit the ball hard, a line drive that went out over the head of the pitcher and was scooped up on two bounces by a teenager with a shaved head.

"Easy double, penis breath," John screamed out, clapping his hands and kicking his feet against the sides of Fat Mancho's car.

"Kick that car again, you little fuck," Fat Mancho said to him, "I'll pull your legs off with my teeth."

"Pull this off with your teeth," John said to him, holding his crotch.

"Ain't big enough to shadow a fly," Fat Mancho said, taking a long drink from his can of beer.

John scooped up the broom handle and stepped in, ready to hit. He planted his feet and squared his shoulders, the broom handle held just above his right ear. The first pitch came in low, to the far side of the sewer cover, fast and hard. John swung and connected, the ball bouncing past the pitcher for a single.

"They gonna take you down, you no-talent fuck," Fat Mancho screamed at the pitcher.

"Just playin' with 'em, Fat Man," the pitcher said. "That's all."

"Lick me," Fat Mancho said, popping the lid off a fresh can of beer.

"He's all yours," I said to Michael, handing him the taped end of the broom handle. "Time to make Fat Mancho proud."

The best way to win at sewer-to-sewer stickball was to hit the ball hard and far. There were no walks and a batter was allowed three swinging strikes. We didn't run any bases, since the street was already crowded enough. So the length the ball traveled determined the type of hit. Anything past one sewer was a single, two sewers counted as a double, past the U-Haul was a triple, and a home run landed somewhere on the 12th Avenue side of traffic. Michael was the only kid on our team to ever hit home runs.

Michael banged the broomstick against the sewer cover and took three hard practice swings. He bent his knees and brought the broom handle to eye level, staring over at the pitcher, the smile now gone from his face.

"You the one I want," the pitcher said to Michael, rolling the spauldeen against his thigh.

"Good thing, 'cause I'm the one you got," Michael said back to him.

"C'mon, Davey," a young woman in a wheelchair shouted out at the pitcher. "Strike this chump out. He's got nothin'."

Michael turned to his left and stared at the woman, her dark hair turned back in a bun, her face tanned and unlined, her arms limp by her sides. A short, overweight old lady stood behind her, elbows resting on wheelchair handles, unfiltered cigarette in her mouth. The young woman was chewing gum, both her legs cut off at the knees, dead flesh half-hidden by a pair of A&S shorts.

"Who is that?" Michael asked.

"His sister," I said, nodding my head toward the Puerto Rican pitcher. "The old lady's the mother."

"Let's go, Mikey," John shouted. "Pound this dufe right on his ass."

"What happened to her?" Michael asked.

"Not sure," I said. "Some kinda cancer. Got her in the legs."

"Strike these scumbags out," the young woman shouted. "They can't touch you, Davey. They can't touch you."

"Swallow your tongue, crip," Fat Mancho said to her from across the street.

Michael stepped in, his legs level, his eyes cornered on the young woman in the wheelchair, waiting for the first pitch. He took a bad swing at a good ball.

"Easy, Mike," I cautioned, standing behind him. I'd never seen an expression like that on his face before. "Take your time. There's no rush."

"She's really good-looking," Michael said, backing away from the sewer.

"What the fuck you lookin' at, little dick?" the woman in the wheelchair screamed at Michael.

"And she's nothin' but charm," I said.

Michael swung at the second pitch too early, the broom handle touching his shoulder by the time the ball was in my hands.

"Look alive, Mikey," John shouted. "Hit your pitch."

"You can take him," Tommy screamed. "You can take him, Mikey."

"Skinny Irish bastard," Fat Mancho said. "What the fuck's he doing?"

"Forget the girl, Mikey," I pleaded. "Worry about her brother."

But he couldn't forget her.

Michael swung and missed at the third pitch.

He dropped the broom handle on top of the sewer and

walked over to the back of Fat Mancho's car, hands in his pockets, watching the woman in the wheelchair, his ears deaf to the groans of the people by his side.

The pitcher pumped his fist in the air, waved to his teammates, and blew kisses across the street to his sister.

"Told you he ain't shit, baby," the woman in the wheelchair said.

"You could've just helped her cross a street," I said to Michael, watching Tommy taking his practice swings. "Maybe get her an ice cream. You didn't have to blow the game."

"It ain't over," Michael said. "Tommy can win it."

"Tommy closes his eyes when he swings," I said. "You're the one who could've won it and you didn't."

"Tell me you wouldn't of done the same?" Michael said.

"You think she gives a shit?" I asked.

"No," Michael said. "I know she doesn't."

"So?"

"So nothin'," Michael said.

"Now we're the fuckin' Salvation Army," I said, turning away, Fat Mancho behind me, staring at us both.

"You ever wonder why there ain't a Salvation *Navy*?" John asked.

I didn't know why he'd done what he did. No, that's not exactly right. I *knew* why he'd done it, I just didn't *understand* why he'd done it.

"This fuck's so stupid, he should be watered," Fat Mancho said, watching Tommy at the plate.

Tommy swung at the first ball he saw, sending a one-bouncer right at the pitcher, who caught it with the palm of his hand. He then turned and tossed the ball over the roof of a warehouse.

"Game's over, losers," the pitcher said. "Cough up the cash. A buck each."

"You beat them, baby," the woman in the wheelchair said, pushing herself closer to her brother.

Michael collected the money, folded the singles, and handed them to the Puerto Rican pitcher.

"Nice game," Michael said, staring at the pitcher's sister in the wheelchair.

"Fuck me," the pitcher said.

Five minutes later we were sitting in front of Fat Mancho's store, drinking Pepsi from bottles, watching the pitcher wheel his sister down toward 11th Avenue.

"He ain't better than you," Fat Mancho said.

"He was today," I said.

"You little punks let him be," Fat Mancho said. "All 'cause Irish here got a thing for crips."

"Stay away from this," Michael said. "It doesn't matter to you."

"You boys are soft," Fat Mancho said. "Like bread. It's gonna catch up. And when it does, it's gonna hurt. Bad."

"Hold the talk, Fat Man," John said. "What happens is our business."

"You gotta *stay* tough to be tough," Fat Mancho said. "Guys smell it when you're weak. Eat you like a salad."

"Bread and salad," Tommy said. "Everything's a meal with you."

"I ain't clownin'," Fat Mancho said. "This is serious. You wanna be hard, you can't play at it."

"Take it easy," I said. "It was just a stickball game."

"Goin' soft is a habit," Fat Mancho said. "Hell to break. You gotta keep yourself mean. And cut your life around it. It's the only way for little punks like you."

"This is like hangin' out with fuckin' Confucius," John said.

"Be funny, limp dick," Fat Mancho said. "No skin sliced from my ass. This is just free advice, me to you. Take it or throw it."

"Thanks a lot, Fat Man," Michael said. "We'll think about it."

"You do that, Irish," Fat Mancho said. "You fuckin' do that."

In truth, we were all a little surprised by Michael's actions. It was not his way to show vulnerability, especially to someone he didn't know. It was also not his style to purposely lose at anything for anyone's sake. It is something John or Tommy would have done without hesitation and something I might have done if I had given it any thought. But for Michael to do it caused us all to pause. We always saw him as the strongest among us, the one least willing to budge.

None of us liked to lose, and yet here we had just lost and we didn't know the reason why. Michael sensed our uneasiness but said nothing. In his mind, losing that game and handing a feeling of victory to a girl in a wheelchair was more than the right thing to do. It was more than a courageous thing to do. It was the *only* thing to do.

14

SUMMER 1967

THE TEMPERATURE TOPPED OUT AT 98 DEGREES ON THE
day our lives were forever altered. It was the middle of a summer when the country's mood plunged into darkness. Race
riots had already rocked 127 cities across the United States,
killing 77 people and putting more than 4,000 others in area
hospitals, and neither side seemed ready to give up the battle.

Along with the turmoil came change.

Thurgood Marshall was appointed to the Supreme Court
by President Lyndon Johnson after Justice Thomas C. Clark
resigned. In return, Ramsey Clark, the son of the retired justice,
was named to the attorney general's post.

The Six-Day War was fought in the Middle East.

The New York World Journal Tribune folded and *Rolling Stone*
published its first issue. *Bonnie and Clyde* brought crowds to
theaters and *Rosemary's Baby* kept readers up all night. The
Beatles sang "All You Need Is Love," while "Ode to Billy Joe"
suggested otherwise, playing and playing on the radio. Mickey
Mantle, limping toward the end of his baseball days, hit his
500th home run, and Muhammad Ali, at the height of his boxing achievements, was stripped of the heavyweight crown for
refusing to fight in Vietnam.

We had spent our morning in the cool shadows of a second-floor poolroom on West 53rd Street, watching a craggy-faced lug in a T-shirt and torn jeans rack up a dozen games against four different opponents. As he played, he smoked his way through two packs of Camels and finished off a pint of Four Roses.

"Bet this guy could even beat Ralph Kramden," Tommy said, watching the man side-pocket the six ball.

"Ralph Kramden doesn't play pool," I said. "He drives a bus."

"Not on *The Honeymooners,*" Tommy said. "In that movie."

"*The Hustler,*" Michael said. "That the one you mean?"

"The one where they break Fast Eddie's thumbs," John said.

"You need directions to figure out the way you think," I said to Tommy.

"It wasn't Kramden?" Tommy asked.

"Let's get outta here," Michael said, looking around the smoke-filled room. "We're startin' to smell as bad as this place."

We made a right out of the poolroom, late morning sun warming our shoulders, our attention jointly fixed on lunch. We ran a red light crossing 11th Avenue, dodged a school bus and two cabs, then eased back into a fast walk in front of old man Pippilo's barber shop. At 51st Street and Tenth Avenue we turned left, side by side on the silent streets.

Between us, we had less than two dollars in our pockets.

"Let's go get some pizza," John said. "We can tell Mimi we'll pay him down the road."

"Mimi charges for *water,*" Tommy said. "He ain't gonna go for any IOUs."

"We can grab something at home," I said. "Leftovers."

"The only leftovers in my house are dirty dishes," John said.

"And week-old bread," Tommy said.

"Why not hot dogs?" Michael asked. "We haven't hit the cart in a couple of weeks."

"I don't know, Mikey," Tommy said. "That cart guy ain't like the others. He gets pretty crazy when you take him off."

"Tommy's right," I said. "Last week, he chased Ramos and two of his friends all the way to the piers. Almost cut one of 'em."

"A hot dog ain't worth bleedin' over," John said.

"We can eat hot dogs or we can eat air," Michael said. "You guys choose."

"Air's probably safer," Tommy said.

"May even taste better," John said.

"Whose turn is it?" I asked.

"Yours," Michael said.

"You think he'll recognize me?" I asked.

"I hope so," Tommy said. "I'm really hungry."

The scam was simple. We'd done it dozens of times before, with almost as many vendors. We picked it up from an Irish crew on 48th Street who used it every summer to score free Puerto Rican ices.

I was to walk up to the hot dog cart and order what I wanted. The vendor would then hand me my hot dog and watch as I ran off without paying. This left the vendor with two choices, neither very appealing. He could stand his ground and swallow his loss. Or he could give chase. This second choice forced him to abandon the cart, where my friends could feast in his absence.

The hot dog vendor at this corner was tall and slender and in his mid-twenties, with thick dark hair and a round, bulbous nose. A recent addition to Hell's Kitchen, his English was as poor as his clothes, ragged blue shirt and jeans, front pockets frayed at the edges. He owned a Yankee warm-up jacket and soiled cap and wore them on colder days.

The vendor worked the far corner of 51st Street and Tenth Avenue, standing under the partial shade of a red and yellow Sabrett umbrella, selling cold sodas, hot dogs, and sausages to an array of passing customers—local merchants, longshoremen and truckers, schoolchildren. Seven days a week, late morning to early evening, he was there, plying a trade that was all too easy for us to ridicule.

We never saw the vendor as a man, not the way we saw the other men of the neighborhood, and didn't care enough about him to grant him any respect. We gave little notice to how hard he worked for the few dollars he earned. We didn't know about the young wife and two kids he left in Greece and how he hoped to build for them a new foundation in a new country. We didn't pay attention to the tedious twelve-hour days he endured, slicing buns and sifting through chunks of ice through cold spells and heat waves. All the time stamping his feet on hard ground to keep the blood flowing.

We never saw the tiny, airless fourth-floor room he lived in, a forty-minute walk from his station, its only comfort a tattered collection of pictures from home, crudely taped to the wall nearest the worn mattress of his bed. We never saw the hot stove, topped by empty cans of Campbell's pork and beans. Or the crumpled packs of Greek cigarettes, tossed in a corner trash bin, gifts from his wife, his only stateside pleasure.

We didn't see any of that.

We saw only a free lunch.

"Mustard and onions," I said, avoiding the vendor's suspicious look. "No soda."

He nodded, wary, his eyes over my shoulders, looking for hidden shadows.

"I know you," he said, accusation more than question.

I shrugged and smiled.

"Can I have two napkins?" I asked, reaching my hand out for the hot dog. "Onions get messy."

The vendor pulled a second napkin from its canister and wrapped it under the bun. He hesitated for an instant, his hand out toward mine, our eyes fixed. We both sensed a wrong about to happen, though we were ignorant of its eventual weight. He shifted his feet and handed over the hot dog. I took it from him and ran.

I scooted past Tommy Mug's dry cleaners and Armond's shoe repair. The vendor, the anger behind his months of frustration broken beyond any reasonable point, gave chase, a wood-handled prong fork in one hand.

As I ran, slivers of red onions flew off the top of the hot dog, dotting my cheek and the front of my white T-shirt. I cut past the P.A.L. entrance and turned the corner at 50th Street.

He was close on me, arms and legs moving in their own furied rhythm, the fork still gripped in one hand, his breath coming in measured spurts.

"Pay my money, thief!" he shouted after me. "Pay my money *now*!"

Michael, John, and Tommy were on their second hot dogs, leaning casually against the side of the cart, faces turned to the sun.

"How long you think he'll be?" John asked, wiping brown mustard from his lower lip.

"Shakes or the hot dog guy?" Michael asked.

"You got one, you got the other," Tommy said. "That guy looked pissed enough to kill."

"Gotta catch him to kill him," John said. "Don't worry."

"These things are heavier than they look," Michael said, standing now, hands gripping the cart's wooden handles.

"The heavy shit's underneath," Tommy said. "Where nobody can see it."

"What heavy shit?" John asked.

"The gas tanks," Tommy said. "The stuff that keeps the food hot. Or maybe you thought the sun made the water boil."

"Think we can push it?" Michael asked. "The three of us?"

"Push it where?" John asked.

"Couple of blocks away," Michael said. "Be a nice surprise

for the guy when he gets back from chasing Shakes not to find his cart."

"What if somebody takes it?" Tommy said.

"You gotta be pretty dumb to steal a hot dog cart," Michael said.

"Ain't we doin' that?" John asked.

"We're just *moving* it," Michael said. "Making sure nobody *else* steals it."

"So, we're helpin' the guy out," Tommy said.

"Now you're listening," Michael said.

THE VENDOR TIRED AT 52nd Street and 12th Avenue.

He was bent over, hands on his knees, the fork long since discarded, face flushed, his mouth open and hungry for breath. I was on the other side of the street, against a tenement doorway, hair and body washed in sweat. My hands were still greasy from the hot dog I held for most of the run.

I looked over at the vendor and found him staring back at me, anger still visible, his hands now balled up and punching at his sides. He was beat but not beaten. He could go ten minutes more just on hate alone. I decided against a run toward the piers, choosing instead to double back and head for neighborhood safety. By now, I figured, the guys should have downed enough hot dogs and sodas to satisfy Babe Ruth's appetite.

I took three deep breaths and started running toward 51st Street, traffic moving behind me. I turned my head and looked back at the vendor, his body in the same position as it was a block earlier. I slowed when I reached the corner and allowed myself a smile, content that the chase, while not over, had drifted to my favor.

If I got to the cart fast enough, I might even have time for a hot dog.

Michael, John, and Tommy were standing at the corner of

50th Street and Ninth Avenue, tired from having pushed the cart up the one long block. They stopped in front of a florist, a short woman, her hair in a bun, clipping stems from a handful of roses, watching them with curiosity.

"Let's have a soda," John said, sliding open the aluminum door and plunging a hand into dark, icy water. "A Dr. Brown sounds about right."

"I'll take a cream," Tommy said.

John handed Tommy a sweaty can of soda. "How about you, Mikey?"

"I don't want anything," Michael said, looking down the street, arms across his chest.

"What's wrong?" Tommy asked, taking a slurp from his soda.

"Shakes is taking too long," Michael said. "He should've been back by now."

I STOPPED AT THE LIGHT at 51st Street and Tenth Avenue and looked for my friends and the hot dog cart.

The vendor was one avenue down, running again at a full pace, his stride seemingly stronger than ever. I bent over to tie my laces and caught a glimpse of him.

"Give it up," I whispered. "Let it go."

I stood and continued to run, this time toward Ninth Avenue. My sides hurt and my legs were starting to cramp. I was light-headed, my throat dry and my lungs heavy. I ran past Printing High School, the yard empty except for two rummies drinking coffee and smoking cigarettes, thinking of ways to score their first drink of the day. I dodged past a heavyset woman tugging a shopping wagon piled with groceries and jumped two garbage-can lids tossed to the side by a passing sanitation crew.

Then, halfway up the block, the vendor still on my trail, I saw the hot dog cart being pushed toward Eighth Avenue by my friends. They were hunched low and moving easy, walking within the shadows of the arches of the old Madison Square Garden, as calm and steady as if they were out walking a dog.

The vendor saw them too.

"Stop them!" he shouted, not breaking stride. "Stop them! Stop the thieves!"

In a neighborhood where silence in the face of crime is a virtue and blindness a necessity, no one moved.

I ran as fast as burnt lungs and tired legs would permit and reached my three friends as they went past a poster announcing the much-heralded rematch between World Wrestling Federation champion Bruno Sammartino and challenger Gorilla Monsoon.

"You're only supposed to take the hot dogs," I said when I got to them, my hands holding a side of the cart. "Not the wagon."

"Now you tell us," John said.

"Just leave it here," I panted. "You guys are lookin' to push somethin', push me. I can't take another step."

"No, not here," Michael said, pointing to our right. "Up there. Over by the subway station."

"The guy's comin' fast, Mikey," John said. "I don't think we got time to make it to the subway."

"I got a plan," Michael said.

I turned around and saw the vendor gaining on us by the second. "I'm sure he's got one too," I said, helping to lift the cart onto the sidewalk, toward the top step of the IRT subway station.

"I don't even *like* hot dogs," John said.

THE PLAN, AS IT turned out, was as simple and as dumb as anything we had ever done. We were to hold the cart on the top edge of the stairwell, leaning it downward, and wait for the vendor. We were to let go the second he grabbed the handles and leave the scene as he struggled to ease the cart back onto the sidewalk.

To this day, I don't know why we did it. But we would all pay a price. Everyone. All it took was a minute, but in that minute everything changed.

People who've been shot always recall the incident as if it happened to them in slow motion, and that's how I'll always remember those final seconds with the hot dog cart. The action around me moved at quarter speed and the background was nothing but haze—quick hands, fleeing legs, scattered bodies, all shaped in dark, nasty blurs.

The moment arrived for me and my friends on a day and time when Mickey Mantle was crossing the plate with a home run we would have all been proud to witness.

MICHAEL HELD THE CART the longest, his arms bulging at the strength needed to keep it from falling down the steps. John had slipped on his side, his back against the station's wooden banister, both hands sliced by the wooden handles. Tommy fell to his knees, desperately grabbing at one of the wheels, his knees scraping concrete. I held both my hands to the base of the umbrella stand, grip tight, splashes of hot water showering my arms and face.

The vendor was a few feet behind us, on his knees, his hands spread out across his face, his eyes visible.

"It's not gonna hold!" Tommy said, the wheel slipping from his grip.

"Let it go," Michael said.

"Don't stop now!" I said. "We can't stop now!"

"Let it go, Shakes," Michael urged, his voice a surrender to the inevitable. "Let it go."

Watching the cart tumble down the stairs was as painful as

trying to keep it from going down. The noise was loud, numbing, and eerie, two cars colliding on an empty street. Hot dogs,
onions, sodas, ice, napkins, and sauerkraut jumped out in unison, splattering against the sides of the stairwell, bouncing and
smacking the front of a Florida vacation poster. One of the rear
wheels flew off halfway down the landing. The umbrella stand
split against the base of the stair wall.

Then came the loudest noise, one that rocked the entire
subway station. It was a sound no one expected to hear.

A crunching sound of wood against bone.

It is a sound I have heard every day of my life since.

* * *

JAMES CALDWELL WAS A SIXTY-SEVEN-YEAR-OLD RETIRED
printer. He had been married to the same woman for thirty-six
years, had three grown children, all daughters, and four grandchildren, three of them boys. He had spent his morning in
Lower Manhattan, visiting with one of those daughters, Alice,
newly wed to a junior executive working for a midtown ac-
counting firm. He had stopped in a bakery in Little Italy to buy
his wife a box of her favorite pastries, which he carried in his
left hand. On doctor's orders, Caldwell had turned his back on
a two-pack-a-day cigarette habit less than a week earlier. He
refused to give up his Scotch, however, a drink he liked straight
up, ice water on the side, a bowl of pretzels at the ready.

He was chewing two pieces of Juicy Fruit gum and was digging into his front pants pocket for enough loose change to buy
the late edition of the *Daily News* when the cart landed on him,
barreling in at chest level. His hands reached out to grab the
sides of the wagon in a futile attempt to ward off its runaway
power.

The cart was a destructive missile, taking with it all in its
wake. That wake now included the body of James Caldwell,

who had no bigger plans for the rest of his day than reading the sports pages.

Together, both cart and man came to rest as one, slamming against a white tile subway wall. The cart crumpled, wheels rolling off in opposite directions, handles splintered, boiling water and pieces of ice crashing on top of Caldwell's bloody head, looking no bigger than a hairless tan ball, lodged against the sharpest edge of the wagon.

The silence after the crash was as numbing as the noise during it.

We held our positions, feet cemented in place. No one spoke, and the three of us choked back tears. We heard the wail of sirens and prayed they were headed our way. I looked down at the wreckage and saw the lower half of Caldwell's legs twitching under the weight. Thin lines of blood mixed with dirty hot dog water to form a puddle in one corner.

The smell of excrement filtered through the air.

Michael turned to me and, for the first time since I'd known him, I saw fear on his face.

John and Tommy didn't move, their bodies trembling, faces ashen, both unnerved enough to pass out. The four of us felt much older than we had less than an hour earlier, the ticking of our personal clocks accelerating with the speed of the unfolding incident.

To our left, a thin, middle-aged woman in a checkered housedress and white apron, strands of long, dark hair hiding the anger fanning her eyes, crossed the street in a run and stood at the top stair of the subway station. Hands on her hips, shoulders hunched in a tight pattern, she stared down at the scene.

"My sweet Jesus," she shouted, turning her gaze toward us, her voice a sharp, loud, high pitch. "What have you boys done? What in God's name have you boys done? Tell me, now, what have you done?"

"I think we just killed a man," Michael said.

15

THAT AFTERNOON, THE POLICE ISSUED AN ORDER OF immediate custody, a juvenile arrest warrant, against the four of us. We were charged with a series of crimes: reckless endangerment; assault in the first; possession of a dangerous instrument; assault with intent; misdemeanor assault; petty theft. We were each assigned PINS status, branding us persons in need of supervision. We were also tagged as youthful offenders, Y.O. on the streets. The label came with the luxury of keeping our records sealed and the knowledge that Y.O.'s were seldom dealt adult-length sentences, even by the harshest family court judge.

While James Caldwell lay in critical condition in the intensive care unit of St. Clare's Hospital, clinging to life on a respirator, we were remanded into our parents' custody. The shock of the day still had not worn away as we moved with great speed and little care through the system of arrest and booking, our eyes and ears closed to the sobs and screams surrounding us. We were in another world. Above the action. Our parents cried and cursed, the cops were stone-faced, Caldwell's family wanted us dead, and the whole neighborhood, it seemed, was waiting for us outside the station house. We'd always been on the other side looking in at the guys getting busted. Now it was us. We were the ones they pointed at. The ones they talked about. We were the guilty ones now.

* * *

MY FATHER HAD JUST SLAPPED ME, HARD, ACROSS MY face. I stared at him; he was slumped on a chair next to the kitchen table, wearing only briefs and a T-shirt. His face was red, his hands were twitching, his eyes welled with tears. My mother was in a back room, facedown on her bed, crying.

My parents had always granted me free reign, confident in my ability to steer clear of street jams, believing I was not the type to bring trouble knocking at the front door. This freedom also served to keep me out of view of their daily physical and verbal battles.

I lost that freedom the instant the hot dog cart crashed against the body of James Caldwell.

"I'm sorry, Dad," was all I could manage to say.

"Sorry ain't gonna do you much good now, kid," my father said, softening. "You gotta face up to what you did. The four of you."

"What's going to happen to us?" I asked, my voice breaking, tears falling down my cheeks.

"The old man lives, you might catch a break," my father said. "Do a few months in a juvenile home."

I could barely ask the question. "And if he doesn't?"

My father couldn't answer. He reached out his arms and held me, both of us crying, both of us afraid.

* * *

OVER THE NEXT SEVERAL DAYS, HELL'S KITCHEN, WHICH, in the past, never failed to embrace its criminals, seemed a neighborhood in shock. It wasn't the crime that had hands raised to the sky, but the fact that Michael, John, Tommy, and I had committed it.

"You guys were different," Fat Mancho told me years later. "Yeah, sure, you fooled around, busted balls, got into fights, shit like that. But you never went outta your way to hurt anybody. You were never punks. Until you did the job with the cart. That was an upstate number and that's something nobody figured on."

By the day, two weeks later, when we stood before a family court judge, we knew that James Caldwell was going to make it out of the hospital alive. The news had been relayed to us by Father Bobby, who counseled all the families involved.

During the time between our arrest and scheduled judgment, I was not allowed to associate with my friends, be seen in their company, or talk to them by phone. We were each kept under close family scrutiny, spending the bulk of our days buried inside our apartments. Father Bobby visited each of us daily, bringing with him a handful of comics and a few words of encouragement. He always left a little sadder than when he arrived.

Our crime had not been terrible enough to make any of the papers, so our notoriety did not move further than the neighborhood. Still, we couldn't help but feel like public enemies. There were whispers behind my mother's back whenever she went out for groceries or headed off to church. John's mother missed so many days of work she was close to losing her job. When Michael was sent out on a fast errand, a beer bottle was tossed his way. Tommy was denied entry to a local movie theater.

"Your kind ain't welcome," he was told. "Not here. Not in my place."

"I didn't do anything to you," Tommy said.

"You got a problem with what I done?" the theater manager asked. "Call the cops."

During those two long, frightening, and tedious weeks, I left my apartment on just three occasions.

The first two, I went to church with my mother.

The third, I went to see King Benny.

* * *

I POURED MYSELF AN ESPRESSO FROM A TWO-CUP POT, King Benny staring across the table. It was a late Sunday afternoon and a transistor radio resting against the window behind me was tuned in low to a Yankee game. Two men, wearing dark slacks and sleeveless T-shirts, sat outside the club on wooden chairs.

I drank my coffee and listened to Phil Rizzuto call the game, taking it into the bottom half of the eighth inning, Yanks down by three runs. King Benny's hands were spread flat on the table, his face a clean-shaven mask.

"They suck this year," he said, lifting a finger in the direction of the radio.

"They sucked last year," I said.

"Gets to be a habit," he said. "A bad habit. Like going to jail."

I nodded and lowered my head, averting his gaze.

"We didn't mean to hurt anybody," I said.

"You didn't mean it don't make it not happen."

"We didn't go out looking to hurt is what I meant," I said.

"Few do," King Benny said.

"How long do you think we'll get?"

"A year," King Benny told me, and it made my knees go weak. "Maybe more. Depends on the mood the judge is in."

"I hear the one we got is tough," I said. "Likes to set examples."

"They're all tough," King Benny said.

I drank some more coffee and scanned the room, framing it

in my mind, not wanting to forget its look, its stench, its feeling of safety. King Benny's foul-smelling club was a second home to me and, like the library, had become a place to escape the harshness of the life I knew.

It was an escape to the quiet company of the single most dangerous man in Hell's Kitchen.

"Your father tell you what to expect?" King Benny asked. "Tell you how to handle yourself?"

"He hasn't talked much," I said. "He's pretty upset. Most of the time, he and my mom just sit and cry. Or they fight. One or the other."

"I can't help you up there," King Benny said, leaning closer to me, his eyes tight on my face. "Or your friends. You're gonna be on your own in that place. It won't be easy, Shakes. It's gonna be hard. The hardest thing you and your friends are ever gonna have to do."

"My father thinks that too," I said. "That's why he's crying."

"Your father *knows* that," King Benny said. "Only he don't think you're ready for it. Don't think you can take it."

"Do you believe that?"

"No," King Benny said. "I don't. There's a part of you that's a lot like me. A small part. That should be enough to bring you back alive."

"I better go," I said, pushing the cup to one side. "I'm not allowed to stay out alone too long."

"When do you leave?"

"I see the judge on Thursday," I said, looking at the man I had grown to love as much as my own father. "That's when we find out where we go and for how long."

"Your parents be with you?"

"My father," I said. "I don't think my mother can handle it. You know how she gets."

"It's better that way," King Benny said. "She shouldn't see you in a courtroom."

"Will you still be here when I get back?" I asked, my voice choked, my eyes focusing on the two men outside, trying not to let King Benny see me cry.

"I'll *always* be here," he said. "Doing what I always do."

"What *do* you do here?" I asked, a smile at the center of my tears.

King Benny pointed to the empty espresso pot.

"I make coffee," he said.

16

M Y FRIENDS AND I STOOD BEHIND A SCARRED OAK table in the middle of a high-ceilinged, airless room, hands at our sides, staring straight ahead. We were dressed in the only good clothes we owned, the dark jackets, dark slacks, white shirts, and sky-gray ties standing out against the cream-colored courtroom walls of New York State's Division of Family Justice.

John and I were on the right side of the table, next to our lawyer, a short, doe-eyed man who had trouble breathing through his nose. His hair was slicked down with gel and the tail of his white shirt was popping out the back of his brown pants.

Michael and Tommy stood to his left.

None of us looked at him and none bothered to listen to a word he uttered.

Our families were behind us, held apart by a wooden barrier and two court officers. My father sat in the first row of benches, directly behind me, his sad, angry presence like hot air on my neck. We had talked very little on the subway ride downtown. He assured me all would go well, that no one beyond the neighborhood would know where I was, and that maybe, just maybe, all this was for the good, that it was a lesson waiting to be learned.

"Be like goin' to camp," my father said as the train careened toward Chambers Street. "Plenty of fresh air, lots of runnin' around, decent food. And they'll keep you in line. Maybe teach you and your friends some discipline. Do what I couldn't do."

"I'm gonna miss you, Dad," I said.

"Save that shit," my father said. "You can't think like that. You gotta be like a stone. Can't think about anybody. Can't worry about anybody. Except yourself. It's the only way, kid. Believe me, I know what I'm talkin' about here."

We rode the rest of the way in silence, wrapped in the noisy company of the rattling car.

I was two months shy of my thirteenth birthday and about to leave home for the first time in my life.

* * *

"HAVE THE DEFENDANTS BEEN MADE AWARE OF THE charges against them?" the judge asked.

"Yes, they have, your honor," our lawyer responded, sounding as low-rent as he looked.

"Do they understand those charges?"

"Yes, they do, your honor."

In truth we didn't understand. We were told the night before our appearance that the charges against us would be lumped together under the umbrella tag of assault one, which constituted reckless endangerment. The petty theft charge would be dropped in everyone's case but mine, since my action was what precipitated all that followed.

"It's the best I could do," our lawyer told us, sitting behind a cluttered desk in his one-room office. "You have to admit, it's better than getting hit with attempted murder. Which is what the other side wanted."

"You're a regular Perry Mason," John told him seconds before his mother cuffed the side of his face.

"What does it *mean* for the boys?" Father Bobby asked, ignoring the slap and the comment.

"They'll do a year," the lawyer said. "Minimum. Lorenzo may get a few months more tacked on since he initiated the action. But then, he may get less time since he was last on the scene. That's the only open question."

"It wasn't his idea," Michael said. "It was mine."

"The idea doesn't matter as much as the act," the lawyer said. "Anyway, I should be able to convince the judge not to tack on any extra time given how young Lorenzo is."

"They're *all* young," Father Bobby said.

"And they're *all* guilty," the lawyer said, closing a yellow folder on his desk and reaching for a pack of cigarettes.

"Where?" Father Bobby asked.

"Where what?" the lawyer said, a menthol cigarette in his mouth, his hands coiled around a lit match.

"Where will they be sent?" Father Bobby asked, his face red, his hands gripping his knees. "Which home? Which prison? Which hole are you going to drop them in? That clear enough for you?"

"Wilkinson's," the lawyer said. "It's a home for boys in upstate New York."

"I know where it is," Father Bobby said.

"Then you know what it's like," the lawyer said.

"Yes," Father Bobby said, the color drained from his face. "I know what it's like."

I LOOKED OVER MY SHOULDER, to the left, for a quick glance at the members of the Caldwell family, sitting in a group in the first two rows behind the prosecutor's table. Old man Caldwell was home, recuperating from his numerous wounds. According to a medical statement filed with the court, he would never again gain full use of his left leg and would suffer from dizziness and numbness in his other limbs for the rest of his life. His hearing and vision had also been affected.

Each of us had written him a note, delivered by Father Bobby, telling Mr. Caldwell and his family how sorry we were.

Each note went unanswered.

"Do any of you wish to say anything before sentence is passed?" the judge asked, moving aside a sweaty glass of ice water.

"No, sir," each of us said in turn.

The judge nodded, looking at his notes one last time. He was in his late fifties, a short, stout man with a head full of thick white hair and brown eyes that revealed little. He lived in a Manhattan housing complex with his second wife and two dogs. He had no children, was an avid poker player, and spent his summer vacations fishing off the dock of his Cape Cod home.

He cleared his throat, sipped some water, and closed the folder before him.

"I'm sure by now you boys have been made aware of the severity of the crime you committed," the judge began. "It was a crime which combined a careless disregard for one man's place of business, in this case a hot dog stand, with a criminal attitude toward another man's safety and well-being. The result left one man ruined and another nearly dead. All for the price of a hot dog."

It was hot in the room and I was sweating through my shirt and jacket. I kept my hands clasped in front of me while staring straight ahead. I heard the mumblings of those behind me, the people on my right fearful of the judge's words, the people on the left anticipating the punishment to come. John's mother, sitting next to my father, whispered the prayers of the rosary, her fingers moving slowly down the row of beads.

"Mr. Kratrous has been forced to give up his business and his dream of building a home here. He returns to his native Greece, his belief in our way of life torn apart by the wanton and remorseless act of four boys intent on thievery. Mr. Caldwell is an even more tragic case. Left for dead by a prank gone asunder, his life will never be what it was prior to that fateful day. He will suffer each and every single moment he has left on this earth, drugged with medications to numb the pain, walking with the aid of a cane, fearful of leaving his house. And all this for what? So four boys could sit back and share a laugh, enjoy a joke caused by the pain of others. Well, the joke backfired, didn't it?"

It was nine-forty in the morning when the judge pushed back the sleeves of his robe, took another drink of water, and sent us to what he called a home for boys and what everyone else called a prison.

He took us one at a time, starting with the Count.

"John Reilly," the judge said. "The court hereby sentences you to be remanded for a period of no more than eighteen months and no less than one year to the Wilkinson Home for Boys. In prior agreement with the attorneys for both parties, the term is to begin effective September one of this year."

Behind me, John's mother let out a low scream.

"Thomas Marcano," the judge said, shifting his attention to Butter. "The court hereby sentences you to be remanded for a period of no more than eighteen months and no less than one year to the Wilkinson Home for Boys. In terms agreed upon by counsel, your sentence is to begin on September one of this year."

"Michael Sullivan," the judge said, his tone turning harsher, convinced he was addressing the group ringleader. "The court hereby sentences you to no more than eighteen months and no less than one year to the Wilkinson Home for Boys. In terms agreed upon by counsel, your sentence is to begin on September one of this year. I might add, were it not for the intervention of Father Robert Carillo of your local parish, who spoke in glowing terms on your behalf, I would have sentenced you to a much stiffer punishment. I still have my doubts as to your inherent goodness. Only time will serve to prove me wrong."

I wiped at my upper lip and forehead, waiting for my name to be called. I turned around and saw my father sitting with his eyes closed, his arms folded, the top of his bald head wet with sweat.

"Lorenzo Carcaterra," the judge said, the contempt in his voice no less than it had been for my friends. "In your case, the court will take into account the fact that you are the youngest of the four and arrived on the scene after the theft of the cart had already occurred. With that in mind, the court hereby sentences you to serve no more than one year and no less than six months at the Wilkinson Home for Boys. In terms agreed upon by counsel, you will begin your sentence on September one of this year."

The judge rested his head on his high-backed chair and stared out at us in silence. He tapped the edge of a case folder with the fingers of his right hand, his face an empty canyon, a small, nondescript man made large by the weight of judicial power.

"I hope," he said in conclusion, "you make good use of your time at Wilkinson. Learn a trade, perhaps, or further your education. If not, if you turn the other way and ignore the possibilities available to you, then I can guarantee you will stand before me again, guilty of another violent act. And I assure you, next time I won't be as kind as I was today."

"Thank you, your honor," our lawyer said, sweat lines streaking the sides of his face.

———

"LOOK AT THE SCUMBAG," my father said to Father Bobby, sitting in the row behind him, his voice loud enough to reach the bench, watching the judge head back to his chambers. "Look at him smile. Puts four kids away for a year and he smiles. I oughta break his fuckin' jaw."

Father Bobby leaned over and put a hand on my father's shoulder.

"Easy, Mario," Father Bobby said. "This isn't the place and now's not the time."

"It's never the place," my father said. "And it sure as shit ain't *never* the time."

Our lawyer reached over the barrier and put out a hand toward Father Bobby, his low voice barely audible over the din coming from the Caldwell family side of the courtroom.

"It went as well as could be expected," the lawyer said.

"For you, maybe," Father Bobby said.

"They could have gotten a lot more time," the lawyer said. "For what they did, a lot more time."

Father Bobby stood and leaned on the barrier, his Roman collar off his neck and in his right hand.

"This isn't a game," Father Bobby said. "It's not about deals or less time or more time. It's about four boys. Four boys whose names you didn't even bother to learn. So don't be so quick to pat yourself on the back."

"I did my job," the lawyer said.

"The sworn oath of the mediocre," Father Bobby said.

"You could have done better with them yourself, Father," the lawyer said. "Then you wouldn't have needed the services of a shit like me."

Father Bobby sat back down, his eyes catching mine, his face ashen and pained.

"It won't be so bad," the lawyer told him. "After all, it's not like everybody who spends time at Wilkinson ends up a criminal."

The lawyer turned away and cleared off the top of the defense table, shoving a handful of manila folders inside his tattered brown bag and snapping it closed.

"Some of them even find God and become priests," the lawyer said, turning again to face Father Bobby. "Don't they?"

"Go to hell," Father Bobby said.

Outside, a light summer rain began to fall.

BOOK TWO

"Live then, beloved children of my heart, and never forget that, until the day God deigns to reveal the future to man, the sum of all human wisdom will be contained in these two words: Wait and hope."

—THE COUNT OF MONTE CRISTO

1

HAD BEEN IN MY CELL FOR LESS THAN AN HOUR WHEN the panic set in. To fight it, I closed my eyes and thought of home, of the neighborhood, of the streets where I played and of the people I knew. I imagined a hydrant spreading its cold spray over my face, felt the stitches of a baseball in my hand, heard soft music floating off a rooftop. I wasn't yet thirteen years old and I wanted to be in those places, back where I belonged. I wanted everything to be the way it was before the hot dog cart. I wanted to be in Hell's Kitchen and not in a place with cold walls and a tiny cot. A place where I was too afraid to move.

It was dark and I was hungry, the dank air heavy with the smell of cleaning fluids. I didn't like tight places or dark rooms and my cell was both. Its walls were cracked and peeling, a torn photo of James Dean taped to one. I hated to be alone, to be without books to read or baseball cards to sort through, forced to stare at a thick iron door that was locked from the outside. The steady rumbling sounds that came out of the other cells were difficult to ignore, making me long for those peaceful hours when I would sit in Sacred Heart Church and find solace in its silence.

It doesn't take very long to know how tough a person you are or how strong you can be. I knew from my first day at

Wilkinson that I was neither tough nor strong. It takes only a moment for the fear to find its way, to seep through the carefully constructed armor. Once it does, it finds a permanent place. It is as true for a hardened criminal as it is for a young boy.

* * *

THE FIRST GUARD I MET INSIDE WILKINSON WAS SEAN Nokes, who was then twenty-five years old. He stood inside my cell, his legs pressed close together, a black baton cupped in both hands. He had a thick, ruddy face and close-cropped blond hair and he wore sharply creased brown slacks, thick-soled black shoes, and a starched white button-down shirt with a black name tag clipped to the front pocket. His eyes were cold, his voice deep.

"Toss your old clothes to the floor" were the first words he said to me.

"Here?"

"If you're expecting a dressing room, forget it. We don't have any. So lose the clothes."

"In front of you?" I asked.

A smile cracked the side of Nokes's face. "For the time you're here, day or night, you do *everything* in front of *someone*. Piss, shit, shower, brush your teeth, play with yourself, write letters home. Whatever. Somebody's gonna be looking. Most times, that somebody's gonna be *me*."

I tossed my shirt to the floor, unzipped my pants, and let them drop past my knees. I stepped out of the pants, kicked them aside, and, wearing only my white cotton briefs, white socks with holes in both heels, and a laceless pair of Keds, looked back up at Nokes.

"*Everything,*" Nokes said, still standing in stiff military posture. "Here on, the only clothes you wear are state issued."

"You want me to stand here naked?" I asked.

"Now you're catching on. I knew you Hell's Kitchen boys couldn't be as dumb as people say."

I took off my underwear, kicked off my sneakers, and balled up the white socks, dropping them all on the pile beside me. I stood there naked and embarrassed.

"Now what?"

"Get dressed," Nokes said, nodding his head toward the clothes that had been left on my cot. "Assembly's in fifteen minutes. That's when you'll meet the other boys."

"Are my friends on this floor?" I asked, taking two steps toward the cot and reaching for a folded green T-shirt.

"Friends?" Nokes said, turning away. "You got a lot to learn, little boy. Nobody's got friends in this place. That's something you best not forget."

* * *

THE BUS RIDE UP TO THE WILKINSON HOME FOR BOYS had taken more than three hours, including two stops for gas and a short bathroom break. Lunch was eaten on board: soggy butter sandwiches on white bread, lukewarm containers of apple juice, and Oh Henry! candy bars. Outside the temperature topped 90 degrees. Inside, it was even hotter. The old air conditioner hissed warm air and half the windows were sealed shut, dust lines smearing their chipped panes.

The bus was old, narrow, and dirty, painted slate-gray inside and out. Half the thirty-six seats were taken up by boys younger than I was; none was older than sixteen. There were three guards along for the ride, one in the front next to the driver and two in the back sharing a pack of smokes and a skin magazine. Each guard had a long black nightstick and a can of Mace looped inside his belt. The guard up front had a small handgun shoved inside the front band of his pants.

Four of the boys were black, two looked to be Hispanic, and the rest were white. We sat alone, occupying every other seat, our feet chained to a thin iron bar that stretched the length of the bus. Our hands were free and we were allowed to speak, but most seemed content to stare out at the passing country-side. For many, it was their first trip beyond New York City borders.

Michael sat two rows ahead of me and John and Tommy were close behind to my left.

"This is like the bus Doug McClure drove in *The Longest Hundred Miles*," John said to a pock-marked teen across the aisle. "Don't you think?"

"Who the fuck is Doug McClure?" the kid said.

"Not important," John said, turning his attention back to the sloping hills of upstate New York.

* * *

EARLIER THAT MORNING, WE HAD SAID OUR GOOD-BYES to relatives and friends outside the courtroom across from Foley Square. My father hugged and held me until one of the guards told him it was time for us to go.

"Treat him right," my father told the guard.

"Don't worry," he answered. "He'll be okay. Now, please, step away."

I walked from my father and into a line forming near the bus. The crowd around us drew closer, older hands reaching out for a final touch, mothers crying softly, fathers bowing their heads in angry silence. I saw John's mother lay a strand of ro-sary beads over his head, her knees buckling from emotion. Michael and Tommy stood behind me on the line, their eyes staring at empty spaces; no one was there to see them off.

I looked to my left and saw Father Bobby standing next to an open-air parking lot, his back pressing a light pole. I nodded in his direction and tried but couldn't bring myself to smile. I watched as he flicked his cigarette to the sidewalk and walked toward the bus.

I wished he wasn't there. I wished none of them were there. I didn't want *anyone*, let alone people I cared about, to see me get on a bus that was going to take me to a place I could only think of as a jail. Father Bobby especially. I felt I had let him down, betrayed his trust in me. He tried to help us as much as he could—sent a stream of letters to the judge, hoping to get the charges dropped or reduced; argued to have us assigned to another institution; begged to have us placed in his custody. None of it worked and now he was left with only prayer.

He stood across from me, his eyes saddened, his strong body sagging.

"Will you write to me?" he asked.

I wanted so much to cry, to put my arms around him and hold him as close as I had held my father. I fought back the tears and tried to swallow, my mouth dirt-dry.

"Don't worry," I managed to say. "You'll hear from me."

"It'll mean a lot," Father Bobby said, his voice as choked and cracked as mine.

He stared at me with wet eyes. Years later I would realize what that look contained, the warnings he wished he could utter. But he couldn't tell me. He didn't dare risk making me even more frightened. It took all the strength he had not to grab me, to grab all of us, and run from the steps of that bus. Run as far and as fast as we could. Run until we were all free.

"Would you do me a favor?" I asked him.

"Name it."

"Check on my mother and father," I said. "These last few weeks, they look ready to kill each other."

"I will," Father Bobby said.

"And no matter what you hear, tell 'em I'm doin' okay," I said.

"You want me to lie?" Father Bobby said, a smile breaking through the sadness, one hand on my shoulder.

"It's a good lie, Father," I said. "You can do it."

Father Bobby moved from the bus and watched as I boarded, his eyes scanning the faces of the other boys already in their seats. He pulled another cigarette from his shirt pocket and lit it, inhaling deeply. He then went over to my father and stood by his side until the bus closed its doors and pulled away from the curb. Then the two men—one a priest, the other an ex-con—walked with heads down and hands inside their pockets toward a nearby subway station for the ride back to the only place either one ever trusted.

2

THE WILKINSON HOME FOR BOYS HELD 375 YOUTHFUL offenders, housed in five separate units spread across seven well-tended acres. It had two large gyms, a football field, a quarter-mile oval track, and one chapel suitable for all religions.

From the outside, the facility resembled what those who ran it most wanted it to resemble—a secluded private school. One hundred guards were on hand to monitor the inmates. The majority were local recruits only a few years older than their oldest charges. For them, this was a way-slop on a path to other jobs in law enforcement or government. A two-year tour of duty at Wilkinson, which was the average stay for most guards, always looked good on a résumé.

The teachers, groundskeepers, handymen, cooks, and main-tenance crews were also local hires. This served the dual func-tion of keeping labor costs low and secrecy high. No one was going to do damage to one of the largest employers in the area, regardless of what they might see or hear.

The facility was run by a warden and his two assistants.

The warden, a disinterested and overweight man in his late forties, was more concerned with appearances than the reality of life inside Wilkinson. He lived with his wife and two chil-dren in a large house less than a five-minute drive from the main gate. He left his office every afternoon at four and was never at his desk any earlier than ten. His young assistants, who both hoped one day to run facilities of their own, kept similar schedules.

The guards were in charge of the day-to-day operations. They ran the drills, which started with a six A.M. wake-up and a twenty-minute breakfast and ended with a nine-thirty lights-out. Each day was a series of whistles directing us to our next station—classroom, gym, showers, meals, clinic, library, and field work.

Michael, Tommy, John, and I were assigned to the second tier of group C in the third and smallest of the buildings dotting the property. We were each placed in a private twelve-foot cell that came equipped with a cot and a spring mattress, a toilet with no lid, and a sink with only a cold water faucet. The iron door leading into the room had three bars across the center and a slide panel at its base. Above the sink was a small window, its glass entwined with wire, which offered a view of what seemed to me to be an always colorless sky.

We were allowed a shower every three days and were given clean clothes every Friday morning; the dirty laundry was thrown into a hamper wheeled by a white-haired man with a limp. To avoid confusion, our green shirts, white pants, white socks, and dark blue sneakers were stenciled with the first two letters of our last name. Those old enough to shave did so under a guard's supervision. Beards and mustaches were not permitted. Neither were portable radios or any type of recording device. There was only one television per building and that was usually watched by the guards.

Once a month, a movie was shown in the main hall and all 375 inmates were required to attend.

There were four guards assigned to each floor, with one, in our case Nokes, designated group leader. The three men working with Nokes were named Ferguson, Styler, and Addison. We were never told their first names, nor were we encouraged to ask. None was older than his mid-twenties, and they seemed to be close friends.

Ferguson was tall and angular, with feminine hands and a thin face that quickly betrayed his thoughts. He was the only son of a slain New York State trooper and was on the waiting list for both the New York City and Suffolk County police departments. He had just completed his first year at Wilkinson and was both distrusted and disliked by the juveniles. He had a flash temper and a brute strength that went against his physical appearance. "You could see it in him from the first day, from the first time you laid eyes on the guy," John said. "He had the kind of temper that was either going to kill or going to get him killed. Or both."

Styler was using his job at Wilkinson to finance his way through law school. He was short but muscular and made as much use of the gym as any of the inmates. On his evening breaks he would do chin-ups on the railing bars, his body dangling over the second level of the tiers, openly daring any juvenile to make a move. Styler was always in a foul mood, brought on by the dual demands of work and school and the frustration of spending time at a job he viewed with contempt. He was a poor kid who looked down on other poor kids. They only reminded him of where he came from and how far he had to go to get away.

Addison was a graduate of a local high school who wanted nothing more than a steady job that paid well, offered good benefits, and a twenty-year pension. He took every civil service test he found out about and was on the waiting list for eight police and fire departments throughout the area. He was the youngest of the guards assigned to us and also the loudest, eager to flex verbal muscles by barking out orders. We had seen many men like him in Hell's Kitchen. He had little else in life but his mundane job. Off the job, he took a lot of shit; on the job, he shit on everyone.

At first look there were no surprises to Addison. There were no surprises to any of them. But that was a first look, and for once we had no idea what to look for.

*   *   *

I WAS SITTING NEXT TO JOHN, OUR BACKS UP AGAINST THE gym wall, our legs stretched out, shirts drenched with sweat, watching six black inmates play an intense game of three-on-three basketball. We were only in the middle of our third day at Wilkinson. It already felt like three months.

I watched a muscular teen in full sweats hit a corner jumper, my eyes looking beyond him at the cement walls that kept us prisoners. Nothing that had happened during my first days at the home had helped ease my anxiety. The food was tasteless, the sleeping conditions horrid, and the atmosphere in the yards and classrooms charged. There was always a sense of impending danger, and I just couldn't envision living a full year of my life in such a way.

As bad as it was for me, it was worse for John. The tight quarters gave weight to his claustrophobia and worsened his asthma attacks. He wasn't eating and couldn't drink the milk that was served at every meal, reducing his liquid intake to the tepid water he sipped from playground fountains. His skin was pale, his nose always seemed to be runny, and he looked as frightened as I felt.

"Is this how you Hell's Kitchen boys spend your days?" It was Nokes. He was standing above us, facing the game, a black baton in his hand. "Watching niggers shoot baskets?"

"We're takin' a break," John said. "That's all."

"I *decide* when you get a break," Nokes said, a smirk on his face.

It didn't take long for Sean Nokes to make his presence among us felt. He was one of those men who enjoyed the power he held and who looked to cause trouble at every turn. He was in the middle of his second year at Wilkinson and had been married less than six months. He lived in a two-bedroom third-floor apartment less than a five-mile drive from the home. He sent a small portion of his paycheck to his widowed mother in nearby Rochester and was captain of the guards' bowling team. He smoked heavily and his breath often smelled of bourbon.

Nokes talked and acted tough, especially around the inmates, but I always got the feeling that on his own, without the back-up guards and the power of his position, he wouldn't amount to much. In a fair fight, on a Hell's Kitchen street corner, any one of us could probably take him. I *knew* Michael would bring him down, maybe even Janet Rivera. But for now we were locked in his house, forced to play according to his rules.

"Get back out there," Nokes said, pointing an end of the baton toward the crowded courts, *"Now."*

I shrugged, turned to John, and said, "One more game won't kill us." Then I got up and, as I did, brushed one of my shoulders against the side of Nokes's uniform.

Nokes, inches behind me, lifted his baton and swung it down hard, against my lower back. The pain was sharp, intense, and numbing. The force brought me to one knee.

Nokes's second shot landed against the center of my back and was quickly followed by a third, a swing that was hard enough to crack bone. I was down on both knees now, gasping for breath, staring into the eyes of a black teen with a gel Afro. He looked back, still and silent, except for the basketball bouncing at his side.

I heard John scream from behind me. "What are you doing? He didn't do anything to you!"

"He touched my uniform," Nokes said calmly. "That's against institute rules."

"He didn't touch you," John said, his entire body trembling. "And if he did, he didn't mean it."

"Stay outta this," Nokes told him.

"You didn't have to hit him," John said, a touch of Hell's Kitchen to his tone. "Don't hit him again."

"Okay." Nokes's voice softened, but his eyes stayed hard. "Help him up. Take him back to his cell." When John hesitated, Nokes said, "Go ahead, pick him up. Don't be afraid."

"I'm not afraid," John told him.

Nokes just smiled.

BACK IN THE CELL, John helped ease me down on my bunk and covered my legs with a folded blanket.

"I can't believe he hit you like that," John said.

"He's hit before," I told him.

"How do you know?"

"While I was down, I looked over at the others. None of them seemed surprised."

And now I wasn't either. I understood what Father Bobby had wanted to tell me but couldn't. I realized the weight of my father's words. I figured out what was behind all of King Benny's veiled warnings. They had tried to prepare me, prepare us all. But none of them, not even King Benny, could have envisioned the full extent of the horror we would face.

* * *

WE FELT THEIR PRESENCE BEFORE WE HEARD THEM. John had lingered, making sure I was all right, delaying his return to the harsher world outside the cell. Somehow, when it was just us, we could make believe that things were fine. But things weren't fine and would never be again.

Nokes stood in the cell doorway, his arms folded across his

chest, a crooked smile on his face. Behind him stood Ferguson, Styler, and Addison, black batons at their sides. Nokes led them into my cell. Addison closed the door behind him. They didn't say anything except when John, as fearlessly as he could muster, asked them what they wanted.

"You see?" Nokes said with a laugh. "See how tough this Irish punk is?"

Ferguson and Styler moved past Nokes and each grabbed one of John's arms. Addison instantly went up behind him and wrapped a thick cloth around John's mouth, knotting it at the back. Nokes stood over me, one of his knees pressed against my chest. I looked away from him, my eyes toward John, both our faces betraying our terror.

"Undo his pants," Nokes said.

John's pants slipped down around his ankles, white legs shining under the glare of the outside light.

"Hold him tight," Addison said to Ferguson and Styler. "I wouldn't want him to slip and hit his head."

"We got him," Ferguson said. "Don't worry."

"Okay, Irish," Nokes said. "Let's see how tough you really are."

Addison beat against John's back, rear, and legs with his baton, the blows causing the skin to swell immediately and my friend's eyes to well with tears. His back turned beet-red and the thin muscles of his legs bent under the pounding. Each blow brought a low moan from John's mouth, until the fifth blow caused him to lose consciousness. Still, Addison didn't stop. He lifted his baton higher and brought it down with even more force, his face gleaming with sweat, his eyes filled with pleasure at the pain he was inflicting. He finally stopped after a dozen shots had found their mark, pausing to wipe rows of sweat from his brow with the sleeve of his shirt. Ferguson and Styler still held John's arms, all that was keeping him from dropping to the floor.

"Think he's had enough?" Nokes asked me.

"Yes," I said, staring up at him.

"Yes what, you guinea fuck."

"Yes, sir," I said. "I think he's had enough."

Nokes and I watched in silence as the trio pulled John's pants up and undid the gag around his mouth. Then John was dragged out of my cell, back to his.

Nokes walked around my cell, hands behind his back, head down.

"See things my way," he said to me. "*Do* things my way. Don't fight us. And there'll never be another problem like there was today. If not, you Hell's Kitchen boys may never get outta here alive. It's something to think about, isn't it?"

It was the end of our third day at the Wilkinson Home for Boys.

3

I T WAS NOT A GROUP OF INNOCENT YOUNG BOYS AT
Wilkinson. Most, if not all, of the inmates belonged there.

Our population was composed of the toughest kids from
the poorest and most dangerous areas of the state, a number of
them riding out their second and third convictions. All were
violent offenders. Few seemed sorry about what they had done
or appeared on the brink of any rehabilitation.

A few of the inmates enjoyed their stay, viewing it as a break
from the pressured street world they inhabited. Others, ourselves included, marked off the days on the walls against our
bunks, scratching lines against concrete, much like we had seen
actors do in many a prison film.

Most of the convicted were there on assault charges, more
than half of them drug-related. Cocaine had just begun to sink
its sinister fangs into poor neighborhoods, quickly replacing
the more tranquil heroin as the drug of choice among the way-
ward.

Blacks and Hispanics were the first among the poor to taste
the drug's power, to feel its need and, as a result, their crimes,
previously bordering on the petty, had taken a more vicious
direction. Unlike their suburban compatriots, they had no parents with crammed wallets who could be counted on when the

urge for the powder grew strong. And so they turned to the defenseless to support their habits and desires.

The Italian and Irish poor, in 1967, still found their troubles through drink and bravado. Street fights were quick to turn into vendettas when the cork was out of the bottle. A sizable portion of the white inmates were serving time on assault charges, almost all fueled by booze and revenge. The others were nabbed for foiled attempts at robbery, committed either while drunk or in the company of older men.

My friends and I fell uncomfortably in the middle. We were there on assault charges, caused neither by drunkenness nor anger.

We were there because of pure stupidity.

There were few solid friendships at Wilkinson. A handful of alliances existed, all of them uneasy. Blacks and whites, as in any penal institution, separated themselves by color. Ethnic groups paired off, neighborhood factions looked to stay together, friends on the street tried to cover for each other.

It was the guards' function to break through the allegiances, to cause dissent, to eliminate any barriers to their own power. Up against a lone individual, the guards easily maintained control. Up against a united group, it would not be so easy.

My friends and I were one of many groups who tried to stick together. That was one reason we were singled out by the guards in our block, Nokes and Styler in particular. They also knew we were an easier problem to solve than other groups, many of which numbered far more than four members. It might be hard, even dangerous, for Nokes and his crew to do battle with the tougher, more seasoned inmates. Keeping those groups in line was merely a part of their job. Recreation came in the form of me and my friends.

We were regarded, from the beginning, as a group that could be toyed with, partly because of our ages, partly because of the simple nature of our crime, and partly because we didn't belong to an already existing gang. With other inmates, other groups, the guards drew a line and waited for that line to be crossed before they attacked.

With us there never was a line. With us Nokes and his crew could go on the attack at any moment, for any reason.

For us there were never any rules.

4

FALL 1967

I T WAS THE MORNING OF MY THIRTEENTH BIRTHDAY.
Our first month at Wilkinson had passed without further
incident. Except for Butter—Tommy—my friends and I had
lost a few pounds, due to the quality of the food and our inability to sleep through the night. My father had warned me
that the noise inside a prison was, initially, the hardest adjust-
ment, and he was right. The moans and groans, the constant
coughs, the occasional screams, the flushing toilets, the music
from hidden radios—none of it ceased until sunup.

I was walking in the middle of a line of eight, coming out
of a morning match session taught by a sleepy-eyed former
drug addict named Greg Simpson. The classes at Wilkinson
were, at best, mediocre. Most were overcrowded, often num-
bering close to forty students, the majority of them as openly
bored as the teachers. English and history were still my favorite
classes and, while neither of the teachers could hold a torch to
Father Bobby, they at least attempted to get some points across.
My friends and I welcomed the homework assignments, since
they gave us something to do in our cells besides stare at the
walls or listen to the constant cries.

We were on the first tier, Michael in front of me, John

bringing up the rear, all heading for the Ptomaine Tavern, as the inmates had nicknamed the mess hall.

"Hold the line," Nokes barked out from my left. "Carca-terra, Sullivan, Reilly, step out. The rest of you, mouths shut and eyes forward."

We had, ever since the beatings John and I had taken, kept our distance from Nokes and his cohorts. We had withstood their steady barrage of verbal abuse, ignored their nudges, slaps, and taunts. It was certainly our safest play and, as we saw it, probably our only play.

We stood at attention, arms brushing the sides of the iron rail, eyes straight ahead.

Nokes eased his body in alongside mine and, with a broad smile on his face, ordered the three of us back to our cells. He knew it was my birthday and began to tease me about it. He told me his was coming up later in the week and Styler's was soon after that. I tried to avoid his gaze, his breath coming on me heavy and strong. He looked drunk, his footing unsteady, his face red, eyes slightly glazed. Whatever was going to happen, I knew it wasn't going to be good.

Nokes stepped away from me and moved toward Michael. He stared at him for a few seconds and then tapped him lightly on the shoulder with the end of his baton, the smile still on his face. He told us he had planned a birthday party, a special celebration we would all enjoy. While Nokes talked, his speech slurred by the booze, a few of the other inmates on line began to giggle.

John and I were too scared to move and had to be pushed along by Nokes. John turned to look at me, his face pale with apprehension. Michael walked with his head down, hands at his sides, powerless to help the friends he had always been there to protect.

We didn't know what Nokes had in store for us, but we knew enough not to expect a cake, balloons, and party hats. The four of us had been locked inside the walls of Wilkinson long enough to expect nothing but the unimaginable.

I walked into my cell, Michael still in front of me, and found Styler, Ferguson, and Addison sitting on my bunk, two of them smoking cigarettes. In the corner, wedged in between the bowl and sink, Tommy stood at attention.

Ferguson had his shirt off and kept his back against the wall. He patted Addison on the shoulder and winked, eager for the fun to begin. Ferguson seldom initiated any of the acts against us, but once they began, he joined in with a viciousness that belied his size and demeanor. He fancied himself a comic and was known to slap and kick inmates until they laughed aloud at one of his stories.

I looked around the room, heard the door behind me slam shut, and watched Addison, Styler, and Nokes undo their shirts. My body was wet with sweat and I felt weak enough to faint. I saw Michael open and close his fists and Tommy shut his eyes to all movement. I heard John start to wheeze, his breath coming in small bursts.

Nokes pulled a cigarette from his shirt pocket and asked me if I liked surprises. When I answered no, they all shared a long, loud laugh. Ferguson came off the cot and rubbed the palm of his hand across my face as he asked how old I now was.

"Thirteen," I said.

Addison pointed a finger in Tommy's direction and ordered him to turn and face the wall. Tommy, moving slowly, did as he was told.

Ferguson moved away from me and ordered both John and Michael to do the same. They walked to the wall farthest from the bunk and turned their faces to it.

Nokes, cigarette dangling from his mouth, tossed one arm casually over my shoulders. Addison put out his cigarette and checked his watch, moving back, closer to my bunk, leaving Nokes with all the free room he wanted.

My eyelids moved like shutters, trying to block out the droplets of sweat falling into them. My voice cracked from fear and nerves. "What do you want?" I managed to ask.

"A blow job," Nokes said.

I don't remember much more about that day. I remember being forced down to my knees, closing my eyes, my consciousness, to all but the laughter and jeers. I remember Nokes's sweaty hands holding the back of my head. I remember feeling numb and wishing they would kill me before the night was over.

I never spoke to my friends about it, nor did they ever mention it to me. We tried as best we could to annihilate those moments—which occurred with dulling regularity after that birthday morning—as deep inside ourselves as possible. To this day, no clear picture of the sexual abuse we endured at the Wilkinson Home for Boys has surfaced in my mind. I have buried it as deep as it can possibly go. But it is there and it will always be there, no matter how hard I work at blocking it out. It occasionally surfaces, not during my most violent nightmares, of which there have been many, but in softer moments. It will show itself across more innocent images—a glimpse of a uniform, the sounds of a man's laugh, a darkened room, the clanging of a fence. It lasts for the briefest of seconds. Just long enough to once more send a chill.

The details of those forced sexual encounters have been relegated to a series of stop-action blurs.

I see hands slap bare skin. I see pants torn and shirts ripped apart. I feel hot breath against my neck and strong legs wrapped around mine. I hear groans and frenzied laughter, my back and neck wet from another man's sweat and spit. I smell cigarette smoke and hear mute talk once it's over, the jokes, the comments, the promises to return.

In those blurry visions I am always alone and crying out against the pain, the shame, and the empty feeling the abuse of a body leaves in the tracks of the mind. I am held in place by men I hate, helpless to fight back, held by fear and the dark end of a guard's baton.

What I remember most clearly from that chilly October day was that it was my thirteenth birthday and the end of my childhood.

5

I WAS WALKING NEXT TO MICHAEL IN THE OUTFIELD OF Wilkinson Park, facing empty wooden stands. It was nearing Thanksgiving and the weather was taking a cold turn. We wore thin pea-green jackets above our prison issues, hands shoved inside the pockets of our pants.

We had been inside Wilkinson for two months. Ten months of our sentences remained. In that short span of time, the guards at Wilkinson had beaten our bodies and had weakened our minds. All that was left was the strength of our spirit, and I knew it wouldn't take much longer for that last part to go.

I began to think I might never make it out of Wilkinson, that my life would end within its walls. There were plenty of rumors floating around about inmates found dead in their bunks or in the shower stalls. I didn't know how many of those rumors were true and I didn't care to know. All that mattered to me was that I was being broken down by a system built to break people like me. I slept less than two hours a night and ate no more of the food than I needed. I had lost interest in most things and went through the routine of my day with shuttered eyes, closed to as much around me as possible.

It seemed even worse for my friends. I looked over at Michael, his face tired and worn, his movements slow and tentative, humbled by the beatings and the surroundings. His passion seemed dissolved, his strength sheared. All that was left beneath the sunken eyes and beat-up body was his pride and his concern for our collective safety. I hoped it would be enough to get him through.

John's condition was even worse. He was sickly to begin with, and the constant beatings and rapes combined with the lack of food he could eat had reduced his body to a withered state. He spent more time in the infirmary than he did in class or in the exercise yard. He spoke in a low, raspy voice and was losing that sharp edge of humor that had always sustained him.

Butter looked the same on the outside, his body weight holding steady, his manner seemingly unaffected. But his eyes were lifeless, stripped of any vibrancy, emptied of their spark. He was cold and distant now, his emotions locked, his responses monosyllabic. It was a survival method, the only way he could think of to make it through one more day.

Each of the guards had chosen one of us as a regular target, tagged us as his own personal pet. In my case, it was Addison. He would call on me to run his errands and even had me wash his car once a week. His hatred of me knew no barriers, his abuse no gates. He would spend hours telling me how easy my life was compared to his, how I was lucky to have a father who cared about me and a mother who didn't sleep around. He told me I should appreciate having grown up in New York City and been able to see all the things he could never afford to see. He told me I was lucky to have a friend like him in a place like Wilkinson.

Ferguson had it in for John, whose very presence would set off the guard's explosive temper. He would kick John as he walked by or hit him on the back of the head with his baton. Often the abuse would be rougher, its ugly results visible the next morning when John walked the yard with swollen eyes or puffy lips. Ferguson had a villain's heart and enjoyed whipping the weakest member of our pack. I always felt it was because he was weak himself, constantly ridiculed by Nokes and Styler. He couldn't lash out at them, so he sought an easier target. He found that target in John Reilly.

STYLER CLAIMED TOMMY AS his personal property. He forced him to carry his free weights around the yard and left a pair of shoes outside his cell every night to be shined by morning. He slapped and verbally abused him at will, a muscular man lording his advantage over a chubby boy. Tommy's presence set off in Styler too many reminders of his own impoverished childhood. He thought himself better than Tommy, constantly berating him over the most minor of infractions. He never let a day pass without attacking him in some form.

While Nokes abused us all, he took his greatest pleasure from beating Michael. He saw it as a match between two group leaders and always made sure that the rest of us were aware of his numerous assaults. He relished the cruelty he showered on Michael, forcing him to wipe up puddles of urine and wash the soiled clothes of other inmates. He ordered him to run laps around the playground track late into the night and then would wake him before the morning bell. He would slap and kick him randomly and trip him from behind while he walked the lunch line. It was all meant to make Michael beg him to stop, beg Nokes to leave him alone. But through it all, Michael Sullivan never spoke a word.

All four of the guards used sex as one more vicious tool in their arsenal. The repeated rapes were not only the ultimate form of humiliation, but the strongest method of control the guards could wield. The very *threat* of a rape kept us frightened of them all the time, never knowing when the door to the cell would swing open, always wondering when we would be pulled from a line.

We weren't the first group that Nokes and his crew treated

with such levels of inhumanity, and they weren't the only guards to abuse inmates. All across Wilkinson, young boys were left to the control of the out-of-control guards. And the cruelty was all in the open, done without fear of reprisal. No one spoke out against the abuse and no one reported it. The guards who did nothing other than maintain order in Wilkinson could ill afford to bring attention to the situation; to do so might cost them their own jobs. The support personnel were in similar positions. The warden and his assistants were blind to what went on, at ease with the pretense that they fulfilled a necessary function by keeping kids like us off the streets. In truth, they were probably right in their thinking. After all, not many in town would waste time worrying about the well-being of juvenile offenders.

The town that surrounded Wilkinson was small and weathered. Most of the houses had been built around the turn of the century. There was nothing in the way of industry other than a few parcels of farmland, two dairies, and a large plastics factory that employed nearly half of the 4,000 population. The townsfolk were friendly, the police department was small and honest, and the high school football team was said to be one of the best in the county. There wasn't much money, but there wasn't much to spend it on, either. Church bells rang loud and clear on Sunday mornings and pork picnics were summer weekend staples. The citizens voted Republican every November and kept to themselves year-round. They would seem to have little time or patience for the concerns of boys sent to their town to live behind locked doors.

I stopped walking and stood looking around the fields, a group of inmates to my left playing football, a smaller group to my right huddled in a circle, talking in whispers and hand signals. The wind was blowing cold, the overhead sky dark with thick clouds that buried the autumn sun in shadow.

There were fifteen more minutes to go on our break. I left

Michael to finish his walk and headed toward the library. We all needed to find a place of solace, and I found mine in the pages of John's favorite book, *The Count of Monte Cristo*. I read and reread the novel, sifting through the dark moments of Edmond Dantes's unjust imprisonment, smiling when he eventually made his escape and walked from the prison where he had been condemned to live out his life. Then I would put down the book and say a prayer, looking toward the day when I could walk out of Wilkinson.

6

VISITORS WERE ALLOWED INTO WILKINSON ON ROTATING
weekend mornings, for a maximum of one hour. Only one vis-
itor per inmate was permitted.

Early into my stay, I had written and asked my father not
to come, explaining how it would make it harder for me to do
time seeing him or my mother. I couldn't look at my father
and have him see on my face all that had happened to me. It
would have been too much for either one of us. Michael had
done the same with the interested members of his family.
Tommy's mother could never get it together to visit, satisfied
with the occasional letter he sent telling her all was well.
John's mother came up once a month, her eyes always brim-
ming with tears, too distraught to notice her son's skeletal
condition.

No one could stop Father Bobby from visiting.

News of his Saturday arrival was always presented with a
stern warning, delivered by Nokes, to keep the conversation on
a happy note. He warned us not to tell Father Bobby anything
and that if we did, reprisals would be severe. He assured us that
we belonged to him now and that no one, especially some
priest from a poor parish, could be of any help to us.

* * *

FATHER BOBBY WAS SITTING ON A FOLD-OUT CHAIR IN the center of the large visitors' room. He had placed his black jacket over the back of the chair and kept his hands on his lap. He was wearing a short-sleeve black shirt with Roman collar, black pants, and a shiny pair of black loafers. His face was tense and his eyes looked straight at me as I walked toward him, not able to hide their shock at what he saw.

"You lost some pounds," he said, a trace of anger in his voice.

"It's not exactly home cooking," I said, sitting down across from him at the long table.

Father Bobby nodded and reached out his hands to touch mine. He told me I looked tired and wondered if I was getting the sleep I needed. He asked about my friends and told me he was scheduled to see each of them later in the day.

I didn't speak much. I wanted to tell him so many things, but I knew I couldn't. I was afraid of what Nokes and his crew would do if they found out. I was also ashamed. I didn't *want* him to know what was being done to me. I didn't want *anybody* to know. I loved Father Bobby, but right now I couldn't stand to look at him. I was afraid that he would be able to see right through me, see past the fear and the shame, right through to the truth.

"Shakes, is there anything you want to tell me?" Father Bobby asked, moving his chair closer to the table. "Anything at all?"

"You shouldn't come here anymore. I appreciate it. But it's not a good thing for you to do."

I looked at him and was reminded of everything I missed, everything I couldn't have anymore. I needed to keep those thoughts out of my mind if I expected to survive. I couldn't

fight through those feelings with every visit. If I was going to come out of Wilkinson, I was going to have to come out of it alone.

Father Bobby sat back in his chair, then pulled out a Marlboro and lit it with a butane. He blew a line of smoke toward the chipped ceiling, gazing over my right shoulder at a guard standing at rest. "I stopped over at Attica on my way up here," he told me. "To see an old friend of mine."

"You have any friends *not* in jail?" I asked.

"Not as many as I'd like," he answered, smiling, cigarette still in his mouth.

"What's he in for?" I asked.

"Triple murder," Father Bobby said. "He killed three men in cold blood fifteen years ago."

"He a *good* friend?"

"He's my *best* friend," Father Bobby said. "We grew up together. We were close. Like you and the guys."

Father Bobby took a deep drag on his cigarette and exhaled slowly. I knew he had been a troubled teenager, a street brawler with a bad temper who was always being dragged in by the cops. I felt that was part of the reason he went to bat for us. But it wasn't until that moment that I knew he had served time in Wilkinson.

"We were both sent up here," Father Bobby said, his voice lower, his eyes centered on me. "It wasn't easy, just like it's not easy for you and the guys. This place killed my friend. It killed him on the inside. It made him hard. Made him not care."

I stared away from him, fighting off the urge to cry, grateful that there was one person who cared about me, cared about us, who knew what we were going through and who understood and would respect our need for silence. It was not surprising to me that the person would turn out to be Father Bobby.

It was also a comfort to know it hadn't killed or weakened him, but that somehow, in some way, Father Bobby found the

courage to take what happened and place it behind him. I knew now that if I could get out of Wilkinson in one piece I had a chance to live with what happened. Maybe I would never be able to forget it, just like I was sure Father Bobby had visions of his own hell every day. But I might be able to live my life in step with those painful memories. Maybe my friends could too. All we needed was to find the same strength that Father Bobby found.

"Don't let this place kill you, Shakes," he told me, the bottom of his hands squeezing the tops of mine. "Don't let it make you think you're tougher than you are."

"Why?" I asked. "So I can come out and be a priest?"

"God, no," Father Bobby said with a laugh. "The church doesn't need another priest who lifts from the poor box."

"Then why?" I asked.

His voice softened. "The road only leads back to this place. And it's a road that will kill you. From the inside out. Just like it did my friend."

Father Bobby stood up from his chair, reached his arms out, and gave me a long, slow hug. I didn't want to let him go. I never felt as close to anyone as I felt to him at that moment. I was so thankful for what he had told me, relieved that my burden and that of my friends could be placed, if we needed to, on his sturdy shoulders.

I finally let go and took three steps back, watching him put on his jacket and button it, a Yankee cap folded in his right hand.

"I'll see you in the Kitchen," I said.

"I'm counting on it, Shakes," Father Bobby said before turning away and nodding for the guard to open the iron door leading out.

7

ONCE A YEAR, IN THE WEEKS BETWEEN THANKSGIVING and Christmas, the Wilkinson Home for Boys sponsored a touch football game. Local residents were invited to huddle in the bleachers surrounding the football field, at a price of two dollars a ticket, with the money going back to the town. Children under ten were allowed in free.

But it was never about football. It was about the process of breaking down an inmate. First, the body was taken, ripped apart as if it were a tackle dummy, toyed with as if it were a stage prop. Next a young man's mind was molested, hounded until all he saw was a guard's face, all he heard was a prison whistle, all he feared was to break an unknown rule. Then, to complete the process, the guards would parade their creations onto a football field in front of the good people of a small town and play a game against them. A game they were too sick, too beaten up, too mentally ruined to compete in. All this was to show off the perfect picture of a perfect institution.

The breakdown didn't work with all the inmates. But it worked with enough of them to keep the portrait intact.

The guards assembled their team much in advance, practiced as often as four times a week, and had full use of the fields. The inmates' team was chosen the Monday before the game, eleven reluctant players selected randomly from the various ethnic groups, placed together, and told to play as a unit. They were allowed one two-hour practice, held under strict supervision. It wasn't meant, in any way, to be a fair or equal match. It was just another chance for the guards to beat up on the inmates, this time in front of a paying crowd. And the way those games were played, you didn't need a ref; you needed a doctor.

Nokes was captain of the guards' team during my months at Wilkinson. Addison, Ferguson, and Styler were players. My friends and I knew, without having to wait for a roster sheet, that we would be chosen for the inmates' team. Even Tommy, who had a badly swollen left ankle, the result of a recent battering he received from Styler. The guards were on our case for days, talking football, asking if we played it in Hell's Kitchen, asking who our favorite players were. It was just their way of telling us to get ready for another beating.

WE WERE TWENTY MINUTES into practice, surrounded by guards on the four corners of the field, when I was tackled from behind by a black kid with braces and wine-barrel arms. My face was pushed into the dirt, grass covering my nose and chin. I turned my head and stared at him.

"It's *touch* football," I muttered.

"I touch hard," he said.

"Save it for the guards," I told him. "I'm on your side."

"Don't need nobody on my side," he mumbled, moving back to the huddle.

"It's not bad enough that the guards are gonna hand us our ass," I said, walking with Michael. "We've got these losers thinking they're the Green Bay Packers."

"What's the point of even *having* a practice?" John said, coming up behind us.

"For them." I nodded toward a group of guards at mid-field, arms folded, laughing and nudging one another.

"We're like a coming attraction," Tommy said, walking slowly, trying not to put weight on his damaged ankle.

"Maybe," Michael said, looking at the inmates on the other side of the field. "Shakes, who's the toughest guy out here?"

"How do you mean, tough?" I said.

"Who can talk and have everybody listen?" Michael said.

"Rizzo," I told him. "Tall black guy with the shaved head. The one holding the ball."

"A black Italian?" John said.

"I don't know what he is. I just know his name's Rizzo. He's the main guy down in B block."

"What's he here for?" Tommy asked.

"Manslaughter," I told him. "Involuntary."

"What's that mean?"

"There was a fight," I explained. "He walked away and the other guy was *carried* away."

"There's gonna be another one if we don't get back and play," Tommy said. "Let's not get Rizzo angry *before* the game."

"They say he's got his own crew on the outside," I said. "He's up from Harlem or Bed-Stuy. I forget which. And the guy he killed?"

"What about him?" Michael said.

"His mother's boyfriend. Got a little too friendly with Rizzo's kid sister."

"That's our guy, then," Michael said.

"Our guy for what?" I said.

"I'll tell you after practice," Michael said.

* * *

RIZZO SAT BY HIMSELF IN THE LIBRARY, AT A WOODEN table in the center of the room, turning the pages of a football magazine, the top of his shaved head enveloped in a halo from the glare of the fluorescent lights overhead. I stood to his left, browsing through the library's collection of adventure books, most of them paperback, many missing pages and covers, a few littered with pornographic sketches.

Michael, a copy of *Tom Sawyer* under his arm, walked to the table, pulled back a chair, and sat across from Rizzo.

"Okay with you if I use this chair?" he asked.

"Okay with me if you set yourself on fire," Rizzo said, his voice and body more man than boy. "Okay with me if you die. I don't give a fuck."

"Thanks," Michael said, and sat down.

They read in silence for a few minutes, Michael turning his head once to look back in my direction, his face a blend of concern and confidence.

"Rizzo," Michael said in a whisper. "I need to talk to you. It won't take long."

"How the fuck you know my name?" Rizzo snarled.

"I'd have to be stupid not to know," Michael said. "You the guy everybody points to and stays away from."

"That *was* true," Rizzo said. "Till today."

"We're wasting time," Michael said. "You interested or not?"

Rizzo took a deep breath and stared at Michael, his jaw set, his hands flat on the surface of the table, his eyes the color of lit cigars.

"Tell your friend over there to pull a chair next to you," Rizzo said. "He ain't smart enough to look cool."

Michael smiled at Rizzo and without turning his head called for me to join them.

I walked down the aisle and eased my way toward the table, looking around the library, empty except for a guard standing by the entrance. I nodded at Rizzo as I sat down, a copy of *Scaramouche* in my hand.

"You been in here longer than a year?" Michael asked him.

"Closer to three," Rizzo said. "Should be out come the spring."

"How many of these football games you play in?" Michael asked.

"This one be my second," Rizzo said. "Why?"

"The guards win the first?"

"The guards ain't ever lost one," Rizzo said.

"What if they did?"

"Look, white boy," Rizzo said, sitting straight up in his chair, a tint of anger seeping through the icy veneer. "Don't know what your play was on the street. Don't care. But in here, the guards call the play and the play calls for them to win the game."

"Why?"

"You think they fuck with you now," Rizzo said. "Beat them Saturday and see what happens. Won't be just you. Be all, in every cell block. Now, you tell me, white boy, we all supposed to get our ass split open just so you can look good in a football game?"

"They don't fuck with you," I said, inching closer to the conversation.

"No," Rizzo said. "They don't. But they'll find them a nigger that ain't me and make him eat it double."

"I'm not saying we gotta win," Michael said. "I just don't want to take a beating."

"You do every day," Rizzo said. "Why's Saturday special?"

"On Saturday we can hit back," Michael said.

"You don't need me to hit them back," Rizzo said.

"It won't work unless we're all in it," Michael said. "The only one who can make that happen is you."

"Guards steer clear of me," Rizzo said. "They stay back and let me do my time. I play the game, put a hurt on one of them, it might change my cushion."

"You're still nothin' but a nigger to them," Michael said.

"Easy, white boy," Rizzo told him. "Just 'cause we talkin' don't mean we on the same side."

"They don't hit you or fuck with you like they do us," Michael said, excited now. "They fuck with you another way. They treat you like an animal. A street animal. One they talk about when his back's turned."

"I don't give a fuck what they say about me," Rizzo said.

"Yeah, you do," Michael said. "You give a fuck. 'Else you wouldn't be the man back where you are."

"And puttin' a hurt on the guards is gonna change that?" Rizzo sneered. "That what you think?"

"It won't change a thing," Michael said.

That stopped Rizzo cold. Now he was interested. "Then why, white boy?" he asked. He bolted up and shoved his chair behind him. "If it ain't gonna change nothin'?"

Michael stood up and looked briefly past Rizzo's shoulders at the guard to his right. He then leaned across the table, his eyes tilted up toward Rizzo.

"To make them feel what we feel," Michael said. "Just for a couple of hours."

Rizzo said nothing for the longest time. Then his lips curled up in what I can only assume was a smile.

"Hope you play as good as you talk," Rizzo said, turning to leave.

"I hope so too," Michael said.

IT WAS THE FIRST Saturday in December.

The afternoon sun did little to contain the cold winds whipping around the grounds. The stands were filled with bodies buried under the weight of wool coats, flap-down hats, furry hoods, leather gloves, wrap-around scarves, and thick quilts. The crowd's collective breath broke through the protective barriers of their clothing, sending waves of warm air snaking toward the slate-gray sky.

Vendors sold peanuts, hot chocolate, and coffee from their

stations at the base of the stands. Armed guards circled the perimeters of the field, eyeing the crowd. Another group of guards stood in a straight-line formation behind our bench, watching with smirks as, shivering in our thin pants and sweatshirts, we laced our sneakers tight.

I turned to stare at the crowd, wondering who they would root for and how far they had come just to see a touch football game between a group of guards and a collection of teenage inmates. I also stared at them with a fair amount of envy, knowing that once the game was over, they were free to leave, to return to their safe homes, dinner waiting, our game reduced to nothing more than table conversation.

The guards came out wearing shoulder and elbow pads, the spikes on their cleats shiny and new. A handful were dressed in jeans and the rest wore sweatpants. All of them had on thick cotton sweaters, a few of them with hoods. We were left to play in our prison issues, from sweats to sneakers.

The two captains, Nokes for the guards and Rizzo for the inmates, met in the center of the field for the coin toss, a guard posing as a referee standing between them. Rizzo had insisted on being named captain, feeling it would send the guards an early signal that this was not going to be just another football game. Neither one attempted a handshake, but Nokes offered to skip the toss and let us have the ball first.

Rizzo turned down the request and called for heads. Nokes didn't want any part of Rizzo, well aware of his reputation. But he couldn't back up, not with the other guards watching and not with the warden sitting in the front row of the stands. He offered Rizzo a deal. He would go easy on him and the other three members of his crew who were on the team if he laid down and stayed out of the game. If not, Nokes warned, they would be as rough on them as they planned to be on the rest of the inmates. Rizzo listened to the offer without any show of emotion, his eyes never moving from Nokes's face. He took several deep breaths and then, once again, asked for the coin to be tossed.

The coin came down heads.

Michael was in the center of the huddle, down on one knee, staring at the faces around him. He needed to see how rough the guards were going to be. He called a running play with me getting the ball. If I was touched as the rules called for, then we would be playing fair. But if I was tackled, as we all anticipated I would be, then we were in for a long and probably bloody afternoon. As Michael broke the huddle, Rizzo warned me not to fumble, regardless of how hard I was hit.

I stood behind Michael and next to Juanito, a fifteen-year-old in a T-shirt and torn pants. Tommy and John were on the line alongside Rizzo and a chubby black kid. Four inmates were spread at wideout, two on each side. The guards played four men up front, three in the middle, and four in the backfield.

Nokes and Addison were in the center of the line, both looking straight at me, their breath coming out in clouds, arms swinging at their sides, their bodies tense. Ferguson and Styler were playing deep, in a crouch, the front end of their cleats digging into hard ground.

"Watch out for the pass," Nokes shouted to the guards positioned around him. "Those wideout niggers can really run. Don't let 'em get in front of you."

Michael grabbed the snap, took three steps back, and flipped me the ball. I clutched it to my side, holding it with both hands, and followed Juanito into the line. The guards came off the ball with a grunt-filled fury, Nokes leading the charge. I turned a sharp left, darting from the center of the crowd, looking for an open space.

Three yards in, I was hit on the side by Addison, his arms

around my waist, his weight dragging me down. From the corner of my eye I saw Nokes, bearing down fast, primed to pin me to the ground.

The elbow came out straight and hard, a black blur that was felt before it was seen. It caught Nokes flush on the side of the face and sent him sprawling to the dirt, Rizzo hovering above him, a smile on his face.

"The nigger on the line can really hit," Rizzo said to him. "Don't let him get in front of you."

"All right!" Juanito said, helping me up. "We got ourselves a game now, motherfuckers. We got ourselves a game."

"That's right," Michael said, giving Rizzo a wink. "We got ourselves a game."

For ninety minutes, spread across four quarters and a half-time break, we played the guards in the toughest and bloodiest game of touch football ever seen on the playing fields of the Wilkinson Home for Boys. For those ninety minutes we took the game out of that prison, moved it miles beyond the locked gates and the sloping hills of the surrounding countryside, and brought it back down to the streets of the neighborhoods we had come from.

For those ninety minutes we were once again free.

We were down by a touchdown midway through the fourth quarter, our energy sapped by the cold and brutal tactics employed by the guards in their all-out effort to emerge with a victory.

Michael stood in the center of the huddle, the sleeve of his left arm drenched in blood, courtesy of a cleat-stomping he received from Addison and Styler on a long run shortly before the end of the half. Two thin streaks of blood flowed down the right side of his face. Tommy was breathing heavily, his ankle thick and purple. Johnny was barely able to stand, having been sandwiched a number of times by Nokes and Ferguson out in the middle of an open field.

I sat on my knees, spitting blood from a split lip, my breath coming in spurts, the pain from my rib cage too strong to ignore. I looked around at the others, all of them bleeding and raw. Rizzo's right hand was broken, twisted in a pile-on four plays earlier.

Behind us, the crowd, so clearly rooting for the guards early in the game, sat stunned into eerie silence, stilled by the sight of a field filled with red-tinged grass. The spectators were left with little else to do but watch the drama play itself out.

We had come so far, our energy level as high as the pain we felt in our bodies. We were all tired from the long game and weak from the blows we had taken. A tall kid, standing next to me in the huddle, had blood running down both his legs.

We needed one more play. A big play, one the guards wouldn't expect us to be able to carry out. It would have to be a street play. The kind that ends in a touchdown and a knockout. All the inmates had played in games that ended in blood. But for the guards this was a new experience, and they didn't much care for it.

Rizzo called the play. Michael would fake-pump a pass to a wideout named R.J. and then turn and throw deep, about forty yards downfield, right to the edge of the goal line. Rizzo would be there, step by step with Styler, both of them reaching for the ball. Rizzo's broken right hand was now hanging softly against his waist. It was Styler who had crushed the knuckles and bones and it would have to be Styler who was paid back, which now meant that the play required more than a touchdown to be successful. We came out of the huddle looking at six points for our team and a broken jaw for Styler. It didn't matter which came first.

Michael called for a quick snap and dropped back as far as he could, one arm useless at his side. I stayed next to Juanito, looking to block anyone who crossed our path. The two front lines banged at each other hard, blood, saliva, and tiny pieces of flesh flying through the air. Nokes, bloody and bruised, came in from the left side of the field, leaping over one inmate and reaching both arms out for Michael. I jumped from my feet and met him square on, both of us falling within inches of Michael's legs, just as the ball left his one good hand to head downfield on a spiral.

"You fucker!" Nokes shouted, slapping and punching at me with both hands. "I'm gonna fuckin' kill you!"

"Get off him!" Juanito screamed, pulling at Nokes's hair, grabbing one of his arms. "Get the fuck off him!"

Michael and another guard were pushing at each other. Two of the inmates were squared off against two other guards. Punches and kicks were being tossed up and down the field. Bodies were crumpled on all sides. Shrill alert whistles were going off in every direction. Guards, in uniform, armed with Mace cans and swinging batons, were running onto the playing area. The warden and his assistants were being driven down the sidelines, in a car with siren blaring, coming in from the goalposts to our backs.

Then the crowd, long silenced, erupted.

They stomped their feet against the base of the wooden stands, clapped their gloved hands in a wild frenzy, and screamed out in a uniform chorus of cheers.

Michael fell to his knees and pumped a fist in the air. Downfield, his arms raised to the sky, Rizzo basked in the applause, waiting for the guards to come take him away. He held the football in his good hand, a smile as open and as free as the emotion he felt spread across his face.

Styler's body lay inches from Rizzo. He was faceup, his legs spread, his head at an angle, motionless.

From inside the prison we heard shouts and yells.

The other inmates, forced to watch the game from their cells or outside open gym windows, celebrated the moment, many screaming out Rizzo's name. A number of the players rushed toward Rizzo, hoping to get to him before the guards, to lay a hand on the hero of the yard.

Nokes stood up on one knee, staring at me and Michael, the blood from his nose running into his mouth.

"You're dead," he said. "You are gonna pay for this in ways you never dreamed of. All of you. You're all gonna pay."

"You ain't worth shit, Nokes," Juanito said to him. *"We* always knew it. After today, *everybody* knows it."

"Outta my way, you fuckin' spic," Nokes said, standing on both legs, limping away to join the rest of the guards.

Michael walked up to him, waiting until he was inches away. "Hey, Nokes?"

"What?" Nokes said, turning, the hate in his eyes enough to chill the blood oozing out of our bodies.

"Good game," Michael said.

8

IT WAS MY SECOND DAY IN THE ISOLATION WARD, MY BACK against a damp wall, my knees tight against my chest, sitting alone in darkness. I was brought down to the place the inmates called "the hole" immediately after the game, dragged down by Ferguson and a heavyset guard with a red beard. They threw me face forward to the cold cement floor and watched as I crawled about, looking for a way to lift myself up.

They laughed at me and mocked my movements as I tried to make my way around the room. Then they slammed the door behind them, bolting it from the outside, their heavy footsteps soon an empty and distant echo. There was no bed in the hole. There was no toilet. There was no noise. There was no food. There was no water and there was no fresh air. There was only darkness and large, hungry rats.

In the hole there was only madness.

I inched my way toward a corner of the room, trying to ignore the dust, the blood that still flowed from my football wounds and, most of all, the soft squeaks of the rats moving somewhere in the black of the cell.

I spent my first day in the hole sleepless, moving my legs from side to side, hoping to keep the rats away from my cuts, knowing that sooner or later I would have to give in and close my eyes and they would make their move.

My hours were filled with terror. Any noise, even the slight whine of a floorboard, sent fear through my body. My clothes were drenched with sweat, my face was wet to the touch, my hair matted against my forehead. I took deep, shivering breaths, my eyes open wide, looking out into the stillness that surrounded me, my hands and feet numb from the cold.

I could not distinguish morning from night, dawn from dusk, each passing moment awash in a darkness that promised no rescue. The guards had not brought in any food or water, and the stench of dried urine and feces was overwhelming.

I was not alone in the hole.

I knew that my friends were somewhere down in the depths with me, each in his own cell, each in his own pain, suffering his own demons. Rizzo was there too, brought down by the guards, his other hand broken on his way in. There was no use shouting out to them; the walls and the cell door were much too thick for sounds to slip past.

I knew enough about the hole to know it was the place where the guards put inmates who had trouble adapting to their system. It was where they earned their control. The usual length of time spent in isolation was a week, never more than two. No one came out of it the same.

I had been there only a matter of hours when I began to think about death. It was what I most wished for, the only thing worth praying for to any God willing to listen.

I do not know how long I had been there when I heard the click of the lock, the bolt being pushed back, the handle as it snapped down. The sharp light that filtered in sent the rats scurrying into corners and forced me to shield my eyes. I heard footsteps approach as a large shadow hovered near.

"Thought you might be hungry, football star," a voice said. It was Nokes, standing above me, a large bowl in his hand. "I brought you some oatmeal."

He placed the bowl down by his feet, in the center of the room, sliding it closer to me with the edge of his shoe.

"Looks a little dry though," he said. "Nobody likes dry oatmeal. Tastes like shit."

I heard a zipper slide down, watched him spread his legs and listened as he peed into the bowl of food.

"There," he said when he had finished. "That's better. That should help it go down easier."

He walked out of the room, a set of keys rattling in his hand.

"Enjoy your meal, football star," Nokes said, closing me back into my dark world.

The minute I heard the lock turn and the bolt shut down I rushed for the bowl and ate my first meal in the hole.

* * *

I STARED AT THE RAT, INCHES FROM MY FACE, WATCHING him nibble on the skin of my stretched-out fingers. I was resting flat against the hard surface of the cell floor, my clothes soiled, my body empty of feeling. I had lost any sense of time, any grasp of place, my mind wandering back and forth on the cloudy road between delusion and nightmare. Rats crawled up and down my back and legs, feasting on my cuts and scabs, nestling in the holes in my clothes.

One of my eyes wouldn't open, feeling sticky and swollen to the touch. One of my hands was balled into a tight fist, the fingers locked in place. My lips were swollen and dry and there was steady pain from my neck to the base of my spine. I couldn't compose a complete thought, and when I tried to call up memories, I could see only fragments of faces. I heard the voices of friends and enemies, the thick tones of my father and King Benny, the empty sounds of Nokes and his crew, the gutter accents of Fat Mancho and Father Bobby, floating in and out, words and faces mixing as one.

I felt the open hydrants of Hell's Kitchen on my body, the cool spray of water stripping away summer heat. I tasted Sno-Kones and hot pepper sandwiches and listened to Frankie Valli hit a high note and Dinah Washington ache with the blues. I tossed pennies against the side of a warehouse wall, dropped water balloons on the head of a passing stranger, ran into the winds of De Witt Clinton Park, and fished off the piers of 12th Avenue. Left for dead in that hole of despair, I sought refuge in the safest spot my mind could wander—the streets of Hell's Kitchen.

Only then, during those rare cloudless moments, could I escape my dark surroundings, clear away the dirt and the pain, the rats and the pools of urine.

Only then could I move away from the wails of the walking dead and feel, for a fragment of time, that I was still alive.

* * *

I WAS RELEASED FROM THE HOLE AFTER TWO WEEKS AND sent to the prison infirmary, where my wounds were cleaned, my clothes thrown away, and my meals served on plastic trays. I was carried into the twenty-two-bed ward fifteen pounds lighter than the day of the football game, my body wracked with a high fever and a series of infections.

The medical staff at Wilkinson was a small one, led by an elderly doctor with a chronic cough and three nurses years past their prime. For each, it was a last stop in an otherwise undistinguished career. While they all must have been aware of what went on, they lacked the desire or conviction to question it, let alone bring the abuse to the eyes of a higher authority. They had more to lose than to gain by such confrontation and would be outmanned, outmaneuvered, and outsmarted if they dared.

"You're lucky," I heard the prison doctor say to me. "Another day in there and we wouldn't be any help."

"I wasn't alone," I said, my voice barely above a whisper, my mind still circling around empty spaces.

"They took everyone out," the doctor said.

"Were we all lucky?" I asked.

"No," the doctor said. "Not all."

* * *

RAYS OF SUNLIGHT CAME DOWN THROUGH AN OPEN WINDOW, warming my face, my left eye still sealed shut. The bed and the sheets felt soft against my bare skin, white bandages covering whole sections of my chest, arms, legs, and feet. An IV bag dripped fluid into one of my arms and two plastic tubes were in my nose, feeding me air from an oxygen canister off the side of the bed. Somewhere in the distance a radio played a song I hadn't heard before.

I turned my head to the right and saw Michael in the bed next to mine. His left arm and right leg were in soft casts, his face was puffy and bruised, the rest of his body bandaged as heavily as mine.

"I thought you'd never wake up," Michael said, looking over.

"I never thought I'd want to," I croaked.

"John and Butter are at the other end of the hall," Michael said.

"How are they?"

"Alive."

"Who isn't?"

"Rizzo," Michael said.

"They *killed* him?"

Michael nodded. "They took turns beating him until there wasn't anything left to beat."

Rizzo was dead because of us. We made him think that going up against the guards in a meaningless football game had some value, would somehow make us better than them. That it would give us a reason to go on. And, once again, we were wrong. We had made another mistake. While it is normal in the course of growing up to have lapses in judgment, our errors always seemed to carry a deadly price. We were *wrong* to take the hot dog cart, and that mistake nearly ruined a man and landed us in a juvenile home. We were *wrong* to go to Rizzo and talk him into taking part in our silly plan. That conversation cost him his life.

The mistakes we were making could never be repaired. I could never give James Caldwell back the feeling in his arm or take away his pain. I could never give the hot dog vendor back his business or his dreams. I could never bring smiles back to John and Tommy, return the sweetness that was at the core of their personalities. I could never take the hardness out of Michael and the hurt out of me. And I could never bring Rizzo back to life. A young man was dead because he went deep against the guards and reached for a ball he shouldn't have caught. Who went deep because we asked him.

I looked over at Michael and he stared back at me and I knew we both had the same thoughts raging through our brains. I turned away and laid my head against the pillow, staring at the white ceiling with my one good eye, listening to a voice on the radio talk about holiday sales and threats of snow. I looked down at my hands, the tips of my fingers wrapped in gauze, scratches like veins marking their way across my flesh. My eye felt heavy and tired, the antibiotics and painkillers making me as foggy as a street junkie.

I shut my eye and gave in to sleep.

* * *

IT WAS TWO DAYS LATER WHEN I HEARD THE FOOTSTEPS, familiar in their weight.

"Hello, boys," Nokes said, standing between our two beds, a smile on his face. "How we feelin' today?"

Michael and I just stared back, watching him swagger up and down, checking our charts, eyeballing our bandages and wounds.

"You should be outta here in no time," Nokes snarled. "It's gonna be good havin' you back. We missed you and your friends. Especially at night."

Michael turned his head, looking down the corridor, checking the faces of the other sick inmates. Juanito was two beds down, his face a mask of cuts, welts, and stitches.

"It's been nice visitin' with you," Nokes said, standing close enough for us to touch. "But I gotta go. I'm on shift. I'll see you soon, though. You can count on that."

Michael motioned for Nokes to stop. "Kill me now," Michael whispered.

"What?" Nokes moved to Michael's side of the bed. "What did you say?"

"Kill me now." It wasn't a whisper this time. It was in a normal tone of voice, calm and clear. "Kill us all now."

"You're fuckin' crazy," Nokes said.

"You *have* to kill us," Michael said. "You *can't* let us out alive."

Nokes was still startled, but he shook it off and replaced his uneasiness with his usual smirk. "Yeah?" he said. "And why's that, tough guy?"

"You can't run the risk," Michael told him.

"What risk you talkin' about?"

"The risk of meeting up," Michael said. "In a place that ain't here."

"That supposed to scare me? That street shit of yours supposed to scare me?" Nokes laughed. "Your friend Rizzo was tough too. Now he's buried tough."

"Kill us all," Michael said. "Or sign yourself up for life in here. That's the choice."

"I've been right all along," Nokes said. "You *are* crazy. You Hell's Kitchen motherfuckers are really crazy."

"Think about it," Michael said to our tormentor. "Think about it hard. It's the only way out for you. Don't take a chance. You can't afford it. You kill us and you kill us now."

9

WINTER 1968

I SQUEEZED THE MOP THROUGH A WOODEN WRINGER, dirty brown water filtering back into the wash pail. I was on the third tier of C block, washing the floors outside the cells. It was my first week out of the infirmary, and my wounds, bound by tight strips of gauze bandages against my ribs and thighs, still ached. After a few strokes with the mop, I rested against the iron railings, my legs weak from days in the hole. It was early morning and the cell block was quiet, inmates either attending classes or exercising in the gym.

I looked around the block, gray, shiny, and still, winter light from outside merging with the glare of overhead fluorescents that were kept on twenty-four hours a day. In its silence, Wilkinson looked serene, cell doors open, floors glistening, steam from large central radiators keeping out the cold winds of winter.

The peace was not meant to hold. Wilkinson was a prison on the brim of a riot. Rizzo had been right. The guards did not take kindly to our playing them even. The day after the game, all inmate privileges were canceled. The late-night beatings and abuse accelerated to the point where no inmate felt safe. The most minor infraction, ignored in the past, was now cause for the most severe punishment.

For their part, the inmates were stirred by Rizzo's death and the conditions in which the rest of the team were released from the isolation ward. Makeshift weapons—zip guns, sharpened spoons stuck into wooden bases, mattress coils twisted into brass knuckles—now appeared in every cell block. The inmates still obeyed every order, but their faces were now masked by defiance.

* * *

I WAS HALFWAY DOWN THE CORRIDOR WHEN I SAW WIL-son on the circular staircase, making his way to the third tier. Wilson was the only black guard in our cell block and the only guard who shunned the physical attacks enjoyed by his co-workers. He was a big man, a onetime semi-pro football player with a scarred knee and a waistline that stretched the limits of his uniform. He smoked nonstop, and always had an open pack of Smith Brothers cherry cough drops in his back pocket. He had a wide smile stained yellow by the smoke, and big hands topped by thick, almost-blue fingers. The inmates called him Marlboro.

Marlboro was older than the other guards by a good ten years and had two younger brothers who held similar jobs at other state homes. In summer months he was known to smuggle in an occasional six-pack to some of the older inmates.

He was also Rizzo's connection to the outside.

"Seem to be doin' a good job," he said when he reached my end of the hall, his breath coming in short spurts, a long stream of smoke flowing out his nose. "You take to the mop real good."

"Some people do," I said. "Some people teach."

"Got that right," he said, laughing, a rumble of a cough starting in his chest.

"How many of those you go through a day?" I said, pointing to the lit cigarette in his hand.

"Three," he said. "Maybe four."

"Packs?"

"We all got habits, son," Marlboro said. "Some that are good. Some that are bad."

I went back to mopping the floor, moving the wet strands from side to side, careful not to let water droplets slip over the edge of the tier.

"How much more time you got?" Marlboro said from behind me. "Before they let you out."

"Seven months if they keep me to term," I said. "Less if they don't."

"You be out by spring," Marlboro said. "Only the baddest apples do full runs."

"Or end up dead," I said.

Marlboro lit a fresh cigarette with the back end of a smolder between his fingers, tossed the old one over the side, and swallowed a mouth of smoke.

"Rizzo was my friend," Marlboro said. "I didn't have a piece of what went down."

"Didn't break your ass to stop it," I said.

"Look around, son," Marlboro said, cigarette clenched between his teeth, veins thick on his bulky arms. "You see a lot of other nigger guards around here?"

"*Guards* is all I see around here," I said.

"I got me a good job," Marlboro said. "Work is steady. Pension, if I make it, a good one. Vacation and holidays are paid, and every other weekend belongs to me and my lady."

"And it keeps you in cigarettes," I said.

"I *hate* what they do to you and the other boys," Marlboro said, cigarette out of his mouth, sadness etched across the stark contours of his face. *"Hate* what they did to Rizzo. That boy was blood to me. But there ain't nothin' I can do. Nothin' I can say gonna change this place."

I put the mop back into the pail and ran it through the wringer, hands on the top end of the handle, eyes on Marlboro.

"You ever hit a kid?" I asked.

"Never," Marlboro said. "Never will. Don't get me wrong. There's some mean sons of bitches in here could take a beatin'. But it ain't what I do. Ain't part of the job. Least not the job I took."

"How do the other guards feel about you?"

"I'm a nigger to them," Marlboro said. "They probably think I'm no better than any of you. Maybe worse."

"They always been like this?"

"Since I been here," Marlboro said. "Goin' on three years come this June."

"How about you and Nokes?" I asked.

"I do my work and keep my distance," Marlboro said. "He does the same."

"What's his deal?" I said.

"Same as the others," Marlboro said. "They don't like who they are. They don't like where they are."

"There's lots of people like that," I said. "Where I live, every man I know feels that way. But they don't go around doing the shit Nokes and his crew pull."

"Maybe they different kind of men," Marlboro said. "Nokes and his boys, they ain't seen much of life and what they seen they don't like. You grow up like that, most times, you grow up feelin' empty. And that's what they are. Empty. Nothin' inside. Nothin' out."

"What about the warden?" I asked, leaning the mop handle against the rail. "The people on his staff. They've *got* to know what goes on."

"But they *act* like they don't," Marlboro said, taking still another drag. "Same as the town folk. *Nobody* wants to know. What happens to you don't touch them."

"So they dummy up," I said.

"That's the jump," Marlboro said. "And don't forget, from where these folks stand, *you* the bad guys. Nokes and his boys, they ain't gonna break into people's homes. Ain't gonna hold 'em up at gunpoint. You the guys pull that shit. That's why you here to begin with. So don't expect no tears. To them that's free, you *belong* inside."

"You've got all the answers," I said to Marlboro, pushing the water pail farther down the center of the floor.

"If I did, I wouldn't need a state check every two weeks," he said. "I just know what I know."

"I've got to finish up," I said, pointing down to the rest of the corridor.

"And I gotta get me some more cigarettes," Marlboro said. "That give us both somethin' to do."

He moved away with a wave, a snap to his walk, his baton slapping against the railing bars. A small pattern of crushed cigarette butts lay in the spot where he had stood.

"You know there's no smoking on the tiers?" I shouted after him.

"What they gonna do?" Marlboro turned to face me, a grin spread across his face. "Arrest me?"

10

MY HANDS WERE FOLDED BEHIND MY HEAD, RESTING against my pillow, a thin sheet raised to my chin. It was late on a Saturday night, one week after Valentine's Day. Outside, heavy snow fell, white flakes pounding the thick glass. I was fighting a cold, my nose stuffed, my eyes watery, a wad of toilet paper bunched in my right hand. My throat was raw and it hurt to swallow.

I thought about my mother, wishing I had a cup of her *ricota* to take away the aches and chills. She would fill a large pot with water and set it to boil, throw in three sliced apples and lemons, two tea bags, two spoonfuls of honey, and a half-glass of Italian whiskey. She boiled everything down until the contents were just enough to fill a large coffee cup.

"Put this on," she would say, handing me the heaviest sweater we owned. "And drink this down. Now. While it's hot."

"Sweat everything right outta you," my father would say, standing behind her. "Better than penicillin. Cheaper too."

I tried to sleep, closing my eyes to the noises coming from outside my cell. I willed myself back to my Hell's Kitchen apartment, sipping my mother's witches' brew, watching her smile when I handed her back an empty cup. But I was too tense and too sick to find rest.

A number of the inmates, as tough as they acted during the

day, would often cry themselves to sleep at night, their wails creeping through the cell walls like ghostly pleas.

There were other cries too.

These differed from those filled with fear and loneliness. They were lower and muffled, the sounds of pained anguish, raw cries that begged for escape, for a freedom that never came.

Those cries can be heard through the thickest walls. They can cut through concrete and skin and reach deep into the dark parts of a lost boy's soul. They are cries that change the course of a life, that trample innocence and snuff out goodness.

They are cries that once heard can never be erased from memory.

On this winter night, those cries belonged to my friend John.

The darkness of my cell covered me like a mask, my eyes searching the night, waiting for the shouts to die down, praying for morning sun. I sat up in my cot, curled in a corner, wiped sweat from my upper lip, and cleaned my nose with the toilet paper. I shut my eyes and capped both hands over my ears, rocking back and forth, my back slapping against the cold wall behind me.

The door to my cell swung open, thick light filtering in, outside noise coming in on a wave. Ferguson stood in the doorway, beer bottle in one hand, baton in the other. He had a two-day growth of beard on his face and his thin head of hair looked oily and in need of a wash. His heavy eyelids always gave him a sleepy appearance and the skin around his thin lips was chapped, a small row of pimples forming at the edges.

"I just fucked your little friend," he said, his speech slurred, his body swaying.

He took three steps into the cell.

I rolled off the cot and stood across from him, my eyes on his, toilet paper still in my hand.

"Take your clothes off," Ferguson said, moving the beer bottle to his lips. "Then get back in bed. I wanna play with you for a while."

"No," I said.

"What was that?" Ferguson asked, taking the bottle away from his face, smiling, his head at half-tilt. "What did you say to me?"

"No," I said. "I'm not taking my clothes off and I'm not gettin' into bed."

Ferguson moved closer, his feet sliding across the hard floor.

"You know what you need?" he said, smile still on his face. "You need a drink. Loosen you up a little. So, have your drink. Then we'll play."

He lifted the beer bottle above my head and emptied it. Streams of cold beer ran down my face and shirt, my mouth and eyes closed to the flow, puddles forming around my feet. Ferguson wiped the beer from my face with the fingers of his hand.

He put his fingers in his mouth and licked them dry.

"There's all kinds of ways to drink beer," he said, throwing the bottle on my cot. "And there's all kinds of ways to fuck."

Ferguson threw his baton on the cot and watched it land inches from the bottle. He turned back to me and undid the buckle of his belt and lowered the zipper of his pants with one hand.

He ran the other hand across my face and chest.

"You're right," Ferguson said in a whisper. "You don't have to take off your clothes, you don't want to. And you don't have to get back in your bed."

"Please, Ferguson," I said, my voice barely audible. "Don't do this."

"Don't do what, sweet thing?" Ferguson asked, his eyes glassy, rubbing my chest harder, bringing his hand lower.

"Don't do what you're doin'," I said.

"But I thought you liked it," Ferguson said. "I thought all you boys liked it."

"We don't," I said. "We don't."

"That's too bad," Ferguson said, his face close to mine, his breath a foul mix of beer and smoke. "'Cause I like it. I like it a lot."

Ferguson ran his hand past my chest and up to my face and along my neck, resting it against the back of my head. He moved even closer to me, placing his face on my shoulder.

"Take my dick out," Ferguson said.

I didn't move, my eyes closed, my feet still, Ferguson's weight heavy against my body, his breath warm on the sides of my face.

"C'mon, sweet thing," Ferguson whispered. "Take it out. I'll do the rest."

I opened my eyes and saw John standing in the doorway.

He had a makeshift knife in his hand.

John moved out of the light and into the darkness of the cell. He was naked except for a pair of briefs, stained red with blood, and one sock drooping down the sides of his ankle. He was breathing through his mouth and kept the knife, held to his hand by a rubber guard, flat by his leg.

"Don't be afraid, sweet thing," Ferguson whispered in my ear. "Take it out. It's ready for you."

"I'm not afraid," I said.

"Then do it," Ferguson said.

"Move out of the light," I said. "It hurts my eyes."

Ferguson lifted his head and grabbed both of my cheeks in his hand, a wild, maniacal smile on his face.

"You *supposed* to keep your eyes *closed*," he said, moving backward, closer to John, dragging me with him. "Didn't you know that?"

We were inches from my cot, my hand close enough to

reach the empty beer bottle and the baton. John was by the side of the bed, the knife still against his leg. Ferguson let go of my face, undid his pants, and took two more steps back.

"All right," he said. "Let's stop fuckin' around, sweet thing. It's time for fun."

I eased down to my knees, my head up, looking into Ferguson's eyes, my hand reaching for the baton to my right.

"That's it, sweet thing," Ferguson said. "And remember, I like it slow. Nice and slow."

Ferguson felt the edge of the knife before he heard John's voice.

"That's how I'm gonna let you die, dip shit," John said. "Nice and slow."

"You little punk," Ferguson said more with surprise than fright. "What the hell you tryin' to do?"

"It's time for me to have a little fun," John said.

"I can have you killed for this," Ferguson said.

"Then I've got nothin' to lose."

I grabbed the baton, jumped to my feet, and held it with both hands. I looked past Ferguson at John, saw something in his eyes that had never been there before.

"You can't cut him, Johnny," I said.

"Watch me, Shakes," John said. "Sit down on your cot and watch me."

"Go back to your cell," I said. "Leave him to me."

"He's not gonna get away with it," John said. "He's not gonna walk away from what he did to me. What he's been doin' to all of us."

"He *has* to get away with it," I said.

"Who says?" John asked. "Who the fuck says?"

"We're gonna get out of here in a few months," I whispered slowly. "If you stick him, we aren't going anywhere."

"Listen to your friend, Irish," Ferguson said. "He's talkin' sense here."

I braced my legs and shoved the fat end of the baton into the center of Ferguson's stomach. I watched him flinch from the blow, his lungs hurting for air.

"Stay outta this, scumbag," I said. "Or I'll kill you myself."

John moved the knife away from Ferguson's neck, stepping back, holding the sharp edge of the blade in the palm of his hand. His face was a portrait of hard hate, emptied of its sweet-eyed charm, a resting place for all the torment and abuse he had endured.

In so many ways he was no longer the John I had known, the John I had grown up with. Wilkinson had done more than beat and abuse him. It had taken him beyond mere humiliation. It had broken him down and pulled him apart. It had ripped into the most gentle heart I had known and emptied it of all feeling. The John Reilly who would turn our clubhouse into a safe haven for lost kittens was gone. The John Reilly who stole fruits and vegetables off supermarket trucks and left them at the apartment door of Mrs. Angela DeSalvo, an elderly invalid with no money and no family, was dead and buried. Replaced by the John Reilly who stood before me now, ready to kill a man and not give it another thought.

"Let it go, John," I said. "He's a piece of shit and he's not worth it."

"Glad to see you got smarts," Ferguson said, getting his wind back, looking up at me. "I'll go easy on you in my report."

"There won't be a report," I said.

"Fuck you mean, there won't be a report?" Ferguson said, the drunken slur of his words replaced by a steadfast anger. "You two assaulted a guard. There's *gotta* be a report."

"Just go, Ferguson," I said, handing him back his baton. "Fix your pants and get the fuck outta here."

"I ain't leavin' before Irish over there hands me the knife," Ferguson said.

"There isn't any knife," I said.

I walked over to where John was standing, the steel look still on his face, his eyes honed in on Ferguson. I rested my hand against the one holding the knife, knuckles tight around the edge of the blade.

"It's okay, Johnny," I said. "You can let go now. It's okay."

"He's not gonna touch me again," John said, the voice no longer that of the boy who cried at the end of sad movies. "You hear me, Shakes? He's not gonna touch me again."

"I hear you," I said, taking the knife from my friend's hand.

I nudged past Ferguson and walked over to my cot. I lifted the thin mattress and put the knife on top of the springs.

"Like I said, Ferguson," I said, turning to face him. "There's no knife."

"I ain't gonna forget you did this," Ferguson said, pointing a shaking finger at both me and John. "You two hear me? I ain't gonna forget this."

"It's a devil's deal, then," I said.

"What the fuck's that mean?" Ferguson said.

John explained it to him. "First one to forget dies," he said.

11

THE ENGLISH TEACHER, FRED CARLSON, STOOD BEFORE the class, his tie open at the collar, his glasses resting on top of his head, a thick piece of gum lodged in the corner of his mouth. He had his back to the blackboard, hands resting on its edge. He was young, not much past thirty, in his first semester at Wilkinson, paid to pass on the finer points of reading and writing to a class of disinterested inmates.

"I was expecting to read thirty book reports over the weekend," Carlson said in a voice that echoed his country home. "There were only six for me to read. Which means I'm missing how many?"

"This here's English class," a kid in the back shouted. "Math's down the hall."

A few inmates laughed out loud, the rest just smirked or continued to stare out the classroom windows at the snow-filled fields below.

"I'm doing my best," Carlson said, his manner controlled, his frustration apparent. "I want to help you. You may not believe that or you may not care, but it's the truth. But I can't force you to read and I can't make you write the reports. That's something only you can do."

"Must be easy to read where you live," an inmate in a thin-cropped Afro said. "Easy to write. It ain't that easy to do in here."

"I'm sure it's not," Carlson said. "But you have to find a way. If you expect to get anywhere once you get out of here, you have to find a way."

"I gotta try stayin' alive," the inmate said. "You got a book that's gonna teach me that?"

"No," Carlson said, stepping away from the blackboard. "I don't. No one does."

"There you go," the inmate said.

"Then I'm just wasting your time," Carlson said. "Is that what you're saying to me?"

"You wastin' *everybody's* time," the inmate said, hand slapping a muscular teenager to his right. "Give it up and keep it home. Ain't no place for what you got here."

Fred Carlson pulled a metal chair from behind the center of the desk and sat down, both hands on his legs, his body rigid, his eyes on the inmate.

He stayed that way until the whistles sounded the end of the period.

"See you Friday, teach," the inmate said on his way out the classroom door. "*If* you still here."

"I'll see you then," Carlson said. "*If* you're still alive."

I WAS WALKING DOWN a row behind four other inmates, a black-edged notebook in my hand, a dull pencil hanging in my ear flap.

"You got a second?" Carlson asked as I passed by his desk.

"I do something wrong?" I asked.

"No," he said, shaking his head and smiling. "I just want to talk to you."

I stood my ground, waiting for the classroom to empty, hands in my pants pockets.

"You did a great job on your book report," Carlson said.

I mumbled a thank-you.

"How come you were able to find the time to do the work?" Carlson asked with a slight hint of sarcasm. "Aren't you worried about staying alive?"

"I worry about it all the time," I said. "That's why I read and write. It keeps my mind off it a while."

"You really seemed to like the book," Carlson said. My report had been on *The Count of Monte Cristo*.

"It's my favorite," I explained. "I like it even more since I been in here."

"Why's that?"

"I told you why in the report," I said.

"Tell me again."

"He wouldn't let anybody beat him," I said. "The Count took what he had to take, beatings, insults, whatever, and learned from it. Then, when the time came for him to do something, he made his move."

"You admire that?" Carlson asked, reaching across the desk for a brown leather bag stuffed with books and loose papers.

"I *respect* that," I said.

"Do you have a copy of the book at home?"

"No," I said. "I've only got the *Classics Illustrated* comic. That's how I first found out about it."

"It's not the same thing," Carlson said.

"There's a librarian in my neighborhood, she knows how much I like the story," I said. "She makes sure the book's always around for me. It's not that big a deal. Not many people look to take it out."

Carlson had his head down, rummaging with both hands through his bag.

"I gotta get goin', Mr. Carlson," I said. "Can't miss morning roll."

"One more minute," Carlson said. "I've got something for you."

"What is it?" I asked.

"This," Carlson said, a hardbound copy of *The Count of Monte Cristo* in his hand. "I thought you might like to have it."

"To keep?"

"Yes," Carlson said.

"Are you serious?" I asked.

"Very serious," Carlson said. "You love a book that much, you should have a copy of your own."

"I can't pay you," I told him.

"It's a gift," Carlson said. "You've received gifts before, haven't you?"

"It's been a while," I said, opening the book, flipping through its familiar pages.

"This one's from me to you," Carlson said. "My way of saying thanks."

"Thanks for what?" I asked.

"For not making me think I'm just spinning my wheels in here," Carlson said. "That *somebody*, even if it is only one student, listens."

"You're a good teacher, Mr. Carlson," I said. "You're just stuck with a bad bunch."

"I can't imagine being locked in here," Carlson said. "For one night, let alone months."

"I can't imagine it either," I said.

"It's not what I thought it would be like," Carlson said with a slow shake of his head.

"I don't think it's what *anybody* thought it would be," I said.

"No, I suppose not," Carlson said.

"Listen, I've got to run," I said. "Thank you again for the book. It means a lot."

"Will the guards let you keep it?" Carlson asked.

"They won't know I've got it," I told him.

"We can discuss the book in class on Friday," Carlson said. "That's if you think the Count can hold their attention."

"He's got a shot," I smiled.

"Any special section I should read from?" Carlson asked, snapping his leather bag shut.

"That's easy," I said, moving toward the door, book in my hand. "The part when he escapes from prison."

12

IT WAS MY FIRST TIME INSIDE THE GUARDS' QUARTERS, a series of lockers, couches, bunks, shower stalls, soda machines, and coffeemakers spread through four large rooms at the back end of C block. The rooms smelled of old clothes and damp tile and the floors were dusty and stained, cigarette butts scattered in the corners. Floor lamps, covers torn and smeared, cast small circles of light, keeping the quarters in a state of semidarkness. Dirty clothes were tossed on the floor and on the furniture. A large framed photo of the Wilkinson Home for Boys, taken during a snowbound winter many years earlier, hung in the main room.

Nokes sat behind a desk, its top cluttered with memos, open binders, a tape recorder, two phones, a handful of magazines, and open packs of cigarettes. A thick toaster-size cardboard box, its center slit open, rested in the middle.

"You asked to see me?" I said, standing in front of him.

"Hang on a second, soldier," Nokes said. "I wanna get the other guys for this."

Nokes lifted the phone off its cradle and pressed a yellow intercom button.

"Get off your asses," he shouted into the speaker. "He's here."

Addison, Styler, and Ferguson walked in from a side room, each in various stages of undress. Ferguson had shaving cream along his face and neck, a straight razor in his hands. Styler, naked except for a pair of white briefs, was smoking a cigar with a plastic tip. Addison held a folded paper in one hand and a slice of pepperoni pizza in the other.

They stood behind Nokes, their attention more on the box than on me.

"You know the rules about mail?" Nokes asked, looking up at me, an unlit cigarette clenched between his teeth. "About what you can get and what you can't?"

"Yeah," I said. "I know them."

"You can't know 'em too fuckin' well," Nokes said, a finger pointing to the open box. "Havin' your mother send all this shit."

"That box's from my mother?" I asked.

"I mean, look at this shit," Nokes said to the three guards surrounding him, ignoring my question. "Where the fuck she think her son is at, the army?"

"What the fuck is this?" Styler asked, his hand pulling out a small jar filled with roasted peppers in olive oil.

"The warden is supposed to clear the mail," I said. "Not the guards."

"Well, the warden ain't around," Nokes said. "And when he ain't around, we clear it."

"None of the shit I see would get past the warden," Styler said. "Ain't none of it on the approved list."

"I'm sure your mama got a copy of that list," Addison said. "It gets sent to all the parents."

"My mother doesn't read English," I said.

"Don't blame us for her being stupid," Nokes said, tossing a jar of artichoke hearts to Styler.

"Those are things she made," I said. "Things she knows I like. She didn't look to do anything wrong."

"Other than have a jackoff for a son," Styler said, opening the jar and putting it to his nose.

"Can I have the box?" I asked. "Please?"

"Sure," Nokes said. "The box is yours. What's in it is ours. That seem fair?"

"Is there anything in there other than food?" I asked, my hands bunched in fists by my sides.

"Just this." Nokes held up a brown set of rosary beads. "Mean anything to you?"

"More than they would mean to you," I said.

"Suppose you'd like to have them, then?" Styler said, his mouth filled with artichoke hearts.

"They belong to me," I told him.

"What do you do with these things?" Nokes asked, fingering the rosary beads in his hand.

"You pray," I said.

"Fuckin' losers like you ain't got a prayer," Styler said.

"Take the food, Nokes," I said. "All of it. Just let me have the beads."

Styler walked around the desk and came up alongside me, one of his arms around my shoulders.

"You gonna let us hear you pray?" he asked me.

"I like to do it alone," I said, my eyes still on Nokes. "It works better that way."

"Like jerkin' off," Addison said.

"Just this once," Styler said, smiling and winking at the other three. "Let us hear you."

"Maybe he needs something to pray about," Nokes said, reaching a hand under the desk, coming up with a black baton.

He gave the baton to Styler, who took it with his free hand, pushing me closer to his side.

"Put your hands on the desk," Styler said to me. "Lay them down flat."

"And start thinkin' up some prayers," Addison said.

MY HANDS WERE INCHES from the box my mother had sent. Styler spread my legs apart and pushed down my pants, tearing off the top button with the force of his effort. Nokes laid the brown rosary beads across both sets of my knuckles. I felt Styler's hands rub against the base of my back, his skin coarse, his manner rough.

"Remember, fucker," Nokes said, eating my mother's peppers with his hands. "We want to hear you pray. Loud!"

Styler put an arm around my stomach and slid the front end of the baton inside me. The pain came in a rush, leg muscles cramping, chest heaving, stomach tied in a knifelike nerve of knots.

"We can't hear no prayers," Nokes said.

"You better start." Ferguson had a terrible smile on his face. "Before Styler there loses his baton up your ass."

"'Our Father,'" I said, my lips barely moving, my breath short, my lungs on fire. "'Who art in heaven.'"

"Nice and loud," Styler said from behind me. "Pray nice and loud."

"'Hallowed be thy name,'" I said, tears falling down the sides of my face. "'Thy kingdom come. Thy will be done.'"

"Don't say come in front of Styler," Nokes said with a loud laugh. "You don't wanna get him excited."

"'On earth as it is in heaven,'" I said, my legs starting to buckle, my body damp with cold sweat. "'And forgive us our trespasses . . .'"

"That part must be about us," Addison said, his eyes wide, his tongue licking at his lips.

"'As we forgive those,'" I said, my hands starting to slide off the desk, knuckles still gripping the rosary beads. "'Who trespass against us.'"

"Louder, fucker!" Nokes said, standing now, holding my face with two hands. "Make like you're in a fuckin' church."

"'And lead us not into temptation,'" I said, the room around me a shifting blur, my arms and legs empty of feeling. "'But deliver us from evil.'"

"Too fuckin' late for that now, loser," Styler said as he released me and let my body crumple to the floor. "Too fuckin' late."

* * *

I WOKE UP IN MY CELL, ON MY COT, MY PANTS STILL wrapped around my knees. I was shivering, sheet and blanket under me, my body numb to movement. The rosary beads were still in my hand, the cross wedged into my palm. I brought the beads to my lips slowly, and kissed them.

I opened my eyes, looked out into the darkness, and cried till the sun came up.

13

SPRING 1968

MICHAEL HIT THE HANDBALL AGAINST THE CEMENT wall, watching it one-bounce its way toward John, who waited for it near the middle of the white divider line. I played off the back line, alongside Tommy, my mind more on the weather than on the game.

It was early afternoon and warm for a mid-April day. The sun was still strong, scattered rays bouncing off the hardened tar floor and onto our arms, legs, and faces. The air was dry, humidity low, soft breeze blowing at our backs.

The handball court was seldom free: the black inmates had co-opted the area as part of their domain. But, for now, they were out of the picture, joined together in organized protest, a reflection of their outrage over the murder earlier in the month of Martin Luther King, Jr. They stayed in their cells and refused to engage in any prison activity, insisting that even meals be brought to them. Initially, the guards reacted as expected, with intimidation and force, but the inmates held firm, anger and pride keeping the rules of the prison at bay. The warden, fearing outside attention, ordered the guards to back off and allow the protest to flame itself out.

The ball came in a dark blur toward Tommy, who took two

quick steps back, balanced his weight, swung his hand, and missed. He turned around, picked up the ball, and tossed it back to Michael.

"I don't get this game," Tommy said. "I don't understand it at all."

"That makes me *really* glad you're on my team," I said.

"What's the point?" Tommy asked.

"We don't *have* any points," I said. "Michael and John, they have all the points. Go ask them."

"It's six to nothing," Michael said, walking toward me, bouncing the ball against the tar, his right hand wrapped in heavy black adhesive tape. "You wanna switch sides?"

"How about we take a break?" I said. "I'm not used to getting this much sun."

"There ain't much shade around here," Michael said.

"Let's go near the trees," I said. "The guards can still see us from there and it's gotta be cooler."

We walked past the wall, wiping sweat from our faces and arms, toward a small chestnut tree with drooping limbs, the duty guard following us with his eyes.

We sat around the tree, our arms spread behind us, legs rubbing against grass, staring out at the square-shaped brick façade of C block, our home these past seven months.

"Nice view," John said.

"Just looks like any other place from here," Tommy said. "It don't look like what it is."

"I'll never forget what it looks like," I said. "Or what it is."

"You might," Michael said. "If you're lucky."

"They give you your release date yet?" Tommy asked me.

"Nokes had the letter from the warden," I said. "He waved it in front of me. Then he tore it up."

"When do you figure?" Michael asked.

"End of June," I said. "Maybe early July. Something like that."

"I wish we were goin' with you," John said, his voice crammed with sadness. "Woulda been nice for us to all walk out together."

"I wish you were too," I said, smiling over at him.

"No use thinking about it," Michael said. "We're gonna do a full year. Not an hour less."

"I could talk to Father Bobby after I get out," I said. "Maybe he could make some calls, shave a month or two off."

"There's nothing to talk about," John said.

"There's *lots* to talk about, Johnny," I said. "Maybe if people knew what goes on in here, they'd make a move."

"I don't *want* anybody to know, Shakes," John said, the center of his eyes filling with tears. "Not Father Bobby or King Benny or Fat Mancho. Not my mother. Not anybody."

"I don't either," Tommy said. "I wouldn't know what to say to anybody that *did* know."

"What about you?" I asked, turning my head toward Michael. "You gonna stay quiet?"

"I can't think of anybody who needs to hear about it," Michael said. "Guys did time in this place or places like it, they know what went on. Those who didn't won't believe it or won't give a shit. Either way, it's nothin' but a waste of time."

"I don't even think *we* should talk about it," John said. "Once it's over."

"I want it buried too, Shakes," Tommy said. "I want it buried as deep as it can go."

"We've got to live with it," Michael said. "And talking makes living it harder."

"People might ask," I said.

"Let 'em," Michael said, standing up, brushing loose grass off the back of his sweats. "Let 'em ask, let 'em think. But the truth stays with us."

"Just be glad you're going home, Shakes," John said. "Forget everything else."

"And try to stay out of trouble till we get back," Michael said.

"That should be easy," I said. "Without you guys around."

"What's the first thing you're gonna do when you get back?" John asked.

"Go to the library," I said. "Sit there for as long as I want. Look through any book I want. Not have to get up when somebody blows a whistle. Just sit there and listen to the quiet."

"Know what I miss the most?" Tommy asked in a sad tone, his face up to the sun, his eyes closed.

"What?" John said.

"Running under an open johnny pump late at night," Tommy said. "Water cold as winter. Stoops filled with people eatin' pretzels and drinkin' beers outta paper bags. Music coming out of open windows and parked cars. Girls smilin' at us from inside their doorways. Shit, it was like heaven."

"Two slices of hot pizza and an Italian ice at Mimi's is heaven," I said.

"Walkin' with Carol down by the piers," Michael said. "Holdin' her hand. Kissing her on a corner. That's hard to beat."

"What about you, John?" I asked.

"I don't want to be afraid of the dark again," John said in a voice coated with despair. "Or hear an open door in the middle of the night. And I don't wanna be touched, don't wanna feel anybody's hands on me. Wanna be able to sleep, not worry about what's gonna happen or who's comin' in. If I can get that, I'd be happy. I'd be in heaven. Or close to it."

"Someday, John," Michael said. "I promise that."

"We *all* promise that," I said.

In the short distance behind us, a guard's whistle blew. Overhead, rain clouds gathered, darkening the skies, hiding the sun in their mist.

14

THE PRISON CAFETERIA WAS CROWDED, LONG ROWS OF wooden tables filled with tin trays and inmates elbowing their way through a macaroni and cheese dinner. Each inmate had twenty minutes to eat a meal, which included time spent on the serving line, finding a seat, and dropping an empty tray on the assembly wheel in the back of the large room. Talking was not permitted during mealtime and we were never allowed to question either what we were given to eat or the amount doled out.

The food was usually at the low end of the frozen food chain, heavy on processed meat, eggs, cheese, and potatoes, weak on vegetables and fruit. Each table sat sixteen inmates, eight to a bench. One guard was assigned to every three tables.

As with every other social situation at Wilkinson, the dining area offered limited opportunities to make friends. The guards were always wary of cliques forming or expanding and moved quickly to split up any such attempts. This left the inmates with no choice but to stick to their original alliances. Living in an atmosphere that stressed survival above all else, random friendships posed too great a risk, for they required a level of trust that no one was willing to concede. It was safer to stay within your own group.

I was fourth on the serving line, standing a few feet behind Michael, empty trays held in our hands. A blank-faced counterman dropped an empty plate on each of our trays, his head rocking up and down, rolling to its own private rhythm. Farther down the line, I grabbed for two spoons and an empty tin cup.

"Can you see what we're having?" I asked Michael.

"Whatever it is, it's covered with brown gravy."

"*All* our meals are covered with brown gravy."

"They must think we like it," Michael said. Then he turned off the line and moved to his left, his tray filled with dark meat, gray potatoes, a small hard roll, and a cup of water, looking for a place for us to sit. He headed for the back of the room, where there were two spots. I followed, right behind him.

The spaces between the tables were narrow, wide enough for only one person at a time to make his way through. The guards stood to the sides, their eyes focused on the tables assigned them. They controlled who left his seat and who sat in his place, all accomplished with hand gestures, nods, and shoulder taps. It was a system that functioned through precision and obedience, guards and inmates merged in an assembly line of human movement. There was no room for error, no space for accidents, no place for a mental lapse.

No time to bring the assembly line to a halt.

Michael was halfway down the row of tables, his eyes focused on two seats in the rear of the room. I was directly behind him, followed by a short teenager with a limp. None of us saw the inmate on Michael's left stand and begin to move out of his row.

Michael moved three steps forward, the edge of his tray barely grazing the arm of the inmate walking toward him on his left. The inmate shot his arm against the tray and sent it skyward, out of Michael's hands and crashing to the floor in full view of a guard.

Michael whirled to face the inmate who called himself

K.C. and who was now standing with a smile on his face and his hands balled into fists. "What the fuck you do that for?"

"You brushed me," K.C. said.

"So?"

"*Nobody* touches me," K.C. said. "I ain't like you and the rest of your fag friends."

Michael swung a hard right at K.C., landing it flush against the much taller boy's jaw. The blow, one of the hardest I'd seen Michael land, barely caused a flinch. Michael looked at me in disbelief and, for a moment, it was almost funny, like something out of a James Bond movie. But K.C. wasn't in on the joke and, as we knew all too well, this was no movie.

K.C. looked to be about three years older than Michael, perhaps eighteen, with broad shoulders, bulked arms, and a crew cut so close it showed little more than scalp. In the few months that he had been inside Wilkinson, K.C. had already razor-slashed another inmate, done time in the hole for his part in a gang rape, and spent a week in a straitjacket after he took a bite out of a guard's neck.

He rushed Michael and they both fell to the floor, shirts and skin sliding against spilled food. K.C. threw two sharp right hands, both landing against Michael's face, one flush to the eye. A circle of inmates formed around them, quietly watching the action, a few holding trays and eating the remains of their lunch. The guard, less than a month on the job, stood off to the side, his face a blank screen.

I held my ground and scanned the circle for other members of K.C.'s crew, watching to see if any weapons were passed over, waiting for one of them to make a move and join their friend against Michael.

K.C. was rubbing a fistful of meat against Michael's face, grinding it into his eyes. Michael shot a hard knee into K.C.'s groin and followed it with a short left to his kidney.

"Your fuckin' life's over," K.C. said, putting his hands around Michael's throat and tightening his grip. "You gonna die here today, punk. Right on this floor."

I tossed my tray aside and jumped on K.C.'s back, punching at his neck and head, trying to loosen his hold. K.C. let one hand go and turned it to me, swinging his punches upward, brushing my shoulder and side. The reduced pressure allowed Michael to take in some fresh breath. K.C. swung his body at an angle, his open hand against my chin, trying to push me off his back. He rolled over with me still clinging to him, his strength taking Michael around with us. I landed on top of the spilled tray, my shirt wet and sticky from the gravy, meat, and potatoes spread across the floor. K.C. was now all flailing arms and legs, kicking and punching at us both with a wild, animal-like intensity. I covered my face with my hands and kept my elbows slapped against my sides, blocking as many of K.C.'s kicks and punches as I could.

Michael did the same.

The crowd inched in closer, sensing that what they wanted to see was about to take place—a bloody finish to the battle.

A sharp kick to the throat stripped me of wind and a wild punch to my jaw forced blood out of my nose. Voices in the crowd, fueled by the rush for the kill, cheered K.C. on.

"Finish him!" someone from behind me shouted.

"Kick him dead!" another said.

"One and two belong to you!" still another screamed. "Step back and just watch 'em die."

The shrill sound of a police whistle brought the shouts to an end.

The crowd parted to let Nokes walk past, each inmate staring at him in silence. Nokes held a can of Mace in one hand and the thick end of his baton in the other. He was chewing a piece of gum and had a cigarette tucked behind one ear. The back of his shirt was streaked with sweat. His eyes moved from me to Michael to K.C. The three of us stood facing him, our bodies washed head to knee in food and blood.

Nokes stood in front of me and took the cigarette from behind his ear, put it to his mouth, and lit it with a closed matchbook. He took in a lung full of smoke and let it out slow, through his nose, his closed jaw still moving to the gum.

"All these months here, they haven't taught you shit," Nokes said. "You're still the same fuckin' clowns you were when you walked in."

Nokes turned from us and faced the inmates behind him. He scanned their faces, running a hand through his hair, cigarette still hanging from his lower lip.

"Back to your seats and finish your lunch," Nokes said to them. "There's nothin' more to see."

"That go for me too?" K.C. said, rubbing his hands against the sides of his pants.

"No," Nokes said, turning back to him. "No, it don't go for you. I want you back in your cell. You're done with lunch."

"Me and you finish this some other time," K.C. said, looking over at Michael. "Sometime real soon."

"Maybe at dinner," Michael said, watching K.C. walk out of the lunchroom.

"You two get any lunch?" Nokes asked, stubbing out the cigarette with the front end of his boot.

"I got to smell it," Michael said. "That's better than eating it."

"How about you finish it now?" Nokes said.

"I'm not hungry," Michael said.

"I don't give a fuck you hungry or not," Nokes said. "You eat 'cause I'm tellin' you to eat."

I started to walk past Nokes, back toward the lunch counter to get a new tray. Nokes put a hand against my chest and held it there.

"Where you think you're goin'?" he asked, his voice louder, playing it up for the inmates watching.

"You said to get lunch," I said, confused.

"You boys don't need to go back on line for food. There's plenty to eat right where you standing."

I stared at Nokes and tried to imagine what had been done to him to make him this cruel, had driven him to the point that his only pleasure came from the humiliation of others. I more than just hated him. I had passed that state months ago. I was disgusted by him, his very presence symbolizing the ugliness and horror I felt each day at Wilkinson. I thought there wasn't much more he could do to me, do to any of us, but I was wrong. There was no limit to Nokes's evil, no end to his torment. And now we were about to take one more plunge into the hellish world he had forced on us.

Michael and I didn't move.

The inmates were pointing and whispering among themselves. A few of them giggled. The guard in the center of the aisle held his position.

"Let's go, boys," Nokes said, smiling now, his anger having found an outlet. "There ain't much more time in the lunch period."

"I'm still not hungry," Michael said.

Nokes immediately brought the back end of the baton down against the side of Michael's head. He quickly followed it with a level blast across his face. The force of the shot sent blood from Michael's nose and mouth spraying onto Nokes's uniform shirt.

"*I* tell you when you're hungry!" Nokes shouted, swinging the baton again, this time landing a sharp blow to Michael's neck. "And I tell you when you're not! Now, get on your fuckin' knees and eat."

Michael dropped to one knee, a shaky hand reaching for a fork, his eyes glassy, the front of his face dripping with blood.

He picked up the fork and jabbed at a piece of meat near his leg, slowly bringing it to his mouth.

"What the fuck are *you* waitin' for?" Nokes asked me. "Get down on your knees and finish your goddamn lunch."

I looked beyond Nokes at the faces of the inmates staring back at me, their eyes a strange mixture of relief and pleasure. They had all been at the edge of Nokes's baton, had all felt his fury, but none would ever move against him for the sake of two prisoners they barely knew. Nokes could have killed us on the floor of that lunchroom and no one would have said a word.

I went down on my knees, picked up a spoon, scooped up a potato slice, and put it in my mouth.

I looked up at Nokes, his shirt drenched and tinged red, his face splattered with Michael's blood.

"Eat faster," Nokes said, swinging his baton against the base of my spine. "Don't think you got all fuckin' day."

Nokes walked between us as we ate, smiling and winking at the other inmates, stepping on the pieces of food we were about to put in our mouths.

"Let's go," he said, pulling the top of Michael's hair and slapping his face. "Nobody leaves here until you clowns are finished with your meal."

Nokes walked to the edge of one of the tables and rubbed his boot on top of a crushed slice of bread. He took a cigarette out of an open pack in the front of his shirt and put it in his mouth. He lit it and sat on the side of the table.

"There's some bread over here," Nokes said, blowing two smoke rings toward the ceiling. "Can't have a good lunch without a slice of bread."

Nokes spread his legs, looked down at the bread, took in a deep breath, and spit on it. He took another drag of the cigarette and wiped at the sweat and blood on his face with the sleeve of his shirt.

"Now, how about you boys crawl over here and get yourself some?" Nokes said.

We were on our knees, chewing our food, our bodies trembling more out of shame than fear. Each humiliation plotted by Nokes and his crew was meant to be a breaking point, to make us crack and finally give in to Wilkinson. We were too young to know that the break line had been passed the minute we entered the prison walls and we were much too stubborn to understand that nothing we did or didn't do would allow us to defeat Nokes while we were still behind those walls.

"I don't see either of you scumbags crawlin'," Nokes said, finishing the cigarette and dropping it down on top of the bread. "Don't make me come drag you on over here."

We went down on our elbows, rubbing against the gravy that was spread across the ground, our faces inches from the food and dirt. Michael's nose was still bleeding and the swelling on his face had forced one eye to shut.

"That's it, now you're startin' to listen," Nokes said. "Show the boys here how to do a good crawl. Show them you know how to follow my rules."

"It's one o'clock, Nokes," Marlboro said, standing behind us, his voice filled with smoke. "Your lunch shift is over."

"I'm not through here yet," Nokes said. "Got a few more things that need cleanin' up before I can leave."

"It's my tour now," Marlboro said calmly, walking past us and moving closer to Nokes. "I'll clean what needs cleanin'."

"Stay outta this one," Nokes said. "This ain't got nothin' to do with you."

"I stayed outta too many as it is," Marlboro said, putting a cigarette to his mouth and lighting it. "This one I'm gonna stay in."

Nokes jumped down from the table, his face as red with rage as his shirt was with blood. He walked up to Marlboro, standing no less than five inches from the taller man's face.

"Don't fuck with me, boy," Nokes said. "I'm *warnin'* you."

"Fuck with me, Nokes," Marlboro said in a calm voice. "I'm *askin'* you."

Nokes continued the stare-down, his eyes locked in on Marlboro. None of the inmates moved, their attention focused on the first visible break in the wall of guard unity. Michael had stopped chewing his food, tossing his fork to the ground, too humiliated to care who would win the battle shaping before him. I held a spoon in my hand, rolling its head against my thigh, my eyes on the floor, wrapped in the silence around me.

Nokes took a deep breath, letting air out through his mouth, and shifted the weight on his feet. He slapped the baton against his open palm, measuring Marlboro, the crease of a smile inching its way to the sides of his face. Marlboro stood his ground without a change in expression, content to let the pressure of the situation percolate at its own pace.

Nokes was the one to back down. His smile faded and he let his head drop so his eyes didn't meet Marlboro's.

"You eatin' into my shift," Marlboro said.

"I'll get out of your way," Nokes said. "For now."

"I take what I can get," the black guard said, walking away from Nokes and over toward us. "Just like you."

Marlboro helped Michael to his feet and looked over at me, the soles of his shoes sliding on the slippery turf smeared with food, spit, and hardened gravy. He nudged his head toward the guard standing in the aisle.

"If you through standin'," Marlboro said to him. "I could use some help."

"What do you need?" the guard said, his eyes darting, checking to see if Nokes was clear out of the room.

"Get the boys on their way," Marlboro said, pointing to the inmates at the tables. "They've seen enough to last till supper time. I'll take care of these two and what needs cleanin' up."

The guard nodded and began to clear out the lunchroom,

one table row at a time. The inmates moved with a quiet precision, eager to leave now that the threat of violence was at an apparent end.

I stood next to Michael and Marlboro, watching the inmates exiting the hall, the three of us knowing there would be a price to pay for all that had happened on this day. Sean Nokes was not the kind of man to let a slight go by or leave an act of torment unfinished. He would go after Marlboro through the system, use whatever clout he could muster to make life difficult for the good man with the bad smoking habit. But he would save his true wrath for me and Michael. We both knew that. What it would be, what it *could* be after all the horrors that he had already initiated, was something neither one of us could envision. All we knew was that it would happen soon and, as with everything Nokes planned, it would be something we would never be able to erase from our minds.

15

SUMMER 1968

JULY 24, 1968, WAS MY LAST FULL DAY AT WILKINSON.
Two weeks earlier, a five-member panel of the New York
State Juvenile Hearing Board had determined that a period of
ten months and twenty-four days was enough penance for my
crime. A written request had been forwarded to the warden,
with all necessary release forms attached. Also included in the
package was the name of my designated control officer, the
four days in August I was scheduled to report to him, and a
psychological profile written by someone I had never met.

The thick manila envelope, sealed with strips of tape, sat on
the warden's desk for three days before he opened and signed it.

"The cook makin' anything special for your last day?" Tommy
asked, walking alongside me in the yard during the middle of
our morning break.

"If he *really* cared, he'd take the day off," I said. "The food in
here has been killin' my insides."

"Two cups of King Benny's coffee will set you straight,"
Tommy said. "No time flat."

"It can't happen soon enough," I said.

"Don't forget us in here," Tommy said, his voice a tender
plea.

I stopped and looked over at him. He still had the baby weight and face, but had changed in so many other ways. His eyes were clouded by a veil of anger and, in place of a swagger, there was now a nervous twitch to his walk. His neck and arms were a road map of cuts and bruises, and his left kneecap had been shattered twice, both above and below the main joint.

It was the body of a boy who had done a man's prison time.

"I won't *ever* forget you," I said, watching the anger briefly melt from his eyes. "In *or* out of here."

"Thanks, Shakes," he said, picking up the walk. "Might help knowin' that one body outta here gives a shit."

"More than one body, Butter," I said. "You'd be surprised."

"It's gonna be a bitch," Tommy said. "These last coupla months."

"It'll be over soon," I said, passing a grunting trio of weight-lifters. "By the time the Yankees drop out of the pennant race, you'll be home."

"Nokes say anything yet about you leavin'?" Tommy asked.

"There isn't much more he can do," I said. "Time's on my side now."

"Until you're out of those gates," Tommy said, "there ain't nothin' on your side."

16

I SAT IN MY CELL, QUIET AND ALONE, IN MY LAST HOURS as an inmate at the Wilkinson Home for Boys. I looked around the small room, the walls barren, the sink and toilet cleaned to a shine, the window giving off only hints of nighttime sky. I had folded the white sheet covering, wedged it under the mattress, and laid against it, my legs stretched out, feet dangling off the end of the cot. I was wearing white underwear and a green T-shirt in the stifling heat.

All my prison issues, except for a toothbrush, had been taken away by the guards earlier that afternoon. In the morning they would be replaced by the clothes I wore on the day I first arrived at Wilkinson. A sealed white envelope containing four copies of my release form rested against one of my thighs. One was to be handed to the guard at the end of the cell block. A second was to be given to the guard stationed at the main gate. A third was for the driver of the bus that would take me back to Lower Manhattan.

The last copy was to be mine, the final reminder of my time behind the bars of Wilkinson.

I reached over, picked up the envelope, opened it, and fingered the four copies of the form. I stared at them, my mind filled with the images of pain and punishment, humiliation and degradation it took to get these forms in hand.

To get back my freedom and send me on my way.

I had walked into Wilkinson a boy. Now I wasn't at all sure who or what I was. The months there had changed me, that was for certain. I just didn't know how or in what way the changes would manifest themselves. On the surface I wasn't as physically ruined as John, or as beaten down as Tommy. I wasn't the lit fuse Michael had become.

My anger was more controlled, mixed as it was with a deep fear. In my months there, I never could mount the courage that was needed to keep the guards at bay, but at the same time I maintained a level of dignity that would allow me to walk out of Wilkinson.

I don't know what kind of man I would have grown to be had I not served time at the Wilkinson Home for Boys. I don't know how those months and the events that occurred there shaped the person I became, how much they colored my motives or my actions. I don't know if they made me any braver or any weaker. I don't know if the illnesses I've suffered as an adult have been the result of those ruinous months. I'll never know if my distrust of most people and my unease when placed in group situations are by-products of those days or simply the result of a shy personality.

I *do* know the dreams and nightmares I've had all these years are born of the nights spent in that cell at Wilkinson. That the scars I carry, both mental and physical, are gifts of a system that treated children as prey. The images that screen across my mind in the lonely hours are mine to bear alone, shared only by the silent community of sufferers who once lived as I did, in a world that was deaf to our screams.

I couldn't sleep, anxious for morning to arrive. It was still dark, the early hours offering little more than thin blades of light filtering into my cell from the outside hall.

I wondered what it would be like to sleep once again in a bed not surrounded by bars, to walk in a room not monitored by alternating sets of eyes. I was anxious to eat a meal of my choosing without fear that the food had been toyed with or tainted.

I thought about the first things I would do once I was back out on the familiar streets of Hell's Kitchen. I would buy a newspaper and check the box scores and standings, see how my favorite players had fared while I was away. I would walk up to the Beacon on West 74th Street and see whatever movie was playing, just to sit once more in those plush seats and breathe air ripe with the smell of burning popcorn. I would go to Mimi's and order two hot slices with extra cheese, stand at the counter, and look out at the passing traffic. I would go to the library next to my apartment building, find an empty table, and surround myself with all the books I loved, running my hands across their pages, holding their torn binders, reading the fine old print.

It was my way of life and I wanted to get back to it.

I never heard the key turn in the latch. Never heard the snap of the bolt. I only saw the door swing open, a crowd of shadows washing across the floor of my cell.

"You should be asleep," Nokes said, his words slurred. He was the first to enter, his uniform shirt off, an empty pint of bourbon in his right hand. "Need all your rest for the big trip back home."

"Told you he'd be up," Addison said, walking in behind Nokes, just as drunk, face, neck, and arms wet with sweat. "These fuckers are like rats. They never sleep."

"What do you want?" I asked as calmly as I could manage.

"I just want to say good-bye," Nokes said. "We all do. Let you know how much we gonna miss havin' you around here."

"We're friends, right?" Styler said, entering the cell, sober and in full uniform, holding John and Tommy by his side. "All of us."

John looked at me with dead eyes, as if he knew what was

going to happen and was trying to shut it out of his mind. Tommy was crying, full tears running down the sides of his face, afraid more for me than for himself.

"Must be hard to leave your friends," Ferguson said, walking in with Michael and locking the cell door behind him. "We've been together for so long."

"Can't leave your friends without a party," Nokes said. "It just wouldn't be right."

Michael, as always, stayed silent, his face, his eyes, his entire body, coiled into one large mask of hate. John and Tommy may have lost their heart, but Michael was in danger of losing his humanity. Everything that was done to him, everything that was said, served only to fuel his hate. By now he had enough fuel to last a lifetime.

"It's over, Nokes," I said, standing up in the crowded room, the heat strong, the air rancid. "Please let it go."

"It ain't over till morning," Nokes said. "It ain't over till the party's over."

"I don't want a party," I said.

"That's too bad," Styler said. "I even went out and got you a gift."

"A special gift," Nokes said. "One you ain't ever gonna forget."

Ferguson and Addison stood next to me and held my arms while Styler reached into his pocket and pulled out a few feet of nylon cord. He tied the cord around my arms, knotting it secure at the back. Styler shoved a wad of tissues into my mouth and held my face as Addison ran thick yellow tape across my lips. Nokes walked over, a wide black belt dangling in one hand.

"Tie his feet too," Nokes said, handing the belt to Styler. "I don't want him to move."

My three friends stood before me, as still as the air, only their eyes betraying their terror. John's lips were trembling and

Tommy kept his head tilted to the ceiling, his mouth mumbling a secret prayer. Michael was a silent statue, his rage at rest.

"We got a full house tonight," Nokes said, leaning over and whispering in my ear, his breath bourbon-coated. "First we take care of your friends. And then we take care of you."

I watched Styler walk over to John and lock a handcuff around one of his wrists. The other half of the cuff was put on Tommy's wrist. Addison did the same to Michael and Tommy, locking the three together.

"Move them up closer," Nokes said, sitting on the cot, one arm hanging over my shoulder. "We wanna get a good look."

Styler pushed the three forward with one hand, lighting a cigarette with the other. Ferguson wiped sweat from his face and forehead with the sleeve of his shirt. Addison stood with his back against the door and giggled.

"Best seats in the house," Nokes said to me. "You won't miss a thing from here."

There was no place for us to go, nowhere for us to run. Our screams would go unheeded. Shouts for the warden would be ignored. No one would listen. No one would care. Fear ruled the night and fear controlled this place.

My friends were facedown on the floor, their pants stripped off and tossed to the side, the three guards on their knees behind them, laughing, sweating, hands rubbing flesh, glazed, watery eyes looking at Nokes, waiting for the nod of his head.

"Everybody's ready," Nokes said to me, squeezing me closer to his side. "Time to drop the ball."

Nokes pushed my head to his shoulder and wiped his mouth with the back of his hand, sweat pouring out of both of us like a light, steady rain.

Styler was slapping John's back, playful taps that echoed off the walls of the small room.

Addison hovered over Tommy, fondling himself and staring at me.

"I'm gonna fuck your friend," he said in a shaky voice. "Every night. Every night you ain't here, I'm gonna fuck your friend."

Ferguson rested his body on top of Michael's, his eyes wide with anticipation.

"Let's go, Nokes," he said. "Stop wastin' time. Let's give 'em what they want."

Nokes pushed us both back against the wall, one of his hands holding my face to the scene before me.

"Go to it," Nokes said, his eyes, his breath, his body on me. "Make it party time."

They tore at my friends, attacked them as if they were animals freed from a cage. The cries, the screams, the shrieks, were all a valued part of their beastly game. I sat there, sweat running down my body and onto the sheet beneath me, and watched three boys be ripped apart, living playthings lost in a garden filled with evil intent.

"You gonna think about this when you're gone," Nokes said, rubbing his arms over my body. "Ain't ya, you little fuck? Ain't ya?"

Nokes leaned over and pushed me facedown on my cot. His hands tore at the few clothes I was wearing, stripping me naked, my arms still bound by the nylon cord. He undid the belt around my legs, folded it, and began to lash at my back and rear with it.

"You're gonna remember this little party, all right," Nokes said as he continued to hit at me with the thick edges of the belt. "You gonna remember but good. I'm gonna see to that. Don't worry, fucker. I'm gonna see to that."

Nokes tossed the belt to the floor and lowered his pants, his breath coming in heavy waves, sweat slicing down off his body. His mouth rested against my ear, his teeth chewing on the lobe.

"This is so you don't forget me," he said again, the weight of his body now on top of mine. "Can't let you do that, sweet thing. You gotta remember me like you gotta remember this night. Forever."

I heard John cry, pitiful moans coming from a well deep inside his soul. I saw Tommy's head bounce like a rubber ball against the cement floor, blood flowing from dual streams above his forehead, his eyes blank, the corners of his mouth washed in foam. I saw Michael's left arm bend across the side of his back until the bones in the joint snapped, the pain strong enough to strip the life from his body.

I felt Nokes pulling at me, hitting me with two closed fists, his mouth biting my shoulders and neck, drawing blood. The front of his head butted against the back of mine with every painful thrust, my nose and cheeks scraping the sharp edges of my cot. One of his knees, the pointy end of his belt now wrapped around it, was wedged against the fleshy part of my thigh, stabbing into it, blood coming out in spurts.

A part of all of us was left in that room that night. A night now far removed by the passage of time. A night that will never be removed from my mind.

The night of July 24, 1968.

The summer of love.

My last night at the Wilkinson Home for Boys.

BOOK THREE

"Lazzaro erased with his hand anything Billy Pilgrim might be about to say. 'Just forget about it, kid,' he said. 'Enjoy life while you can. Nothing's gonna happen for maybe five, ten, fifteen, twenty years. But lemme give you a piece of advice: Whenever the doorbell rings, have somebody else answer the door.'"

—KURT VONNEGUT,
Slaughterhouse-Five

1

FALL 1979

HELL'S KITCHEN HAD CHANGED. THE STREETS WERE NO longer swept daily and graffiti marred many of the buildings. A scattering of low-income high-rises had replaced stretches of run-down tenements, and storefronts now needed riot gates to guard against the night. Many of the Irish and Italian tenants had left the area, heading for the safer havens of Queens and Long Island, and the Eastern Europeans had deserted the neighborhood altogether, moving to Brooklyn and New Jersey. Replacing them were a larger number of Hispanics and a mixture of uptown blacks and recent island immigrants. In addition to these groups, young middle-class couples flush with money arrived, buying and renovating a string of tenements. The young and rich even set about changing the neighborhood's name. Now they called it Clinton.

The old order was in turmoil, guns and drugs replacing gambling and stolen goods as a criminal's best route to a fast dollar. Cocaine use was rampant and dealers dotted the area, openly selling on corners and out of parked cars. Residents fell asleep most nights to the sounds of police sirens. There were many gangs, but the deadliest was Irish and numbered close to forty sworn members.

They called themselves the West Side Boys and they controlled the Hell's Kitchen drug trade. The deadliest gang to invade the neighborhood since the Pug Uglies, the West Side Boys would do anything for money, both within the area and beyond. They hired themselves out to the Italian mob as assassins; they hijacked trucks and fenced the stolen goods; they shook down shopkeepers for protection money; they swapped cocaine and heroin with uptown dealers for cash, and then returned to shoot the dealers dead and reclaim their money. Heavily fueled by drugs and drink, the West Side Boys considered no crime beyond their scope.

They even had their own style of dress—black leather jackets, black shirts, and jeans. In winter they wore black woolen gloves with the tips cut off. They also left their signature on every body they discarded: bullets through the head, heart, hands, and legs. Those they didn't want found were hacked up and scattered throughout the five boroughs of New York City.

* * *

HELL'S KITCHEN WAS NOT ALONE IN THE CHANGES AF-fecting its streets. Similar sounds were being heard in cities and neighborhoods throughout the country and the world. In Atlanta, a serial killer was on the loose, preying on young black children. Eleven people were crushed to death at a Who concert in Cincinnati. Sony introduced the Walkman. The first test tube baby, Louise Brown, was born in a London Hospital. The Camp David Peace Accord was signed and England's Lord Mountbatten was killed by IRA terrorists. Chrysler was saved from bankruptcy by an act of Congress and John Wayne died of cancer.

During all these changes, a few familiar faces remained. King Benny still ran a piece of Hell's Kitchen, working out of the same dark room where I first met him. He openly ignored the drug and gun trade, content with his profits from less violent, if equally illegal, enterprises. He was older, a little wiser, and still as dangerous as ever. Even the West Side Boys conceded him his turf.

Time had not mellowed Fat Mancho either. He still stood in front of his bodega, snarling and screaming at all who passed. But time had also brought him another wife, a new social security number, one more apartment, and another monthly disability check.

BARS AND RESTAURANTS STILL dotted the neighborhood, though many were new, designed to draw an uptown clientele. But the best establishments were old and frayed, and among them, the Shamrock Pub on West 48th Street, with the sweetest Irish soda bread in town, was the finest place to eat in Hell's Kitchen. It was a joint that kept true to the past, where a local could run a tab, place a bet, and even spend the night on a cot in the back. It was also a place where a secret could still be kept.

THE SHAMROCK PUB WAS unusually crowded for a late Wednesday night. Two men in outdated suits, ties undone, sat at the center of a wooden bar that ran the length of the restaurant, each clutching a sweaty Rob Roy, arguing about the economic policies of President Jimmy Carter. An old, raw-faced Irishman in a heavy wool coat sat at the far end of the bar, nursing his third beer, pointedly ignoring their conversation.

Five leather booths faced the bar, each positioned next to a window and lit by lanterns hanging overhead. Four circular tables draped with white tablecloths lined the rear wall. Framed photos of champion race horses hung above them, along with tranquil Irish settings and a color portrait of the restaurant's original owner, a sour-looking Dubliner named Dusty McTweed.

The Shamrock Pub was a neighborhood institution known to all who lived or worked on the West Side. It catered to an odd assortment of locals, publishing types with a taste for ale, beat cops with a thirst, tourists, and, in recent years, to the volatile members of the West Side Boys.

A young couple sat at one of the tables, their backs to the bar, holding hands, a half-empty bottle of white wine between them. Another couple, older, more friends than lovers, sat in a front booth, their attention fixed on their well-done lamb chops and second basket of Irish soda bread.

Two waitresses in their early twenties, wearing short black skirts and white blouses, stood against a side wall, smoking and talking in whispers. They were actresses and roommates, earning enough in tips to pay the rent on a third-floor Chelsea walk-up. One was divorced, the other had a relationship with a long-haul trucker with a drinking problem.

There was one other customer in the restaurant.

A chunky man in his late thirties sat in the last booth. He smoked a cigarette and drank a glass of beer while the meal in front of him cooled. He had ordered the day's special—meat loaf and brown gravy, mashed potatoes, and steamed spinach. He had asked for a side order of pasta, which was served with canned tomato sauce. On top of the sauce he had placed two pats of butter, turning the overcooked strands until the butter melted.

The man had long, thick blond hair that covered his ears and touched the collar of his frayed blue work shirt. His face was sharp and unlined, his eyes blue and distant. The shirt of his uniform was partly hidden by a blue zippered jacket with Randall Security patches on both arms. A .357 Magnum revolver was shoved into his gun belt. A small pinky ring decorated his right hand.

Putting out the cigarette in an ashtray lodged between the glass salt shaker and a tin sugar canister, he picked up his fork, cut into his meat loaf, and stared at the television screen above the bar. The New York Knicks and the Atlanta Hawks were playing their way through a dreary second quarter on the soundless screen.

Outside, a crisp fall wind rattled the windows. The overhead sky threatened rain.

It was eight-fifteen in the evening.

At eight twenty-five P.M., two young men walked through the glass and wood doors. They were both dressed in black leather jackets, black crew shirts, and black jeans. One was bone-thin, with dark curly hair framing his wide, handsome face. He wore black gloves, the fingers on each cut to the knuckle, and a pork-pie hat with the brim curved up. He had a half-pint of bourbon stuffed in one back pocket of his jeans and three grams of coke in a cigarette case in the other. He was smoking a Vantage and was the first one through the door.

The second young man was heftier, his black jeans tight around his waist, the open black leather jacket revealing the bulk of his neck and shoulders. His mouth was hard at work on a wad of chewing tobacco. He wore a longshoreman's watch cap atop his light brown hair. His calf-length black boots had a fresh spit shine, and he walked into the tavern favoring his right leg, damaged in childhood.

The bartender nodded in their direction. He knew their faces as well as most of the neighborhood knew their names. They were two of the founding members of the West Side Boys. They were also its deadliest. The thinner man had been in and out of jail since he was a teenager. He robbed and killed at will or on command and was currently a suspect in four un-solved homicides. He was an alcoholic and a cocaine abuser with a fast temper and a faster trigger. He once shot a me-chanic dead for moving ahead of him on a movie line.

The second man was equally deadly and had committed his first murder at the age of seventeen. In return, he was paid fifty dollars. He drank and did drugs and had a wife he never saw living somewhere in Queens.

They walked past the old man and the couple in the first booth and nodded at the waitresses, who eagerly smiled back. They sat down three stools from the businessmen and tapped the wood bar with their knuckles. The bartender, Jerry, an affable middle-aged man with a wife, two kids, and his first steady job in six years, poured them each a large shot of Wild Turkey with beer chasers and left the bottle.

The thinner man downed the shot and lit a fresh cigarette. He nodded toward the bartender and asked what the two men in suits were discussing. He didn't change expression when he was told of the Carter debate. He leaned closer to the bar, his eyes on the young couple at the table in the rear of the pub, and poured himself and his friend another double shot. He told the bartender to bring the two men in suits a drink and to run it on his tab. He also told Jerry to tell them that Republicans were not welcome in Hell's Kitchen and that either a political conversion or a change in conversation was in order.

The chubby man checked his watch and nudged his friend in the ribs. They were running late for an appointment. A dealer named Raoul Reynoso was holed up at the Holiday Inn three blocks away, expecting to complete a drug deal with them no later than nine P.M. Reynoso was looking to buy two kilos of cocaine and was ready to hand off $25,000 as payment. The two men had other plans. They were going to take his money, put four bullets in his heart, cut off Reynoso's head, and leave it in an ice bucket next to the television set in his room.

The thin man reached over the bar, grabbed a menu, looked at his friend, and shrugged his shoulders. He hated to kill *anybody* on an empty stomach. He gave the menu to his friend and asked him to order for them both. He needed to use the bathroom. The chubby man took the menu and smiled. He had known the thin man all his life, they had grown up together, gone to the same schools, served time in the same prisons, slept with the same women, and put bullets in the same bodies. In all those years, the thin man, without fail, *always* had to use a bathroom before a meal.

The thin man stood up from his stool and finished off his beer. He then turned and walked down the narrow strip of floor separating booths from bar stools, his hands at his sides, his face turned to the street outside. At the end of the bar, across from the rear booth, his eyes moved from the passing traffic and met those of the man eating the meat-loaf special. Both men held the look for a number of seconds, one set of eyes registering recognition, the other filled with annoyance.

"I help you with somethin', chief?" the man in the booth said, his mouth crammed with mashed potatoes.

"Not right now," the thin man said, heading to the back. He smiled down at the man in the booth and told him to enjoy the rest of his meal.

He stumbled into the men's room and ran the cold water in the sink, looking at himself in the mirror. He looked much older than his twenty-seven years, the drugs and drink taking a toll on an Irish face still handsome enough to coax a smile from a reluctant woman. He took off his gloves and checked his hands, calm and steady, the skin raw, the scars across both sets of knuckles white and clear. He put the gloves back on and stepped over to the urinal.

"Reynoso, you're one lucky fucker," he thought to himself. "This piss saved your life."

HE WALKED OUT OF the men's room and past the man in the back booth. He took his seat next to his friend, put a cigarette in his mouth, and poured himself a refill.

"I ordered brisket on a roll," his friend said. "With fries. And two baskets of soda bread. I know you like that shit. That okay by you?"

The thin man's eyes were on the small mirror above the bar, riveted on the man in the uniform finishing his meat-loaf dinner.

"C'mon," his friend said, tapping him on the shoulder. "Let's take the booth behind us. We can spread out all we want."

The thin man turned to face his friend. He asked him to take a look at the last booth in the pub. To take a good look and study the face of the man sitting in it.

His friend turned in his stool and stared at the man in the zippered jacket. His face stayed blank for the few moments it took to link the man to memory, but his eyes betrayed his swirling emotions.

"You sure it's him?" he asked, his voice harsh, his upper lip twitching. "You sure it's really him?"

"You know me," the thin man said. "I never forget a friend."

They stayed at the bar long enough to release the safeties on the guns hidden beneath their jackets. They stood up together and walked toward the booth at the back of the pub, the thin man leading the way.

"Hello," the thin man said, pulling up a chair. "It's been a long time."

"Who the fuck are you guys?" the man in the booth demanded. He didn't seem particularly afraid, merely annoyed at the intrusion. "And who the fuck asked you to sit down?"

"I thought you'd be happy to see us," the chubby man said. "Guess I was wrong."

"I always thought you would do better," the thin man said, looking at the patches on the sleeves of the jacket. "All that training, all that time you put in, just to guard somebody else's money. Seems like a waste."

"I'm askin' you for the last time," the man said, his temper as hot as his coffee. "What the fuck do you want?"

The thin man took off his gloves and put them in the front pocket of his leather jacket. He laid his hand flat on the table, the tips of his fingers nudging the sides of the security guard's empty beer glass.

"See the scars?" he asked. "Look at them. Take your time. It'll come to you."

The guard stared at the thin man's hands, his upper lip wet with sweat, his body tense, sensing danger, feeling cornered.

Then he knew.

The knowledge fell across his face like a cold cloth. He sat back, his head resting against the top of the leather booth. He tried to speak but couldn't. His mouth went dry as his hands gripped the edge of the table.

"I can see how you would forget us," the thin man said softly. "We were just somethin' for you and your friends to play with."

"It's a little harder for us to forget," the chubby one said. "You gave us so much more to remember."

"That was a long time ago," the security guard said, the words coming out in a struggle. "We were just kids."

"We're not kids now," the thin man said.

"Whatta ya want me to say?" the security guard asked, anger returning to his voice. "That I'm sorry? Is that what you want? An apology?"

"No," the thin man said, moving his hands off the table and onto his lap. "I *know* you're not sorry and hearin' you say it won't change a fuckin' thing."

"Then *what*?" the security guard asked, leaning over his empty platter. "What do you want?"

"What I've *always* wanted, Nokes," the thin man said. "To watch you die."

The thin man, John Reilly, and his chubby friend, Tommy

"Butter" Marcano, were on their feet, a gun in each hand. All movement in the pub ceased. The young woman at the back table took her hand off her boyfriend and clasped it over her mouth.

The bartender clicked off the Knicks game.

The two waitresses slipped into the kitchen.

Sean Nokes, thirty-seven, was a security guard with a gambling problem. He was two months behind on his rent and his wife was threatening to leave him and take their daughter home to her mother. He had not fared well since his years at Wilkinson, moving from job to job, small town to small town. He was hoping he had finally turned the corner, working a Manhattan job that paid decent money. He had come to Hell's Kitchen to pay off a debt and stopped into the pub for dinner before heading home to his wife, hopeful of landing one more chance at a reconciliation. He never planned on a Wilkinson reunion.

"Too bad you ordered the meat loaf," Tommy said. "The brisket's real good here. Only you'll never know it."

"You were scared little pricks," Nokes said. "Both of you. *All* of you. Scared shitless. I tried to make you tough, make you hard. But it was a waste of time."

"I had you all wrong, then," Tommy said. "All this time I just figured you liked fuckin' and beatin' up little boys."

"You are gonna burn in hell!" Sean Nokes said. "You hear me! You two motherfuckers! You are gonna burn in hell!"

"After you," John said.

The first bullet came out the back of Nokes's head, the second went through his right eye, and the third creased his temple. Nokes rested with his head back and his hands spread, mouth twisted into an almost comical grimace. Tommy stepped out of the booth and walked over to Nokes's side. He put a bullet into each of his legs and one into each hand. John stood his ground and pumped three slugs into Nokes's chest, waiting for the body jerks to stop each time before pulling the trigger again.

The bartender closed his eyes until the gunfire stopped.

The young couple fell to the ground, hovering for cover under their table.

The couple in the first booth sat frozen with fear, staring at each other, still holding their knives and forks.

The two businessmen never turned their heads. One of them, the pretzels in his hand crushed to crumbs, had wet his pants.

The two waitresses stayed in the kitchen, shivering near the grill, the cook by their side.

The old man in the corner had his head on the bar and slept through the shooting.

John and Tommy put the guns back in their holsters, took one final look at Sean Nokes, and turned to leave the pub.

"Hey, Jerry," Tommy called over. "Be a pal, would ya?"

"Name it," the bartender said, his eyes now open, trying not to look over at the fresh body in the back booth.

"Make those brisket sandwiches to go," Tommy said.

2

IT HAD BEEN ELEVEN YEARS SINCE MY FRIENDS AND I had been released from the Wilkinson Home for Boys.

In all those years we had never once spoken to each other about our time there. We remained caring friends, but the friendship had altered as we traveled down our separate paths. Still, we were friends. By the time of Nokes's murder, the friendship had become less intimate, but no less intense.

Michael Sullivan, twenty-eight, had moved out of Hell's Kitchen shortly after being released from Wilkinson. Never again would he have a problem with the law. Father Bobby called in a handful of chits to get Michael accepted at a solid Catholic high school in Queens, where Michael was sent to live with his mother's sister and her accountant husband. He continued to date Carol Martinez, twenty-seven, until the middle of his sophomore year, when the distance and their evolving personalities finally conspired to cool their longing. But he continued to see his Hell's Kitchen cohorts as often as he could, unwilling to give up the friendship, needing to be with us as much as we needed to be with him.

Michael graduated with honors from high school and moved on to a local university. Then, after a hot and fruitless summer working as a waiter at a Catskills resort, he decided to enroll in a Manhattan law school.

At the time of Nokes's shooting, Michael was rounding out his first six months as a New York City assistant district attorney.

We tried to share a meal once a week, the bond between us difficult to sever. When we were together, often joined by Carol, Michael still held sway. He was always our leader and still the toughest of the group. Only now his strength was of a different sort, not physical and violent like that of John and Tommy, but carried quietly within. The months at Wilkinson had changed Michael in many ways, but they could not strip him of his drive. If anything, the horrors he endured gave a focus to his life, a target toward which he could aim.

He worked out at a gym, two hours every morning, a strenuous mix of aerobics and weights. He didn't smoke and he drank only with dinner. His fellow students and coworkers considered him to be a loner, a reticent man with a sharp sense of humor but a gentle manner. He had grown tall and good-looking, his boyhood freckles giving way to the clear face of a confident man. He had a deep, soulful voice and a twelve-inch scar running across his shoulders.

Michael kept his world private.

He had an apartment in Queens that few were permitted to see. He dated frequently, but never seriously. His loves were kept to a minimum—the Yankees, foreign movies, Louis L'Amour westerns, the silent halls of museums. In a loud city, Michael Sullivan was a quiet stranger, a man with secrets he had no desire to share.

He walked the streets of Hell's Kitchen only occasionally, and then only to visit Father Bobby, who by now had risen to principal of our former grammar school. He loved his work and buried himself in studying the subtle ways the law could be maneuvered.

"There are a thousand different crimes that someone can commit," he said to me shortly before the shooting. "And there are more than a thousand ways to get him out of any one of them."

JOHN AND TOMMY HAD both stayed in Hell's Kitchen, finished grammar school, then attended a technical junior high, close to the neighborhood, for less than the required two years. In that time they continued to do odd jobs for King Benny, took in some numbers action for an Inwood bookie, and occasionally strong-armed players late on loan shark payments. They also began carrying guns.

They never recovered from the abuse of Wilkinson. In our time there, Michael and I realized that we weren't anywhere near as tough as we had thought. John and Tommy, however, came away with an entirely different frame of mind. They would let no one touch them again, let no one near enough to cause them any harm. They would achieve their goal in the most effective way they knew—through fear. It was a lesson they learned at the Wilkinson Home for Boys.

By the mid-seventies, John and Tommy had helped found the West Side Boys, farming the initial five-member group out as enforcers, thugs for hire. As the gang grew, they progressed to more lethal and lucrative action, including moving counterfeit cash and buying and selling large amounts of cocaine. They also took on contract murders. Their specialty—dismembering their victims' bodies and disposing of the pieces throughout the area—evoked fear in even their closest associates.

When they killed, they got rid of everything except the hands.

Those they kept in freezers in a select number of Hell's Kitchen refrigerators, preserved to provide fingerprints on the guns used by the gang. It was a tactic that made it virtually impossible for the police to pin the crew to any one murder.

When prints were checked, the patterns led back to men who were already dead.

Along the way, both John and Tommy got hooked on cocaine and began to drink heavily. They remained best friends and lived in the same West 47th Street tenement, two floors apart. They were respectful toward King Benny, who, recognizing the changing times, gave their operation the space it needed to thrive and survive.

They still joked with Fat Mancho, played stickball in front of his candy store, and helped his bookie operation rake in thousands a week, their powerful support insuring that no one dared back down from a phone-in bet.

I saw them as often as I could, and when we got together, it was easy for me to forget what they had become and remember only who they were. We went to ball games, took long Sunday-morning walks down by the piers, and helped Father Bobby with the basket collections at mass. I seldom asked them about their business and they always teased me about mine.

Like Michael, I moved out of Hell's Kitchen soon after my release from Wilkinson. Father Bobby also pulled some strings for me: I was admitted to a first-rate Catholic high school for boys in the Bronx. By my late teens I was taking night courses at St. John's University in Queens, working a nowhere day job in a Wall Street bank, and wrestling with a fresh set of demons—the discovery that my father was a convicted murderer who had served nearly seven years for killing his first wife. I divided my time between a bed in my parents' Bronx apartment and a two-room basement sublet in Long Island.

One summer afternoon in 1973, I was reading an early edition of the *New York Post* on my lunch hour, sitting on a bench in front of a noisy and crowded outdoor fountain, half a ham sandwich by my side. There, under the heat of a New York sun, I read a Pete Hamill column about former vice president

Spiro T. Agnew. By the time I got to the last paragraph, I knew I wanted to work on a newspaper.

It would take three years before I would land a job as a copy boy for the New York *Daily News,* working the midnight-to-eight shift, sharpening pencils, making coffee runs, and driving drunken editors home after a night on the prowl. By the time of Nokes's death, I had worked my way up to the clerical department, typing movie schedules for the next day's editions.

It was easy work, leaving me with plenty of free time, and most of it was spent in Hell's Kitchen. I still liked the feel of the neighborhood, no matter how much it had changed. I still felt safe there.

I had coffee twice a week with King Benny, once again seeking refuge in the stillness of his club, as much a home to me as any place. Benny's espresso was as bitter as ever, his mood as dark, and he still cheated at every hand of cards we played. The years had made him older, his black hair touched by lines of white, but no one in the neighborhood dared question his strength.

I bought sodas from Fat Mancho every time I passed his store. He ran enough business from that front to fill a mall and was easily spotted in his loud shirts sprayed with colorful birds and palm trees, which his older sister sent over from Puerto Rico. Every time he saw me he cursed. We had known each other for more than twenty years and I remained one of the few people he fully trusted.

On weekends I would drive down and endure two-hour one-on-one basketball games against Father Bobby, more than twenty years older than me and still two steps faster. We all were aging, but Father Bobby always looked young, his body trim, his face relaxed. Whatever problems he had, he handled beneath the silent cover of prayer.

On occasion I would have dinner with Carol, who still lived in the neighborhood and worked as a social worker in the

South Bronx. She had moved with ease from awkward teenager to a young woman of striking grace and beauty. Her hair
was long and dark, her face unlined, covered by only the softest
makeup. She had long legs and spend-the-night eyes that lit up
when she laughed. Her concern for us was undiminished by
the passing years.

Carol was passionate about her work and quiet about her
life, living alone in a third-floor walk-up not far from where we
had gone to school. She dated infrequently and never anyone
from outside the neighborhood. Though I never asked, I knew
she still held strong feelings for Michael. I also knew that when
that relationship ended she had been with John during his
more sober periods. She always had a special affection for John,
could always see the boy he once had been. Whenever we went
out as a group, Carol would walk between Michael and John,
grasping their arms, at ease and in step between the lawyer and
the killer.

These were my friends.

We accepted each other for what we were, few questions
asked, no demands made. We had been through too much to
try to force change on one another. We had been through
enough to know that the path taken is not always the ideal
road. It is simply the one that seems right at the moment.

Wilkinson had touched us all.

It had turned Tommy and John into hardened criminals,
determined not to let anyone have power over them again. It
had made me and Michael realize that while an honest life may
not offer much excitement, it pays its dividends in freedom.

It cost Father Bobby countless hours in prayer, searching
for answers to questions he feared asking.

It made Fat Mancho a harder man, watching young boys
come out stone killers, stripped of their feelings, robbed of all
that was sweet.

Wilkinson even touched King Benny, piercing the protective nerve he had developed when it came to the four laughing boys who turned his private club into their own. It awakened the demons of his own horrid childhood, spent in places worse than Wilkinson, where he was handled by men more fearsome than those who tortured us. It made the hate he carried all the heavier.

None of us could let go of the others. We all drifted together, always wondering when the moment would arrive that would force us to deal with the past. Maybe that moment would never come. Maybe we could keep it all buried. But then John and Tommy and luck walked in on Sean Nokes halfway through a meat-loaf dinner. And for the first time in years, we all felt alive. The moment was out there now, waiting for us to grab it. Michael was the first to realize it. To figure it out. But the rest of us caught on fast. It was what we had been living for, what we had waited years for. Revenge. Sweet, lasting revenge. And now it was time for all of us to get a taste.

3

ICHAEL SAT ACROSS FROM ME, QUIETLY MIXING SOUR cream into his baked potato. We were at a corner table at the Old Homestead, a steak house across from the meat market in downtown Manhattan. It was late on a Wednesday, two weeks after Nokes was killed in the Shamrock Pub.

The second I read about the shooting, I knew who had pulled the triggers. I was as afraid for Tommy and John as I was proud of them. They had done what I would never have had the courage to do. They had faced the evil of our past and eliminated it from sight. Though Nokes's death did nothing to relieve our anguish, I was still glad he was dead. I was even happier when I learned that Nokes not only knew why he died, but at whose hands.

John and Tommy did not remain fugitives for long.

They were arrested within seventy-two hours of the shooting, fingerprinted, booked, and charged with second-degree murder. Police had four eyewitnesses willing to testify—the older couple in the first booth and the two businessmen sitting at the bar. All four were outsiders, strangers to Hell's Kitchen. The restaurant's other patrons, as well as its workers, stayed true to the code of the neighborhood: They saw nothing and they said nothing.

John and Tommy were held without bail.

The two hired a West Side attorney named Danny O'Connor, known more for his boisterous talk than for his ability to win. They pleaded not guilty and admitted to nothing, not even to their lawyer. There seemed to be no connection between the deceased and the accused, and both the press and police shrugged the murder off as yet another drug-related homicide.

"HAVE YOU GONE TO visit them yet?" Michael asked, cutting into his steak. It was the first time either of us had talked about the shooting since dinner began.

"The day after the arrest," I said, jabbing a fork into a cut of grilled salmon. "For a few minutes."

"What did they have to say?" Michael asked.

"The usual small talk," I said. "Nothing with any weight. They know enough not to say anything in a visitors' room."

"What about Nokes?" Michael said. "They talk about him?"

"John did," I said. "But not by name."

"What'd he say?"

"All he said was 'One down, Shakes.' Then he tapped the glass with his finger and handed me that shit-eatin' grin of his."

"How do they look?" Michael asked.

"Pretty relaxed," I told him. "Especially for two guys facing twenty-five-to-life."

"I hear they hired Danny O'Connor to defend them," Michael said. "That right?"

"That's temporary," I said. "King Benny's gonna move in one of his lawyers when the trial starts."

"No," Michael said. "O'Connor's who we want. He's perfect."

"*Perfect?*" I said. "The guy's a fall-down drunk. Probably hasn't won a case since La Guardia was mayor. Maybe not even then."

"I know," Michael said. "That's why he's perfect."

"What are you talking about?"

"You covering this story for the paper?" Michael asked, lifting his beer mug and ignoring my question.

"I'm a timetable clerk, Mikey," I said. "I'm lucky they let me in the building."

"Anybody at work know you're friends with John and Butter?"

"No," I said. "Why would they?"

"You didn't finish your fish," Michael said. "You usually eat everything *but* the plate."

"I'm still used to my old hours," I said. "Eating dinner at five in the morning and breakfast at eleven at night."

"You should have had eggs."

"I *will* have a cup of coffee."

"Order it to go," Michael said, waving to a waiter for the check. "We've got to take a walk."

"It's pouring out," I said.

"We'll find a spot where it's not. Down by the piers."

"There are rats down by the piers," I pointed out.

"There are rats everywhere."

* * *

THE RAIN WAS FALLING IN SOFT DROPS, LOUD BLASTS OF thunder echoing in the distance. We were standing in an empty lot along the gates of Pier 62, West Side Highway traffic rushing by behind us. Michael had thrown his raincoat on over his suit. His hands were stuffed inside the side pockets and his briefcase was wedged between his ankles.

"I'm going in to see my boss in the morning," Michael said, the words rushing out. "I'm going to ask him to give me the case against John and Tommy."

"What?" I looked at his eyes, searching for signs that this

was nothing more than the beginning of a cruel joke. "What are you going to do?"

"I'm going to prosecute John and Tommy in open court." His voice was filled with confidence, his eyes looked square at me.

"Are you fuckin' nuts?" I shouted, grabbing his arms. "They're your friends! Your *friends,* you heartless fuck!"

A smile curled the sides of Michael's lips. "Before you take a swing, Shakes, hear me out."

"I should shoot you just for talking about shit like this," I said, easing my grip, taking in deep gulps of air. "And if anybody else hears it, I'll have to open a freezer door to shake your hand."

"You decide who else knows," Michael said. "Just you. You'll know who to tell."

"You take this case, *everybody's* gonna know!" I shouted again. "And *everybody's* gonna be pissed."

"You'll take care of all that," Michael said. "That'll be part of your end."

"Do something smart," I said. "Call in sick tomorrow. It might save your life."

"I'm not taking the case to win," Michael said. "I'm taking it to lose."

I didn't say anything. I *couldn't* say anything.

"I've got a plan," Michael said. "But I can't do it without you. I can work only the legal end. I need you to do the rest."

I took two steps forward and held my friend's face in my hands.

"Are you serious?" I asked. "You crazy bastard, are you really serious?"

"It's payback time, Shakes," Michael said, water streaming down his face and mixing with tears. "We can get back at them now. John and Tommy started it. You and I can finish it."

I let go of Michael's face and put my hands in my pockets.

"Let's walk for a while," I said. "We stand here much longer, we'll get arrested for soliciting."

"Where to?"

"The neighborhood," I said. "Where it's safe."

* * *

WE HUDDLED IN THE DOORWAY OF MY OLD APARTMENT building, rain now lashing across Tenth Avenue. Down the street, two old rummies argued over a pint of raspberry brandy.

Michael's plan was as simple as it was bold. At nine in the morning he would walk into the office of the Manhattan district attorney and ask for the murder case against John Reilly and Thomas Marcano. He would explain that he was from the same neighborhood as the two shooters and that he understood the mentality of the area better than anyone else in the office. He would tell the D.A. he knew how to keep the witnesses from running away scared, hold the case together, and win it. Other than that, Michael would admit to no connection to either John or Tommy and was counting on me to quell any neighborhood talk about their friendship.

There was also no need to worry about the link with Wilkinson. Like all juvenile records in the state, ours had been destroyed after seven years. In addition, he would have someone alter the Sacred Heart school records to eliminate any evidence of our one-year absence. Besides, for the D.A., it was a can't-miss proposition. There were four eyewitnesses and two shooters with murderous reputations. The perfect case to hand an ambitious young attorney like Michael Sullivan.

Michael took a deep breath and wiped the water from his face. There was more to this, a lot more. I knew Michael well enough to know that Nokes wasn't it for him and that freeing John and Tommy wouldn't do. He needed to go after the other guards. He needed to go after Wilkinson. I felt nervous watch-

ing him, waiting for him to continue, fearful that we would all
be caught and once again be brought to such a place.

He crouched down and laid his briefcase across his knees.
Inside were four thick yellow folders, each double-wrapped in
rubber bands. He handed all four to me. I looked at them and
read the names of the guards who tormented us all those
months at the Wilkinson Home for Boys stenciled across the
fronts. The first folder belonged to Tommy's chief abuser, Adam
Styler, now thirty-four, who had scotched his dreams of being
a lawyer and, instead, worked as a plainclothes cop.

Styler was assigned to a narcotics unit in a Queens precinct.
It didn't surprise me to learn that he was also dirty, shaking
down dealers for dope and cash. He had a major coke problem
that was supported by $3,000 a month in bribe money. The rest
of the folder contained personal information—daily routines;
women he dated; food he liked; bars he frequented. There were
lists of trusted friends and hated enemies. A man's life bound
inside a yellow folder.

The second bundle belonged to my tormentor, Henry Addison. I felt nauseated as I read that Addison now worked for
the mayor of the City of New York as a community outreach
director in Brooklyn. He was good at his job, honest and dili-
gent. But his sexual habits hadn't changed much since our time
at Wilkinson. Addison still liked sex with young boys. The
younger they were, the more he was willing to pay. Addison
belonged to a group of well-heeled pedophiles who would
party together three times a month, paying out big dollars for
all-nighters with the boys they bought. The parties were usually
taped, the kids and the equipment supplied by an East Side
pimp with the street name of Radio.

The third folder belonged to Ralph Ferguson, thirty-three,
the man who helped give John Reilly a killer's heart. He wasn't
a cop, though I'd expected him to be. He was a clerk, working
for a social service agency on Long Island. Ferguson was mar-

ried and had one child. His wife taught preschool during the week and they both taught Catholic Sunday school. He sounded as clean as he was boring. Which is exactly how Michael wanted him to be. Ralph Ferguson was going to be called as a character witness, to talk about his best friend, Sean Nokes. Once he was on the stand, Michael could finally open the door to the Wilkinson Home for Boys.

I moved farther into the hall, trying to keep the folders dry, trying to absorb all that Michael was telling me. He had waited nearly twelve years for this moment, planned for it, somehow *knowing* it would happen, and, when it did, he would be prepared.

He insisted that John and Tommy be told nothing of our plan, that it would play better in court if they didn't know. There was to be no jury tampering. The not guilty we sought had to be a verdict that no one would dare question. Danny O'Connor was to remain as the defendants' attorney. We needed to keep him sober and alert and, since he was going to be as deeply involved as we were, too scared to tell anybody what we were up to.

Michael would relay the information I needed through a system of messengers and drop boxes. I would pass information back to him in a similar manner. He pulled three keys out of his coat pocket and handed them to me. They belonged to lockers at the Port Authority, the 23rd Street YMCA, and a Jack LaLanne health club on West 45th Street. Once I had the packets in hand I would pass them on to O'Connor. I would make sure we weren't seen.

For the plan to succeed, we needed total secrecy and the involvement of only people we completely trusted. My first step was to get to King Benny. He would be our weight, our muscle, and could get us through doors we didn't even know existed. He would put enough fear into Danny O'Connor's heart to gently seal his lips. King Benny would also call off the West Side Boys, who were sure to be gunning for Michael the minute they knew he had taken the case against John and Tommy.

I also needed Fat Mancho to turn over some rocks and Carol Martinez to open some more files.

After this night, Michael would not be available to any of us. The only time we would see him would be in court.

It was a foolproof plan in one respect. If it worked, we would avenge our past and, in the process, bring down the Wilkinson Home for Boys. If it didn't work, if we were caught, people would want to know why we did what we did. Either way, information would get out.

Michael's way, however, insured that John and Tommy would walk with us and share in the victory.

"Is that it?" I asked, gazing down at the folders in my arms. "Is that all you need?"

"Just one more thing," Michael said.

"What?"

He sighed, leaving the best for last. "We've got four witnesses who say they saw the shooting and are willing to testify. We need to knock that number down."

"I'll work on it," I said. "But if you lose more than two, it might get some people nervous."

"I'll take two," Michael said. "If you can get us one for our side."

"One what?" I asked.

"One witness. A witness who'll put John and Tommy somewhere else the night of the murder. *Anywhere* else. A witness they can't touch. Strong enough to knock out whatever anybody else says."

"Don't they have a name for that?" I asked.

"A judge would call it perjury," Michael said.

"And what are we calling it?"

"A favor," Michael said.

4

KING BENNY STOOD BEHIND THE BAR OF HIS CLUB, drinking from a large white mug of hot coffee, reading the three-page letter I had written and left for him in a sealed envelope on the counter. When he had finished, he laid the letter down and walked to the edge of the bar. He looked out at the streets of Hell's Kitchen, the mug cradled in both hands.

"Tony," King Benny said to one of four men sitting around a card table, sorting early morning betting slips.

Tony dropped the slips from his hands, pulled back his chair, and walked over.

"Bring Danny O'Connor to see me," King Benny said, his eyes never leaving the window.

"Danny O'Connor the lawyer?" Tony asked.

"You know more than one Danny O'Connor?" King Benny said.

"No, King," Tony said.

"Then bring me the one you know," King Benny said.

King Benny turned from the window and moved farther down the bar, stopping at the empty sink next to the beer taps. He put down his coffee mug and grabbed a book of matches from the top of the bar. He took one final look at my letter and then dropped it into the sink. He lit a match and put it to the letter and stood there, in silence, watching as it burned.

Then, for the first time in many years, King Benny laughed out loud.

5

"**Y**OU GOT TIME FOR ME, FAT MAN?" I SAID, STANDING in the middle of Fat Mancho's bodega, watching him as he bent over to open a carton of Wise potato chips.

"I'm a busy man, fucker," Fat Mancho said, standing up, hugging his bulky pants above his waist, a smile on his face. "I got a business. Ain't like you paper boys, with time on my fuckin' hands."

"This won't take long," I said, grabbing a pack of Wrigley's Juicy Fruit gum from one of the racks. "I'll wait for you outside."

"You gonna pay me for that, you little prick?" Fat Mancho asked.

"I never did before," I said, putting two pieces in my mouth and walking out into the cool of the day. "Why ruin a good habit now?"

Fat Mancho came out carrying two wood crates for us to sit on and a cold, sweaty Yoo-Hoo for him to drink. I sat down next to him, leaned my back against his storefront window, and stretched my legs. I pointed to the fire hydrant in front of us.

"Kids still use that in the summer?" I asked.

"It still gets hot, don't it?" Fat Mancho said. "That pump's the only beach they know. Just like you fuckers. You all cut the same."

"I need your help, Fat Man," I said, turning to look at him. "A big favor. It would be easier for you to say no. A lot smarter too. And there's no problem if you do."

Fat Mancho downed his Yoo-Hoo in two long gulps and wiped his mouth with the rolled-up sleeve of a green shirt dotted with orange flamingos.

"I bet you *would* like me to say no," Fat Mancho said, laying the bottle by his feet. "Then you can tell your buddies that the Fat Man don't stand up. Don't back his friends."

"Are you callin' me your friend?" I said with a smile. "I'm touched, Fat Man."

"I ain't callin' you shit," Fat Mancho said. "I'm just tellin' you I'm here. You fuckers can't pull off anything alone. You ain't got the brass and you ain't got the brains. There's two of you in jail right now. Ain't lookin' to make it four."

"I guess King Benny's been around to see you," I said.

"Some fuckin' team we puttin' together," Fat Mancho said. "A drunk lawyer on one side, fuckin' kid lawyer on another. A paper boy makin' like Dick Tracy. Four eyeballs swear they saw the whole thing. And the two on trial killed more people than cancer. That motherfucker Custer had a better shot at a walk."

"Nobody's expecting it," I said. "That's the biggest card in our favor."

"This ain't no fuckin' book, kid," Fat Mancho said. "You best remember that. And this goes bad, it ain't a fuckin' year upstate in a kid jail. This is *real*. You get caught on this, you lookin' straight at serious."

"There's no choice," I said. "Not for us."

"They were good boys," Fat Mancho said. "That little fucker Johnny give you his shirt he thought you need it. That other prick, Butter, always chewin' on a mouthful of somethin', his lips covered with chocolate."

He turned to look at me. "But they ain't good boys anymore. They killers now, cold as stone."

"I know," I said. "I know what they were and I know what they are. It's not about that."

"Ain't worth throwin' away a life just to get even," Fat Mancho said. "You and the lawyer got a shot. You can make it out the right way. You ready to flip that aside? Just to get even with three fuckin' guards?"

"I think about what they did every day," I said, looking away from Fat Mancho, my eyes on the street in front of us. "It's a part of me, like skin. When I look in a mirror, I see it in my eyes. Sometimes, I see it in other people's faces. It's a nasty feeling. It's a feeling that makes you think a piece of you is already dead. And there's no way to bring it back."

"Gettin' away with this gonna make you feel all better?" Fat Mancho asked. "Gonna make you forget every fuckin' thing that happened?"

"No," I said, turning back to face him. "It'll just give me something a little sweeter to remember. Somethin' nicer to think about."

"I read that shitty paper you workin' on now," Fat Mancho said, standing and picking up his soda crate. "Read it every day. Still ain't seen your fuckin' name anywhere."

"Be patient," I said. "Someday you will. Just keep on buyin' it."

"I don't buy shit," Fat Mancho said, walking back into his bodega. "I never put any of my money in a stranger's pockets."

"You still married to two women?" I asked him, standing and dusting the back of my pants.

"Two wives and a lady friend," Fat Mancho said. "They can't get enough of what I got."

"Must be good," I said.

"They like it," Fat Mancho said. "That's what counts."

"Thanks, Fat Man," I said, leaning against his doorway. "I owe you. I owe you big-time."

"Bet your ass you owe me, fucker," Fat Mancho said. "And you ain't leavin' this spot till you pay me for that fuckin' pack of gum."

6

I WAS SITTING ON THE HALLWAY STEPS, MY BACK INCHES from the apartment door, a bag holding a six-pack of beer by my side, when Carol Martinez lifted her head and saw me.

"Mug me or marry me, Shakes," Carol said, searching through her open purse for her keys. "I'm too tired for anything else."

"Will you settle for a couple of beers?" I asked, tapping the paper bag.

"If that's your best offer," she said.

"I'll throw in a hug and a kiss," I said.

"Sold," she said.

I stood up and put my arms around her waist and held her close to me, feeling her soft curves, even under the layers of thick jacket and sweater. She looked as pretty as I'd ever seen her.

"You need something, don't you, Shakes?" Carol asked, warm hands rubbing the back of my head and neck.

"I could use a glass," I said. "I hate drinking out of a can."

HER APARTMENT WAS CLEAN and orderly, filled with books and framed posters of old movies. The kitchen had a small table in its center, and a large cutout of Humphrey Bogart in a trench coat smoking a cigarette was taped to the fridge.

"You pour the beer," Carol said, taking off her jacket. "I'll put on some music."

"You got any Frankie Valli?" I asked.

"You're so old-fashioned, Shakes," Carol said with a laugh. "Valli was gone before the pill."

"At least he's alive," I said. "Which is more than I can say for your pal Bogart."

"Bogie's always gonna be cool," she said. "I can't say the same about the Four Seasons."

"Well, don't throw away their albums just yet," I said, handing her a glass of beer, watching as she put a Bob Seger record on the turntable.

"I don't *have* any to throw away," she said, sitting down next to me on the small pull-out couch in the center of the living room.

We sat there quietly, listening to Seger frog his way through "Tryin' to Live My Life Without You," sipping our beer, my head resting against a thick, hand-quilted throw pillow.

"You look tired," Carol said, placing a hand on my knee. "They don't give you time for sleep on this new job of yours?"

"How much do you know?" I asked, turning my eyes toward hers.

"Just what the neighborhood says," Carol said.

"And what does the neighborhood say?"

"That they're going to put John and Tommy away," she said, sadness touching her eyes and voice. "And that their best friend is going to be the one to do it."

"You believe that?"

"It's hard not to, Shakes," Carol said. "I mean, unless we all have it wrong, he did take the fucking case."

"Yeah, he did take the case," I said.

"Then what else is there to say?" she asked, drinking the rest of her beer and trying not to cry.

I sat up and moved closer to her, our hands touching, our eyes on each other.

"You know Michael very well," I said. "Maybe even better than I do."

"I thought I did," Carol said. "I really thought I did. Now I don't know."

"You *do* know, Carol," I said. "You know he loves you. And you know he'd *never* do anything to hurt you or me or Johnny or Butter. Never."

"Then why take the case?" Carol said. "For God's sake, he even went in and asked for it. What the hell kind of friend is that?"

"The best kind," I said. "The kind who will throw whatever he has away, just to help his friends. The kind who never forgets who he is and what he is. The kind who's crazy enough to think he can get away with what he's trying to do."

"What are you telling me, Shakes?" Carol asked.

"You've lived in this neighborhood a long time, Carol. Long enough to know that everything is a shakedown or a scam. Why should this be any different?"

"I'll go get us another beer," Carol said, walking back into the kitchen. By now Bob Seger was singing "Against the Wind." "You want a sandwich with it?"

"You got any fresh mozzarella and basil?" I asked.

"How about a couple of slices of old ham on stale bread?"

"With mustard?"

"Mayo," Carol said.

"You got me," I said.

We ate our sandwiches, drank our beer, and listened to music, the two of us relaxed in each other's company and lost in the valleys of our own thoughts. After many moments had passed, I asked her why she had stopped dating Michael.

"It just happened," Carol said. "He was living in Queens,

working and going to school. I was here and doing the same. We'd go weeks without seeing each other. After a while, it was easier to let it go."

"You still love him?"

"I don't think about it, Shakes," Carol said. "If I did, I'd say yes. But Michael needed to get away from Hell's Kitchen. Get away from the people in it. I was one of those people."

"And you're with John now," I said.

"As much as anybody can be with John," Carol said. "The man I know is not the boy you remember. But there's something special about John. You just have to look harder to see it."

"You visit him?"

"Once a week," Carol said. "For about an hour."

"Good," I said. "Keep that up. Just don't tell him you see me. In fact, don't tell him anything. The more it looks hopeless to him, the better this might work."

"Why not tell him?" Carol said. "Might make things easier."

"He'll put on a tougher act in court if he thinks he's cornered," I said. "I want that little baby face of his looking straight at the jury and I don't want it to look happy."

"Why didn't *you* ever ask me out?" Carol said, a thin hand running through her thick hair.

"You were Mikey's girl," I said. "He got to you first."

"And after Mikey?" she said, her face shiny and clear.

"I never thought you'd say yes," I said.

"Well, you were wrong, Shakes," Carol said.

"Will you say yes to me now?" I said, holding her hand in mine. "No matter what I ask?"

Carol leaned over and put both arms around me and rested her head against my neck.

"Yes," she whispered. "What do you want me to do?"

"Break the law," I said.

7

MICHAEL'S PLAN RELIED HEAVILY ON HELL'S KITCHEN to deliver information and to keep silent. Both were skills the neighborhood had in abundance.

The plan also depended on keeping Michael alive, which meant that word had to get to John and Tommy's killing crew that he was not an open target. Within days of Michael taking the case, the West Side Boys got a visit from King Benny. The King requested that the verbal abuse directed toward Michael continue, but that there never be a death move against him. The hit on Michael Sullivan, if there were to be one, could come only from King Benny.

While the neighborhood, led by King Benny, Fat Mancho, and Carol, worked their end, I received and relayed the information I got from Michael back down the line. In turn, I fed Michael all that he needed to know.

We had set up a simple method of communication.

If Michael was sending, messages were left at work for me to call my nonexistent girlfriend, Gloria. Once I received the signal, I would send one of King Benny's men to pick up an envelope no later than noon of the next day at one of three designated drop spots.

If I needed to get word to Michael, I would have someone from the neighborhood pick up an early edition of *The New*

York Times, script the word *Edmund* on the upper-right-hand corner of the Metro section, and drop it in front of his apartment door. Later that day, Michael would pick up his envelope at an Upper East Side P.O. box.

We spent our early weeks going beyond Michael's files, digging up information that could be used either in a courtroom or on the street against the three remaining guards. We also were working the witnesses, gathering their backgrounds, finding their weak spots. A full folder was also being developed on the Wilkinson Home for Boys, finding former guards, employees, and inmates willing to speak out, hunting down wardens and assistants, locating the names of juveniles who died during their stay there and checking on the given cause of death.

Michael supplied us with a list of questions for O'Connor to ask in court. He also gave us the questions he intended to ask and the answers he expected to receive. Any additional information on the guards or on Wilkinson that he came across was also passed along.

All written messages, once delivered, were destroyed. Phone conversations were permitted only through the use of coded numbers on clear third-party lines. There was never any personal contact between the main participants.

Our margin of error was zero.

Hell's Kitchen, a neighborhood that came to the aid of its allies as quickly as it rushed to bury its enemies, thrived under Michael's plan. The verbal shots at Michael continued, cries of "traitor" and "gutter rat" heard up and down the avenue, but those were bellowed for the sole benefit of strangers. The underground word, the only one that mattered, had spread through the streets with the speed of a late-night bullet—King Benny's "sleepers" were making their play. "Sleepers" was a street name for anyone who spent time in a juvenile facility. It was also a mob phrase attached to a hit man who stayed overnight after finishing a job. There were many "sleepers" in Hell's

Kitchen, but my friends and I were the only four King Benny considered his crew.

"You want a Rolls-Royce, you go to England or wherever the fuck they make it," Fat Mancho said. "You want champagne, you go see the French. You want money, find a Jew. But you want dirt, scum buried under a rock, a secret nobody wants anybody to know, you want that and you want that fast, there's only one place to go—Hell's Kitchen. It's the lost and found of shit. They lose it and we find it."

8

KING BENNY SAT ON A PARK BENCH IN DE WITT CLINton, feeding pumpkin seeds to a circle of pigeons, the late fall sun scanning his back. It was one week past Thanksgiving and three weeks into our work. The weather had begun its turn to New York cold.

He wore the same black outfit he usually wore in his club, ignoring the frigid air much as he ignored everything else. He had a coffee cup resting next to his right leg along with a small bottle of Sambuca Romana.

"I didn't know you liked pigeons," I said, sitting down next to him.

"I like anything that don't talk," King Benny said.

"I heard from Mikey today," I said. "The case goes to trial first Monday in the new year. It'll be a small story in the papers tomorrow."

"You only got two witnesses who are gonna testify," King Benny said. "Two others changed their minds. That won't be in the papers tomorrow."

"Which two?"

"The suits at the bar," King Benny said. "They said they had too many drinks to know for sure who they saw walk in."

"That leaves the couple in the booth," I said.

"For now," King Benny said.

"Everything else is falling into place?" I asked, blowing breath into my hands.

"Except for your witness," King Benny said. "That pocket's still empty."

"I've got somebody in mind," I said. "I'll talk to him when the time's right."

"He good?"

"He will be," I said. "If he does it."

"Make sure, then," King Benny said, tossing more seeds at the pigeons, "that he does it."

"None of this would work without you," I said.

"You'd find a way," King Benny said. "With me or without."

"Maybe," I said. "But I'm glad you're with us on this."

"I don't know if I coulda been any help to you back in that place," King Benny said. "But I shoulda tried." It was the only time he ever alluded to the fact that he knew what had gone on when we were at Wilkinson.

"Things happen when they're supposed to," I said. "It's what you always said to me."

"Good things and bad," King Benny said. "Goin' in, you never know which one you're gonna find. Always be prepared for both."

"And most of the time," I said, "bet on the bad."

"You better go now," King Benny said. "You don't wanna be late for your appointment."

"What appointment?"

"With Danny O'Connor," King Benny said. "He's waitin' for you in Red Applegate's bar. Should be on his second Scotch by now. Get to him before he has a third."

"Is he ready to go along?" I asked.

"He'll go," King Benny said. "He's too young to have his friends drive their cars with their lights on."

9

WINTER 1980

THE COURT OFFICERS LED JOHN REILLY AND THOMAS Marcano into the courtroom, both defendants walking with their heads down and their hands at their sides. They were wearing blue blazers, blue polo shirts, gray slacks, and brown loafers. They nodded at their attorney, Danny O'Connor, and sat down in the two wooden chairs by his side.

The court stenographer, a curly-haired blonde in a short black skirt, sat across from them, directly in front of the judge's bench, her face vacant.

The chairs of the jury box were filled by the twelve chosen for the trial.

Michael Sullivan sat at the prosecutor's table, his open briefcase, two yellow legal folders, and three sharp pencils laid out before him, his eyes on the stenographer's legs. He was in a dark wool suit, his dark tie crisply knotted over his white shirt.

I sat in the middle of the third row. Two young men, both of whom I knew to be part of the West Side Boys, sat to my left. Carol Martinez, eyes staring straight ahead, was to my right. She held my hand.

Judge Eliot Weisman took his place behind the bench. He was a tall, middle-aged man with a square face topped by a

cleanly shaved head. He appeared trim and fit, muscular beneath his dark robes. He was known to run a stern courtroom
and allowed scant time for theatrics and stall tactics. Criminal
attorneys claimed his scale of justice almost always tipped
toward the prosecutor. The assistant district attorneys themselves called him fair, but by no means an easy touch.

Michael knew that Judge Weisman's initial take on John
and Tommy would be one of disdain, a response that would be
further fueled by the facts of the case. Michael also knew that
the evidence against the two defendants would be so heavy that
combined with their history of violence, it would prod Weisman to try to avoid a trial. He expected Weisman to pressure
both sides to work out a plea-bargain agreement.

Three times the judge privately asked both counsels for
such an agreement and three times they refused. John and
Tommy stuck to their not-guilty plea and the judge stuck to
holding them without bail. Michael insisted that the people, as
represented by his office, would want these men prosecuted to
the fullest extent of the law. As the case entered the jury-
selection phase, Judge Weisman did not appear pleased.

At no time during those early weeks in that uncomfortable
courtroom did Michael give any indication of what he planned
to do. He interviewed and selected his jury carefully, as well as
any young assistant district attorney would, asking all pertinent
questions, attempting to weed out, as honestly as possible, any
juror he felt would not or could not deliver a fair verdict. Both
counsels settled on a jury of eight men and four women. One
of the women was Hispanic, as were two of the men. Two other
men were black. Three jurors, two men and a woman, were
Irish.

When mentioning the defendants, Michael always referred
to them by their names to establish their identities and so move
them beyond a pair of anonymous faces. He insisted that pro-
spective jurors gaze at the two men on trial while he catalogued

their reputations and asked anyone fearful of those reputations not to feel compelled to serve. John and Tommy always made a point of looking at Michael, but he carefully averted their gaze, not willing to take the chance that some spectator would notice even a hint of their relationship.

Michael's vision on where he wanted this case to go was very clear.

He was aiming for a guilty.

A charge of guilty against the Wilkinson Home for Boys; a charge of guilty against Sean Nokes, Adam Styler, Henry Addison, and Ralph Ferguson.

Michael sat impassively through Danny O'Connor's unemotional opening statement, listening to the grizzly voiced attorney refer to John and Tommy as two innocent pawns, quickly arrested and just as quickly prosecuted on the slightest threads of evidence. O'Connor would prove, he insisted, beyond any reasonable doubt, that John Reilly and Thomas Marcano did not kill Sean Nokes on the night in question. That, in fact, they were nowhere near the Shamrock Pub at the time of the shooting.

No one was impressed by O'Connor's performance, least of all Judge Weisman, who fidgeted throughout the fifteen minutes it took for his statement. The few reporters covering the case, scattered through the front rows, stopped taking notes after O'Connor's initial remarks. Veteran spectators, accustomed to more volatile defense attorneys, shook their heads in boredom.

"He's not exactly Perry Mason," Carol whispered.

"He got their names right," I said. "For him, that's a great start. Besides, if he wins this case, he'll be bigger than Perry Mason."

Michael stood up, unbuttoned his suit jacket, and walked in front of his table, toward the jury box. He had his hands in his pockets and a friendly smile on his face.

"Good morning," he said to the jurors. "My name is Michael Sullivan and I am an assistant district attorney for the county of Manhattan. My job, like most jobs, I suppose, seems, on the surface, an easy one. I have to prove to you and only to you that the two men who stand accused killed a man named Sean Nokes in cold blood, without any apparent motive. I will present to you evidence and offer into account testimony to prove that. I will place them at the scene of the crime. I will bring witnesses to the stand who will confirm that they were there on that deadly night. I will present to you enough facts so you can then go into the jury room and come out with a clear decision that's beyond a reasonable doubt. Now, I know you all know what that means, since you probably watch as much TV as I do."

Three of the women on the jury smiled and one of the men, a postal employee from the Upper West Side, laughed out loud. "I hear that," he said, pointing a finger at Michael.

"Let me remind one and all that this is a *court*room," Judge Weisman said in a somber tone. "Not a *living* room. With that in mind, will the jurors please refrain from making any further comments."

"My fault, your honor," Michael said, turning to face the judge. "I gave the impression that a response was required. It won't happen again."

"I'm sure it won't, counselor," the judge said, relaxing his tone. "Proceed."

"Look at their faces," I said to Carol, nudging her attention toward the jury box. "Their eyes. They're falling in love with him."

"That's not a hard thing to do," Carol said.

"The past history of these two young men is not important and not an issue in this case," Michael said, turning back to the jury, his hands on the wood barrier, his eyes moving from face to face. "Violent or peaceful, criminal or honest, saints or sinners. None of it matters. What *does* matter is what happened on the night of the murder. If I can prove to you that these two men were the men who walked in, had two drinks, and shot Sean Nokes dead, then I expect no less than a guilty verdict. If I can't do that, if I can't put them there, put the guns in their hands, put the body before them and make you firmly believe that they pulled the triggers, then the weight of guilt is cleanly off your shoulders and on mine. If that happens, I will have failed to do my job. But I will do my best not to fail you and not to fail to find the truth. I will do my best to seek justice. And I know you will too."

10

I WAS TWENTY MINUTES LATE. I HAD TOLD CAROL TO meet me in front of the church at six, but had lost track of time kneeling in prayer in one of the back pews in Sacred Heart. I walked out of the church and saw her sitting on the steps, the collar of her leather jacket lifted against the strong winds whipping up from the river.

"Sorry I'm late," I said. "I was lighting candles."

"Now you've got St. Jude in on this too," Carol said. "Anybody else?"

"Just one more," I said.

"We supposed to meet up with him here?" Carol asked.

"No. He's waitin' for us at his place."

"Which is where?"

"Which is there," I said, pointing a finger at the redbrick building next to the church. "The rectory."

"Oh, my God!" Carol said, her eyes opened wide. "Oh, my God!"

"Not quite," I said. "But it's as close as I could come on short notice."

* * *

FATHER BOBBY SAT IN A RECLINER IN HIS SMALL, BOOK-lined first-floor room, his back to a slightly opened window. He lit a cigarette and took a deep drag, letting the smoke out his nose. He held a bottle of Pepsi in his right hand. Carol sat across from him, her legs crossed, elbow on her knee, chin in the palm of her hand.

I sat on a windowsill in the corner of the room that looked down on the school yard, hands in my pockets, my back brushing white lace curtains.

"How was court today?" Father Bobby asked, his voice tired.

"Like the first round of a fight," I said. "Everybody just feeling each other out."

"How do the boys look?"

"Like they wished they were someplace else," Carol said. "I think that's how we all felt."

"I've been in this parish nearly twenty years," Father Bobby said, flicking cigarette ash into his empty bottle of soda. "Seen a lot of boys grow into men. And I've seen too many die or end up in jail for most of their lives. I've cried over all of them. But this one, this one's been the hardest. This one's cost me every prayer I know."

Father Bobby knew that it wasn't the streets that had chilled John Reilly and Thomas Marcano. And it wasn't the allure of drugs or gangs that led them to stray. You couldn't blame their fall on the harsh truth of Hell's Kitchen. There was only one place to blame.

"You did what you could, Father," I said. "Helped me. Michael too. We'd all be on trial today, wasn't for you."

"It's the sheep that strays that you most want back," Father Bobby said.

"It's not too late, Father," I said, moving away from the window and closer to his side. "We still have a chance to bring in a couple of stray sheep. One last chance."

"Is that one chance legal?" Father Bobby asked.

"Last chances never are," I said.

"Is King Benny behind this?"

"He's in it," I said. "But he's not calling the shots."

"Who is?"

"Michael," I said.

Father Bobby took a deep breath and leaned forward in his chair.

"There's a bottle of Dewar's in the middle drawer of my desk," Father Bobby said. "I think we're going to need some."

* * *

I TOLD FATHER BOBBY EVERYTHING. IF HE WAS GOING to be involved, he deserved to know what he was getting into. If he wasn't going to help, I still trusted him enough to know that the truth would move no farther than his room.

"I should've smelled it," Father Bobby said. "The minute Michael went for the case, I should have figured something was up."

"It's a good plan," I said. "Mikey's got it all covered. Every base you look at, he's got it covered."

"Not every base, Shakes," Father Bobby said. "You're still short something, or else you wouldn't be here."

"Don't shit a shitter," I said with a smile.

"That's right. So, spill it. Where do you come up short?"

"A witness," I said. "Somebody to take the stand and say they were with John and Tommy the night of the murder."

"And you figured a priest would be perfect?" Father Bobby said.

"Not just any priest," I said.

"You're asking me to lie," Father Bobby said. "Asking me to swear to God and then to lie."

"I'm asking you to help two of your boys," I said. "Help them stay out of jail for the rest of their lives."

"Did they kill Nokes?" Father Bobby asked. "Did they walk into the pub and kill him like they say?"

"Yes," I said. "They killed him. Exactly like they say."

FATHER BOBBY STOOD UP and paced the small room, his hands rubbing against the sides of his legs. He was still dressed in the black street garments of a priest, short-sleeve shirt under his jacket, keys rattling in a side pocket.

"This is some favor you're asking me," Father Bobby said, stopping in the center of the room, staring at me and Carol.

"We know, Father," Carol said.

"No," Father Bobby said. "I don't think you do."

"You always said if there was ever anything I needed to come and ask you," I said.

"I was thinking more along the lines of Yankee tickets," Father Bobby said.

"I don't need Yankee tickets, Father," I said. "I need a witness."

Father Bobby undid the top button of his shirt and peeled out the Roman collar beneath it. He held the collar in both hands.

"This is my *life*," Father Bobby said, holding up the collar. "It's all I've got. I've given everything to it. *Everything*. Now, you two come walking in here with some plan that asks me to throw it away. To throw it away so two murderers can walk free. To kill again. And you ask me that as a favor."

"Two lives should be worth more than a Roman collar," I said.

"What about the life that was taken, Shakes?" Father Bobby asked, standing inches from my face. "What's that worth?"

"To me, nothing," I said.

"Why not, Shakes?" Father Bobby asked. "Tell me."

I sat in the chair next to the desk, Father Bobby and Carol on the other end of the room. I stared at the shelves crammed with the books I had read as a child and the many more I wanted to read. I held an empty glass in my hand, struggling to recall the faces and images that had, for so long, been safely buried.

Faces and images I never wanted to believe were real.

I sat in that chair and told Father Bobby what was in my heart. It was the first and only time I had ever told anyone—until then—exactly what the life of Sean Nokes was worth.

I spoke for more than an hour, my words weighed with anger and urgency, letting Father Bobby and Carol know the things I never thought I would be telling anyone. To Father Bobby, it was a shock, a jolt of pain straight to his heart. Carol had been close enough to Michael and John to suspect, but the specifics stunned her, made her sit bolt upright and took her breath away.

I told them about the Wilkinson Home for Boys.

I told them about the torture, the beatings, the humiliation.

I told them about the rapes.

I told them about four frightened boys who cried themselves to sleep and who prayed to Father Bobby's God for help that never came. I told them about endless nights spent staring into darkness, rats owning the corners, keys rattling jail cell locks, nightsticks swinging high in the air, a guard's grip, a boy's scream.

I told them everything.

And when I was done, Carol said quietly, in almost a whisper, "Now you tell me, Father. What would a good priest do?"

* * *

FATHER BOBBY STARED STRAIGHT AHEAD, AS HE HAD for the past hour, only his eyes registering any change. He blew out a mouthful of breath and then looked toward the ceiling, his hands resting on the soft edges of his chair.

"It's getting late," he finally said. "You should go. You both look tired."

He stood up and placed a hand on my arm.

"I've got a decision to make," Father Bobby said. "All I can do is pray that it's the right one."

"It will be, Father," I said. "Whichever way you go."

"The boys were on target about you," Father Bobby said, reaching out for Carol and holding her in his arms.

"About what?" Carol asked, lifting her head.

"They always said you had balls," Father Bobby said. "And they were right."

"I'll take that as a compliment," Carol said. "Especially coming from a priest."

11

MICHAEL SMILED AT THE WITNESS, A DARK-HAIRED, handsome woman from New Jersey. She had her legs crossed under the chair, her skirt pleated, her white blouse buttoned to the throat. Her hands were folded on her lap.

"Mrs. Salinas, how often have you had dinner at the Shamrock Pub?" he asked.

"Just that one night," she answered, her voice assured, speaking in the manner of a woman with nothing to hide.

"What night would that be?" Michael asked.

"The night of the murder," she said.

"What time did you get there?"

"Near seven-thirty," Mrs. Salinas said. "I met a friend for dinner."

"What's the name of your friend?"

"David," she said. "David Carson."

"Who was the first to arrive?"

"I was," she said. "But only by a couple of minutes."

"You waited for Mr. Carson outside?"

"No," she said. "By the coatrack. As I said, it wasn't much of a wait."

"Okay," Michael said. "You and Mr. Carson go in, sit down, order a drink, start catching up on your day. That right?"

"Pretty much," Mrs. Salinas said. "We hadn't seen each other for a few weeks. David had been away on a business trip."

"Who decided to eat at the Shamrock Pub?"

"I did."

"Why?"

"I read about it in a magazine," she said. "They said it was colorful."

"And was it?"

"Up until the shooting," Mrs. Salinas said.

I looked over at the defense table and caught a smirk from John and a smile from Tommy. Their lawyer, head down, was furiously scrawling notes on a legal pad.

"What's he taking notes for?" Carol whispered. "He knows the questions he's supposed to ask."

"Maybe he forgot them," I said. "Left them on a barstool."

"She's good," Carol said, indicating Mrs. Salinas.

"We want her to be," I said.

"Had Mr. Carson ever been there before?" Michael asked now. "With or without you?"

"No," she said. "It was the first time for both of us."

"Where were you seated, Mrs. Salinas?"

"In a booth," she said. "The one closest to the door."

"Was that by choice?"

"Yes," she said. "All but one of the booths was free, so we could have sat anywhere. But David likes fresh air and I don't mind it either."

"Do you remember what you ordered?"

"I asked for the lamb chops," she said. "It was one of the specialties mentioned in the magazine. David had his usual."

"For those of us not familiar with Mr. Carson's eating habits, could you tell us what his usual consists of?" Michael asked, throwing Mrs. Salinas a wide smile.

"Steak," she said. "David *always* orders steak, baked potato, and a tossed salad."

"Did you have anything to drink?"

"We ordered a bottle of red wine," Mrs. Salinas said. "A Chianti, I believe."

"That's all?"

"Yes," she said. "That's all."

"Did you notice the number of people in the pub?"

"There were only a few scattered about," she said. "It was quiet. A good place to meet someone and talk."

"Did you notice the victim, Sean Nokes?"

"No," she said. "I did not."

"You didn't even see him when you walked in?" Michael asked.

"No," she said. "Our table was right near the coat check and I didn't bother looking around."

"Your attentions were focused on Mr. Carson," Michael said.

"Yes, they were," Mrs. Salinas said. "As I said, I hadn't seen him for a while."

"Which way were you facing?" Michael asked. "Which side of the booth were you sitting on?"

"The one facing the rear of the pub," she said.

"The side facing down the row of booths?"

"Yes."

"The side facing Mr. Nokes's booth," Michael said.

"I believe so," Mrs. Salinas said. "Yes."

"But you couldn't see him from where you were sitting?"

"I wasn't looking to see him," she said. "I knew there was someone sitting in the rear booth. I just didn't notice."

"Did you notice the two men who walked in shortly after you sat down for dinner?"

"I heard them come in," she said. "You couldn't help but hear them."

"Why's that?"

"They were loud," she said. "They caused a commotion. I'm sure everyone noticed."

"Did you see their faces when they came in?"

"No," she said. "Not when they came in."

"Why not?"

"I was talking to David," she said. "When I finally looked up, they had moved past me."

"Did you notice their faces when they went to the bar?"

"From the side," she said. "I could see them in profile."

"Both of them?"

"Yes," Mrs. Salinas said, the confidence in her voice never wavering. "Both of them."

"Did you see them approach the booth where Mr. Nokes was sitting?" Michael asked.

"I noticed it," she said. "Yes."

"Did you hear what was said between them?"

"No," she said. "I didn't."

"Did you see them pull out their guns?"

"No," she said.

"Did you hear the shots?"

"Yes," Mrs. Salinas said. "I heard the shots."

"What did they do after the shooting?" Michael asked.

"They walked out of the pub," she said. "As if nothing had happened."

"Did you see their faces then?"

"Yes," she said. "I looked up as they walked by."

"Are you positive of that, Mrs. Salinas?"

"Yes," she said. "Very positive."

"And are the two men you saw in the Shamrock Pub in this room today?"

"Yes," Mrs. Salinas said. "They are."

"Can you point them out to me, please?"

"They're sitting right over there," Mrs. Salinas said, aiming a finger at John and Tommy.

"Your honor, will the record reflect that Mrs. Salinas identified defendants John Reilly and Thomas Marcano as the two men in question."

"Noted," Judge Weisman said.

"I have no further questions," Michael said.

"Counselor?" Judge Weisman said, lifting an eyebrow in Danny O'Connor's direction. "Are you ready to proceed?"

"Yes, your honor," Danny O'Connor said. "The defense is ready."

"It better be," Carol whispered.

* * *

DANNY O'CONNOR WAS WEARING A CHARCOAL-GRAY SUIT that needed cleaning and a white shirt tight around his neck. His shoes were scuffed and his blue tie stopped at an Oliver Hardy length.

"He's got that Columbo look down," I muttered. "All he's missing is the cigar."

"It's probably in his pocket," Carol said. "Still lit."

"Good morning," Danny O'Connor said to Mrs. Salinas.

"Good morning," she said.

"I just have a few questions," he said. "I won't take up too much more of your time."

"Thank you," she said.

"You said you had only wine to drink with dinner," O'Connor said, looking away from Mrs. Salinas and making eye contact with the jury. "Is that correct?"

"Yes," she said. "That's correct."

"Are you sure about that?" O'Connor asked. "Are you sure that was all you ordered, one bottle of wine?"

"Yes," she said. "A bottle of red wine."

"Had you had anything to drink prior to that?"

"What do you mean, prior?" Mrs. Salinas asked.

"At lunch, maybe," O'Connor said. "Did you have anything to drink at lunch?"

"Yes, I did," she said. "But that was hours earlier."

"What did you have, Mrs. Salinas?"

"I went shopping and stopped for lunch at a place on Madison Avenue," she said.

"I didn't ask where you went," O'Connor said. "I asked what you had to drink at lunch."

"A martini," she said.

"And what else?"

"And some wine," she said.

"How much wine?"

"One glass," she said. "Maybe two."

"Closer to two?" O'Connor asked.

"Yes," Mrs. Salinas said, her cheeks turning a light shade of red. "Probably two."

"What time did you have lunch, Mrs. Salinas?"

"Objection, your honor," Michael said without standing. "What Mrs. Salinas did on the day of the murder has nothing to do with what she saw the night of the murder."

"How much she had to drink does, your honor," O'Connor said.

"Overruled," Judge Weisman said.

"What time, Mrs. Salinas," O'Connor said, "did you have lunch?"

"About one-thirty," she said.

"And what did you have for lunch?"

"A salad," she said.

"A martini, two glasses of wine, and a salad," O'Connor said. "Is that correct?"

"Yes," Mrs. Salinas said, her eyes looking to Michael for help. "Yes, that's correct."

He gave her none.

"And then you had wine at dinner," O'Connor said. "About six hours later. Is that right?"

"Yes, that's right," she said.

"How much wine did you have to drink by the time my clients allegedly walked into the Shamrock Pub?"

"Two glasses," she said, anger now undercutting the confident tone.

"Do you drink this much every day, Mrs. Salinas?"

"No," she said. "I do not."

"So would you say four glasses of wine and a martini in a six-hour period is a lot for you to drink?" O'Connor asked.

"Yes, it is," Mrs. Salinas said.

"Are you married, Mrs. Salinas?" O'Connor asked.

"Yes, I am," she said.

"Happily?"

"As happy as anyone married for fifteen years can expect to be."

"I've been divorced twice, Mrs. Salinas," O'Connor said, smiling at the jury. "Fifteen years sounds like a lifetime to me. How happy would that be?"

"I'm still in love with my husband," Mrs. Salinas said.

"Objection," Michael said. "This line of questioning is out of order."

"I'll allow it," Judge Weisman said, looking at O'Connor. "But get to your point."

"Yes, your honor," O'Connor said. "Thank you."

The defense attorney now walked alongside the jury, one hand inside the pocket of his wrinkled pants, his thin brown hair combed straight back.

"What is your relationship with Mr. Carson?"

"I've already said."

"Tell me again," O'Connor said. "Please."

"We're friends," she said. "Very old and dear friends."

"Is Mr. Carson a friend of your husband's as well?" O'Connor asked.

Mrs. Salinas paused and pursed her lips before she answered.

"No," she said. "He isn't."

"Mrs. Salinas, what were you talking about at dinner?"

"The usual," she said. "Catching up on things."

"What things?"

"His family," she said. "Mine. Things like that."

"And did you and Mr. Carson have any plans beyond dinner?" O'Connor asked.

"What do you mean?" Mrs. Salinas asked.

"I mean, was your evening going to end with just a dinner?" O'Connor asked.

"No," she said, her eyes cast down. "It wasn't."

"Sounds romantic," O'Connor said.

"Objection," Michael said. "The twice-divorced counsel seems to have an overactive imagination."

"Sustained," Judge Weisman said. "Let's get on with it, Mr. O'Connor."

"Had you ever heard a gun fired, Mrs. Salinas?" O'Connor asked, shifting his questioning and walking closer to the witness stand. "Prior to the night in question, that is."

"No, I hadn't," she said.

"How would you describe the sound?"

"Loud," she said. "Like firecrackers."

"Did the sound frighten you?"

"Yes, very much," she said.

"Did you close your eyes?"

"At first," she said. "Until the shooting stopped."

"Did you think the men who did the shooting were going to kill everyone in the pub?"

"I didn't know what to think," she said. "All I knew was that a man had been shot."

"Did you think *you* might be shot?" O'Connor asked. "Shot dead by two cold-blooded killers?"

"Yes," Mrs. Salinas said, nodding her head firmly. "Yes, I did."

"Yet, despite that fear," O'Connor said, "despite the risk to your life, you looked at their faces as they left the pub. Is that right?"

"Yes," she said. "Yes, that's right."

"*Is it?*" O'Connor said, his voice rising. "Did you really look at their faces?"

"Yes."

"Did you, Mrs. Salinas, really *look* at their faces?" O'Connor asked, now standing inches from her.

"I glanced at them as they walked by," she said. "But I *did* see them."

"You *glanced,*" O'Connor said, his voice hitting a higher pitch. "You didn't *look*?"

"I *saw* them," Mrs. Salinas said.

"You *glanced* at them, Mrs. Salinas," O'Connor said. "You *glanced* at them through the eyes of a frightened woman who may have had too much to drink."

"Objection, your honor," Michael said, his hands spread out in front of him, still sitting in his chair.

"No need, your honor," O'Connor said, clearly relishing his first dance in the spotlight. "I have no further questions."

"Thank you, Mrs. Salinas," Judge Weisman said to the now-shaken woman. "You may step down."

"Looks like Columbo did his homework," Carol said.

"Today anyway," I said, my eyes on John and Tommy, watching them wink their approval at O'Connor.

"Have you got time for lunch?" Carol asked.

"I'll make the time," I said.

"Where would you like to go?"

"How about the Shamrock Pub," I said. "I hear it's colorful."

12

THE DETECTIVE IN THE FRONT SEAT KEPT THE ENGINE running, his hands on the steering wheel, a container of coffee by his side, the lid still on. I sat in the back, opposite the driver's side, a heavy manila envelope on my lap. Another detective sat to my left, looking out the window, watching the wind whip shreds of garbage down Little West 12th Street. The defogger was on and all four windows of the late-model sedan were open a crack, letting in thin streams of January air.

It was six-fifteen on a Sunday morning and the downtown streets were empty.

"So, you gonna show me?" the detective to my left asked, pointing down at the envelope. "Or you just gonna ride the suspense?"

His name was Nick Davenport. He was twenty-eight years old and a sergeant in the Internal Affairs Division of the New York City Police Department. It is the unit responsible for dealing with corrupt cops.

"You've got to agree to a couple of things first," I said. "Then we deal."

"Frankie, what is this shit?"

"Hear the kid out, Nick," the detective in the front seat said. "It'll be worth your time. Believe me."

The detective in the front seat, Frank Magcicco, worked out

of a homicide unit housed in a Brooklyn precinct. He grew up in Hell's Kitchen and remained friendly with many of the people who lived there. He was a first grade detective with an honest name and a solid reputation. He was thirty-three years old, owned a two-family house in Queens, had two preschool children, and was married to a woman who worked part-time as a legal secretary.

He was also King Benny's nephew.

"Okay," Nick Davenport said. "What's it gonna cost?"

He had a blue-eyed, boyish face hidden by a three-day stubble and an older man's voice. He'd been on the force seven years, two as a patrolman in Harlem and two working plainclothes in Brooklyn, before making the move to I.A.D. He was cold to the fact that most cops hated anyone associated with Internal Affairs and ambitious enough to want to make captain before he hit forty. He knew the fastest way up that track was to reel in the maximum number of dirty cops in a minimum amount of time.

"I don't want any deals cut," I said.

"How so?" Davenport asked, shifting his body.

"You don't offer him *anything*," I said. "You don't use him to finger other cops. You bring him in and you bring him down."

"That ain't up to me," Nick said. "Once a case starts, a lot of other people get involved. I can't shut 'em all out."

"I heard you can," I said toward Frank in the front seat. "But maybe I heard wrong. Maybe I should take this to somebody else."

"Where'd you find this fuck?" Nick asked Frank, chuckling as he pulled a cigarette from his shirt pocket.

"I were you, I'd do what the kid says," Frank said, staring out through the windshield, sipping his coffee. "You make this one, you're gonna be havin' breakfast once a month with the commissioner."

"Okay, Eliot Ness," Nick said to me. "You got it. He won't

be offered any deals. No matter how much he talks, no matter who he fingers. No deals. Anything else?"

"Two more things," I said.

"Let me hear 'em," Nick said.

"He gets convicted, he gets state time," I said. "I don't want him sent to one of those cop country clubs. He's gotta do prison time."

"You got a real hard-on for this guy," Nick said. "What's your beef with him?"

"There's one more thing," I said. "You wanna hear it or not?"

"I can't wait," Nick said.

"It's simple," I said. "Nobody knows who fed you the information. How you got it. How you found it. And I mean *nobody*."

"How *did* you get it?"

"It fell into my lap," I said. "Just like it's falling into yours."

"That it?" Davenport asked, tossing his cigarette out through the crack in the window. "That's all you want?"

"That's all I want," I said.

Davenport stared at me for a few moments and then turned to look back outside. One hand rubbed the stubble on his face, one foot shook nervously back and forth.

"You okay with this, Frank?" he asked the detective in the front seat.

"I'm here, ain't I?" Frank said, watching him in the rearview mirror.

"Okay, Mr. Ness," Davenport said, putting out his hand. "You and me got ourselves a deal."

I handed him the thick envelope. Inside was the file that Michael had given me on former Wilkinson guard Adam Styler, plus additional information dug up in the past three months by King Benny and Fat Mancho.

"Christ almighty!" Davenport said, sorting through the material. "You got everything in here but a confession."

"I thought I'd leave that to you," I said. "And my preference is that you beat it out of him."

"Dates, times, phone numbers," Davenport said, his eyes wide, a smile spread across his face. "Get a load of this, Frankie, there's even surveillance photos. This piece of shit's pulling in about five grand a month. Rippin' off pushers. Has been for about three years."

"More like four," I said.

"He ain't gonna see five," Davenport said. "I'll tell you that right now."

"Do you have enough to get a conviction?" I asked.

"That ain't up to me, kid," Davenport said. "That's up to a jury."

"Then show the jury this," I said.

I reached into my jacket pocket and pulled out a plastic bag. In it was a snubnose .44 revolver and three spent shells.

"Whatta ya got there, Ness?" Davenport asked, taking the bag.

"Three weeks ago the body of a drug dealer named Indian Red Lopez was found in an alley in Jackson Heights," I said. "There were three bullets in his head and nothing in his pockets."

"I'm with you so far," Davenport said.

"That's the gun that killed him," I said. "Those are the shells."

"And what's behind door number three?" Davenport asked.

"The prints on the gun belong to Adam Styler," I said.

"Do me a favor, would ya, Ness?" Davenport said, putting the gun in his pocket.

"What?"

"I ever make it onto your shit list, give me a call," he said. "Give me a chance to apologize."

"You'll find a woman's name and phone number in the folder," I said. "Pay her a visit. Her English isn't too good. But it's good enough to tell you she saw Adam Styler put the gun to Lopez's head and pull the trigger."

Davenport lit a fresh cigarette, folding the spent match in his hand. He put Styler's folder back together and slid it into the envelope.

"I'll take it from here, Ness," Davenport said, putting out his hand. "You did your part."

"You need anything else, Frank knows how to reach me," I said, shaking hands.

"Want us to drop you off anywhere?" Frank asked, turning to face me.

"No, it's okay," I said. "I'll get out here."

"Say hello for me," Frank said.

"I will," I said, opening the car door. "And thanks, Frank. Thanks for all your help."

"Take care of yourself, kid," Frank said, winking at me as I got out of the car. "Water gets choppy out your way."

"I'll do what I can," I said, leaving the car and closing the door behind me.

"Hey, Ness," Davenport said, sliding over to where I had been sitting and rolling down the window.

"What?" I said, standing by the curb.

"You ever think of becoming a cop?" he asked, smiling.

"And leave the good guys?" I said with a laugh. "Never happen."

13

B Y THE END OF THE FIRST WEEK OF THE TRIAL, MICHAEL
had done all that could be expected of an assistant district attorney seeking a conviction in the murder case of People vs.
Reilly and Marcano. He had presented a detailed drawing of
the interior of the Shamrock Pub, giving the jury a picture to
go along with the verbal scenario. He had a replica made to
scale, with little wax figures representing the patrons and employees. He then showed the jury how it was possible for two
wax figures to walk into the pub, sit at a bar, have a few drinks,
move to the rear booth, shoot dead another wax figure, and
leave the pub without a problem.

He just never put faces on the two wax figures.

He had the crime scene photos blown up, with Nokes's
riddled corpse surrounded by two plates of jelled food and a
cold cup of coffee, then displayed them for the jury. He had a
forensics expert detail the make and caliber of the gun that
killed Nokes and encouraged the coroner to drone on about the
bloody manner of his death.

He just never had a weapon, the murder weapon, to show
them.

The officers at the scene all testified as to what they found
when they first arrived at the Shamrock Pub on the night of
the shooting. They ran through the statements presented to

them by those present. Michael then brought on the detectives assigned to the case, two veteran cops who combined those statements with other information they gathered to bring in John Reilly and Thomas Marcano.

He just never gave the jury a motive for the murder.

Michael kept to the plan, a plan that called for the action to stay simple.

He had left doubt in the minds of the jury. He had given them dozens of facts, but no weapon, no motive, and, more important, no prints that would put John and Tommy at the scene that night. The gloves they wore helped some. Jerry the bartender quietly took care of the rest. Michael had brought two eyewitnesses to the stand, but both were shaky and one, David Carson, had his back to the shooting and saw nothing but leather jackets and blurred faces come in and out of the Shamrock Pub.

Danny O'Connor did his part as well, asking the questions he was told to ask and occasionally throwing in pertinent queries of his own. His sloppy attire and lack of finesse played well with the working-class jury Michael had helped to select. He came off as a seasoned pro, a ruffled man of the people who had seen his share of victories and defeats. He talked to them and never lectured, but always made time, when the moment called for it, for a touch of Irish drama.

Michael had been right. Danny O'Connor was perfect.

At two-thirty P.M., a half hour before the close of the Friday session, Michael Sullivan prepared to announce the final witness in his prosecution of case docket number 778462. Judge Weisman asked him to hold the witness until Monday morning, as Michael knew he would. He agreed and wished both the judge and jury a pleasant weekend, then sat down, the first part of his job nearly finished.

He looked about five years older than he did when he and I met on that rainy night nearly four months earlier. The tension of his task, the hours we were all keeping, the uncertainty about the outcome, all weighed heavy. If the plan worked, it would be everyone's success. If it failed, the fault would fall to Michael.

We still didn't know if we had Father Bobby locked in as a witness and wouldn't know until he walked into that court-room. We decided it would be best for him to deal directly with O'Connor and not risk being seen talking to either me or Carol. If Father Bobby were to take the stand, we wanted it to be as late into the trial as possible, allowing the impact of his testimony to stay with the jury as they headed into the delib-eration room.

Father Bobby Carillo, a priest with the best outside jump shot on the West Side, remained the key to a plan that called for all involved to get away with murder.

14

KING BENNY STOOD IN FRONT OF HIS CLUB, HANDS folded at his back, eyes staring straight ahead. Three of his men huddled close by, stamping their feet against the cold. The door to the club remained open, the lilting sound of Doris Day singing "Que Sera, Sera" easing its way onto the street.

It was King Benny's favorite song.

"I see you've still got a thing for Doris Day," I said, coming up next to him.

"She's a good woman," King Benny said.

"You like her movies?" I asked.

"I don't go to movies," King Benny said. "C'mon, let's take a walk."

We crossed 11th Avenue and walked down 52nd Street. I kept my head down and my collar up, the wind blowing hard, the air now cutting sharp as ice. King Benny was, as usual, dressed in black shirt, slacks, and jacket. His hair was slicked back and his bum leg dragged, but he walked with a slight jaunt and seemed not to notice the weather.

"This guy Addison," King Benny said. "The one works for the mayor."

"I know him," I said.

King Benny went after Henry Addison with a vengeance. It went beyond mere business. King Benny took Henry Addison and made it personal. He knew that he was part of a young, well-to-do crowd that paid lots of money for sex parties with little boys. It didn't take King Benny long to find out who supplied those boys and how much their bodies were worth. The East Side pimp with the street name of Radio gave up everything—names, dates, videotapes, and photos. Enough material to cost Henry Addison a cushy city job that was handed to him by a friend in the mayor's office.

It took King Benny even less time to find out that unlike his other friends, Henry Addison didn't have much money. So he was forced to borrow for his pleasure. This put him in debt to the kind of people who charged interest in return for their loans.

"He's gonna quit his job in two weeks," King Benny said.

"Why's that?"

"He don't want nobody to know the kind of guy he is," King Benny said. "Don't want nobody to see pictures of him they shouldn't see."

"He knows this?"

"He will," King Benny said.

"That it?" I said.

"The boys he buys for parties are expensive," King Benny said, taking a handkerchief from his back pocket and wiping the edge of his nose. "Addison makes good money. He don't make real money."

"What's he owe?"

"Eight grand," King Benny said. "With a heavy vig."

"To who?"

"Three small-timers downtown," King Benny said. "They were letting him pay it off for a piece a week. Until this morning."

"What happened this morning?"

"They were paid off," King Benny said. "In full."

"Who paid 'em?"

"Henry Addison's chits belong to me now," King Benny said.

"You hate debts," I said.

"I hate Henry Addison," King Benny said.

We stopped at the corner of 52nd Street and 12th Avenue. I looked over at King Benny and saw in his dark eyes the dangerous void that he usually hid so carefully. It was an emptiness his enemies had good reason to fear.

It was an emptiness about to be filled with Henry Addison.

His black sedan was across the street, one of his men behind the wheel, the windows up, the engine running. We walked slowly toward the car.

"We going for a ride?" I asked him.

"I am," he said. "You're going home. To sleep, in case anybody ever asks."

"Where are you going?"

"Pick up my money," King Benny said.

"Take me with you," I said. "I want to be in on this."

"Go home," King Benny said. "We're in the dirty end of the field now. That's where I play. And I like to play alone."

King Benny watched as his driver opened the back door of the sedan. He looked over at me and nodded.

"You're a good kid," King Benny said. "You always were. Don't let this change it."

* * *

THE LIVING ROOM WAS DARK, THE ONLY LIGHT COMING from two bare windows and the glimmer of a floor lamp. All the furniture was new, two black leather couches taking up one end, a white shag pull-out sofa shoved against the opposite wall. In the center of the room was a long butcher-block table surrounded by four black leather chairs on rollers. There was a framed wall poster of Dr. J hanging on one wall and a cardboard cutout of Earl "the Pearl" Monroe leaning against a door that led to the small kitchen. The room smelled of fresh paint and incense.

A tall, reed-thin black man sat in one of the black leather chairs, his feet flat on the floor, his hands folded and resting on the butcher-block table. He was wearing a black turtleneck and black leather slacks. He had a Rolex on his left wrist and a diamond pinky ring on his right hand. He wore black Gucci loafers and no socks.

His mother named him Edward Goldenberg Robinson, after her favorite actor. To continue the Hollywood connection, Eddie Robinson took the street name Little Caesar as he made his way up the ranks of the lucrative drug trade. He was Brooklyn's number-one mover among black dealers and was rivaled only by the remains of the infamous Nicky Barnes's crew for power over the entire city. He earned close to $50,000 a day on cocaine, raked in another $25,000 on heroin, and skimmed a ten percent fee off any marijuana that sold on his streets.

Eddie Robinson was thirty-six years old and had already fathered six kids with three different women. His oldest child, a son, was twelve years old and attended a private school in upstate New York, where he lived with his mother. Little Caesar named his son Rizzo after his youngest brother, who died while in the custody of the Wilkinson Home for Boys.

"You alone?" Eddie Robinson asked King Benny, who was sitting on the other side of the butcher-block table.

"Got a guy downstairs," King Benny said. "In the car. Your guy shoulda told you before you let me in."

Eddie Robinson smiled and turned toward the thick-muscled black man in a sweatsuit standing in a corner by the window.

"Bip can't talk," Eddie Robinson said.

"Smart move," King Benny said.

"I'm not looking for partners," Eddie said, thick mustache highlighting his thin face. "If that's your reason for the meet."

"I don't want a partner," King Benny said.

"Then what?" Eddie Robinson said.

"I want you to give me some money," King Benny said.

"How much money?"

"Eight thousand dollars," King Benny said.

"I'll play along," Eddie Robinson said with a smile. "Say I give you the eight grand. How long before you pay it back?"

"I'm not paying it back," King Benny said, reaching a hand into his jacket pocket and taking out a folded piece of paper. "Somebody else is."

"This somebody somebody I know?" Eddie Robinson said, taking the paper from King Benny and placing it in his own pocket.

"Your little brother knew him," King Benny said.

"Rizzo?" Eddie Robinson asked, a sudden deadness to his voice. "How did he know Rizzo?"

"The man was a guard at an upstate home," King Benny said. "Was there the same time as Rizzo. Before and after he died."

"Bip," Eddie Robinson said, not moving his eyes from King Benny. "Count out eight thousand and put it in an envelope."

King Benny and Eddie Robinson stared at each other in silence, waiting for Bip to walk into the kitchen and come back out with a white envelope. Bip handed the envelope to Eddie Robinson.

"You go back a long time, old man," Eddie Robinson said as he passed it on to King Benny.

"Old men always do," King Benny said.

"Ran with the guineas back when the guineas were tough," Eddie Robinson said.

"Ran when I could run," King Benny said.

"Maybe you and me can do some business," Eddie Robinson said. "Close us a deal."

"We just did," King Benny said, putting the envelope in the side pocket of his jacket and turning to leave the room.

"I'll look up our friend soon," Eddie Robinson said as King Benny walked away. "And collect the money he owes me."

"He owes you somethin' more than money," King Benny said, standing in the entryway, his face in the shadows. "Something worth more."

Eddie Robinson stood up from his chair, hands spread out before him. "Ain't nothin' worth more than the green."

"This is," King Benny said.

"What, old man?" Eddie Robinson said. "What's this guy owe means more to me than dollars?"

"He owes you Rizzo," King Benny said. "He's the man that killed your brother."

King Benny walked past the light, opened the apartment door, and disappeared.

15

"YOU HAVE A WITNESS FOR US, COUNSELOR?" JUDGE Weisman asked Michael.

"Yes, your honor," Michael said.

"Let's get to it, then," Judge Weisman said.

"Your honor," Michael said. "The prosecution would like to call Ralph Ferguson to the stand."

I TOOK A DEEP breath and turned to my right, looking at Ferguson as he walked down the center aisle of the courtroom. Twelve years had passed, but I still recognized the sound of his walk and the slight feminine manner in which he moved his shoulders. He had gained some weight and lost some hair and appeared uncomfortable in his baggy blue blazer.

The last time I saw Ralph Ferguson I was tied up in my cell, my mouth taped shut, Sean Nokes holding me down, watching him rape and beat one of my friends. It was a night of terror that Ferguson probably dismissed soon after it happened. It is a night that for me has never ended.

Michael kept his head down as Ferguson walked past, heading for the stand to be sworn in by the bailiff. Michael and Ferguson had not yet met. He had another attorney in his office handle Ferguson's deposition and the initial Q & A, not wanting to tip his hand before he and O'Connor were to question the former guard in open court.

Ralph Ferguson and Sean Nokes had remained friends beyond their years at Wilkinson. They spent vacations together hunting deer in upstate woods and long weekends in a rented cabin by a lake fishing for bass. They drank beer and whiskey, talked about old times, and made plans for the future. They hoped one day to go in as partners on a bait and tackle shop in central New Hampshire.

The unhappily married Nokes often visited the happily married Ferguson and his wife, Sally, staying in the spare room in the small tract house they owned in the Long Island town of Freeport. Ferguson had been best man at Nokes's first wedding, a union that had lasted less than a year. Nokes was godfather to Ferguson's only child, his four-year-old daughter, Shelley Marie.

On the surface, Ralph Ferguson was a model citizen. Pee-Wee soccer coach. A dedicated employee who never missed a day and helped organize company parties. He even handled the Sunday collections at his church.

A perfect character witness.

Ferguson fidgeted on the stand, too nervous to focus his attention on Michael, gazing instead at the faces of the jury and the spectators.

John and Tommy sat quietly, staring at him with open contempt.

"Doesn't look so tough up there, does he?" I whispered to Carol.

"Nobody does," she said.

"He looks like anybody," I said. "No one would ever know he did the things he did."

"Sit tight, sweetheart," Carol said, slowly rubbing my arm.

"They're gonna know today. Everybody's gonna know. Saint Ferguson is about to fall on his ass."

"Good morning, Mr. Ferguson," Michael said, buttoning his jacket and standing on the far side of the witness stand. "I'd like to thank you for coming. I realize it's a long trip for you."

"I'm sorry I had to do it," Ferguson said. "I'm sorry it had to be for something like this."

"I understand," Michael said, his voice coated with sympathy. "You and the victim, Sean Nokes, were good friends. Is that right?"

"We were *great* friends, yeah," Ferguson said. "The best. You'd have to look hard to find a better friend."

"How long did you two know each other?"

"About fourteen years," Ferguson said.

"How often did you see each other?"

"We got together as much as we could," Ferguson said. "I'd say about ten, maybe twelve times a year. On weekends, holidays, vacations. Things like that."

"Would you say you were his best friend?"

"His closest, that's for sure," Ferguson said. "We could talk to each other, you know. Talk about things that only good friends talk about."

"What sort of things?" Michael asked, walking past the defense table, his head down.

"Normal stuff," Ferguson said, shrugging. "Women sometimes, sports during football season, our jobs all the time. Nothin' you would call deep. Just talk. Plain talk between friends."

"What kind of man was Sean Nokes?" Michael asked.

"He was a good man," Ferguson said. "Too good to be shot dead by a couple of street punks."

"Objection, your honor," O'Connor said, standing. "Statement is one of opinion, not fact."

"He was *asked* his opinion," Michael said.

"Overruled," Judge Weisman said. "Please continue."

"When you say Sean Nokes was a good man, how do you mean that?" Michael asked, moving closer to the witness stand. "Did he give money to charities, adopt stray pets, shelter the homeless? Tell us, please, Mr. Ferguson, how Sean Nokes was a good man."

"Nothing like that," Ferguson said, a smile creasing his nervous exterior. "Sean just cared about you. If you were his friend, there's nothing he wouldn't do for you. I really mean that. There was nothing."

"Did he have any enemies you were aware of?"

"You mean, other than the two who killed him?" Ferguson asked.

"Yes," Michael said with a smile. "Any enemies other than the two who killed him?"

"No," Ralph Ferguson said. "Sean Nokes had no enemies."

"Thank you, Mr. Ferguson," Michael said, turning his back to the stand. "I have no further questions, your honor."

"Mr. O'Connor," Judge Weisman said. "He's your witness."

"Can you tell us how you and Sean Nokes first met, Mr. Ferguson?" O'Connor asked, sitting in his chair, elbows on the defense table.

"We worked on a job together upstate," Ferguson said.

"As what?"

"We were guards at the Wilkinson Home for Boys," Ferguson said.

"What is that?" O'Connor asked. "A prison?"

"No," Ferguson said. "It's a juvenile facility for young boys."

"Young boys who have broken the law," O'Connor said. "Is that correct?"

"Yes, that's correct," Ferguson said.

"And your function was what?"

"Standard stuff," Ferguson said. "Keep the boys in line, see they got to their classes on time, keep an eye out for trouble, put them down for the night. Nothing exciting."

"As guards, were you and Mr. Nokes allowed to use force to, as you say, keep the boys in line?" O'Connor asked, pushing his chair back and standing by the side of his desk.

"What do you mean, force?" Ferguson asked, looking over at Michael.

"I mean, were you allowed to hit them?"

"No, of course not," Ferguson said.

"Were any of the boys hit by any of the guards?" O'Connor asked, walking around his desk, arms folded at his chest. "At any time?"

"I'm sure something like that may have happened," Ferguson said, sweat starting to form around his neck. "It was a big place. But it wasn't a common practice."

"Let's narrow the place down, then," O'Connor said. "Did you or Mr. Nokes ever hit any of the boys under your care at the Wilkinson Home?"

Both Judge Weisman and Ferguson stared at Michael, waiting for the obvious objection to the question.

Michael sat at his desk and kept his eyes on Ferguson, not moving.

John and Tommy turned and gave Michael a quick glance, one filled with curiosity and confusion.

"Would you like me to repeat the question, Mr. Ferguson?" O'Connor asked, walking toward the witness stand.

"No," Ferguson said.

"Then answer it," O'Connor said. "And remember, you're under oath."

"Yes," Ferguson said. "A few of the boys we considered to be discipline problems were hit. On occasion."

"And these discipline problems, how were they hit?" O'Connor asked.

"What do you mean, how?" Ferguson asked.

"Fist, open hand, a kick," O'Connor said. "A baton, maybe. What was the best way, Mr. Ferguson, to calm a discipline problem?"

"It depended on what the situation called for," Ferguson said.

"And who determined that?"

"The guard on the scene," Ferguson said.

"So you and Sean Nokes would decide in what way a discipline problem would be dealt with," O'Connor said. "Is that correct?"

"Yes," Ferguson said. "That's correct."

"That's a lot of power to have over a boy," O'Connor said. "Isn't it?"

"It came with the job," Ferguson said.

"Did torture come with the job?" O'Connor asked.

"No, it did not," Ferguson said.

"But boys were tortured, weren't they?" O'Connor said, his face turning a shade of red. "*Weren't* they, Mr. Ferguson?"

The spectators all leaned forward, waiting for Ferguson's answer. Judge Weisman poured himself a glass of water and rolled his chair back, his angry eyes focused on Michael.

"On occasion," Ferguson said, looking as if he were about to faint.

"Who tortured them?" O'Connor asked.

"The guards," Ferguson said.

"*Which* guards?" O'Connor asked.

"I can't remember all of them," Ferguson said.

"Remember one," O'Connor said.

Ferguson wiped his lips with the back of his hand. He looked over at Michael, who sat in his chair, hands folded before him. He looked at John and Tommy, who stared back impassively. He put his head back and took a deep breath.

"Sean Nokes," Ferguson said.

O'Connor waited for the courtroom murmurs to quiet. He watched as Judge Weisman lifted his gavel and then placed it back down, as troubled as everyone else by the testimony he was hearing.

I looked over at Carol and saw tears streaming down her face. I put my arm around her and moved her closer.

"Let me ask you, Mr. Ferguson," O'Connor said, standing next to him, one hand in his pocket. "Was there any sexual abuse at the Wilkinson Home for Boys?"

"Counselor," Judge Weisman said to O'Connor. "This line of questioning better lead someplace having to do with this case."

"It will, your honor," O'Connor said, keeping his eyes on Ferguson.

"For your sake," Judge Weisman said.

"Answer the question, Mr. Ferguson," O'Connor said. "Was there any sexual abuse at the Wilkinson Home for Boys?"

"Yes," Ferguson said. "I heard that there was."

"I'm not asking if you *heard*," O'Connor said. "I'm asking if you *saw*."

"Yes, I saw," Ferguson said in a low voice.

"Did you and Sean Nokes ever force yourselves on any of the boys?" O'Connor asked, taking two steps back, his voice hitting full range. "Did you and Sean Nokes *rape* any of the boys at the Wilkinson Home? And again, I remind you that you are under oath."

The courtroom held the silence of the moment, no moving, no coughing, no crumpling of paper. All eyes were on the witness stand. The twelve heads of the jury were turned at an angle. John and Tommy sat at attention. Carol gripped my hand as Michael looked above the bench at the painting of blind justice gripping her sword.

"Counselors," Judge Weisman said, breaking the silence. "Approach the bench. *Now*."

Michael and O'Connor moved to the sidebar, on the end farthest from the witness stand.

"What the *hell* is going on here?" Judge Weisman asked Michael, temper flashing above his calm demeanor.

"Well, your honor," Michael said, glancing over at Ferguson. "It looks like I called the wrong character witness."

"And what are you going to do about it?" Judge Weisman asked.

"Nothing, your honor," Michael said. "There's nothing I can do."

"Or maybe, counselor," Judge Weisman said, "you've already done enough."

The lawyers returned to their positions.

"Please answer the question, Mr. Ferguson," Judge Weisman ordered.

"Yes," Ferguson said in a choked voice, tears lining his face.

"Yes *what*?" O'Connor asked.

"Yes, boys were raped," Ferguson said.

"By you and Sean Nokes?" O'Connor said.

"Not just by us," Ferguson said.

"By *you* and *Sean Nokes*?" O'Connor said, repeating the question, raising his voice even louder.

"Yes," Ferguson said.

"On more than one occasion?" O'Connor asked.

"Yes," Ferguson said.

"With more than one boy?"

"Yes," Ferguson said.

"Now, do you still think Sean Nokes was a good man, Mr. Ferguson?" O'Connor asked.

"He was my *friend*," Ferguson said.

"A friend who raped and abused boys he was paid to watch over," O'Connor said. "Boys who could maybe grow up and become an *enemy* of such a *good* man."

"Are you finished?" Ferguson asked, his eyes red, his hands shaking.

"Not just yet," O'Connor said.

"I want it to be over," Ferguson said, wiping his eyes and looking at the judge. "Please, your honor, I want it to be over."

"Mr. O'Connor?" the judge asked.

"This won't take long, your honor," O'Connor said.

"Proceed," Judge Weisman said.

"Sean Nokes spent a lot of time at your home, is that right?" O'Connor asked.

"Yes," Ferguson said.

"As much as a week at a time, is that also correct?"

"Yes," Ferguson said.

"And you have a child, is that correct?"

"Yes," Ferguson said. "A daughter."

"In all the time your *good* friend Sean Nokes spent in your home, all the days, all the hours, did either you or your wife ever allow him to be alone with your daughter?" O'Connor asked. "At *any* time? For *any* reason?"

Ferguson stared at O'Connor, his fear evident, his body leaning toward the judge's bench for support.

"No," he finally said. "No, we never did."

"Why was that, Mr. Ferguson?" O'Connor asked. "If he was such a *good* man."

"Objection, your honor," Michael said for the first time, looking at Ferguson. "Question doesn't call for an answer."

"Counselor's right, your honor," O'Connor said. "I withdraw the question."

"Witness is excused," Judge Weisman said.

"Thank you, your honor," Ferguson said, stepping down from the stand.

"Mr. Ferguson, if I were you, I wouldn't stray too far from home," Judge Weisman said. "People will need to talk to you. Do you understand?"

"Yes, your honor," Ferguson said meekly, his eyes darting from John to Tommy and then to Michael, slowly, finally re-coiling in recognition. "I understand."

Michael waited until Ferguson walked out of the court-room and then stood up.

"The prosecution rests its case, your honor," he said. "We have no further witnesses."

"Thank God for that," Judge Weisman said.

16

FAT MANCHO BOUNCED A SPAULDEEN AGAINST THE GROUND, his eyes fixed on the brick wall in front of him. He was wearing a long-sleeve wool shirt, a Baltimore Orioles baseball cap, scruffy blue jeans, and hightop PF Flyers.

I stood five feet to his left, wearing a leather jacket, two black wool gloves, and a pull cap. My jeans felt stiff in the windy cold and my sneakers and thin white socks weren't enough to prevent the late Sunday afternoon chill from seeping through.

Carol stood with her back to the chain-link fence separating the open lot from the sidewalk. She was on her third cup of coffee and had two thick winter scarves wrapped around her neck.

"Most people play handball in the summer," I said to Fat Mancho, rubbing my hands together. "It's easier to see the ball without tears in your eyes."

"I give a fuck about most people," Fat Mancho said.

"What do you have planned for after the game," I asked. "A swim?"

"Your balls all twisted up 'cause you gonna lose the game," Fat Mancho said. "And you one of them fuckers that can't live with losin'."

"Freezing, Fat Man," I said. "I'm one of those fuckers who can't live with freezing."

Fat Mancho slapped the ball against the wall, a hard shot, aimed low, with a heavy spin to it. I took three steps back and returned the hit. Fat Mancho was ready for the return, crouched down, hands on his knees, not wearing gloves, his eyes on the ball, looking like an overweight third baseman who forgot his Old-Timer's Day uniform.

His right hand whipped at the ball, sending it higher than the serve, faster, forcing me to move back, the soles of my sneakers slipping on a thin slab of ice. I watched as the ball bounced over my head.

"That's six for me, loser," Fat Mancho said. "Two for you."

"You never *play* this game," I said, my breath coming heavy. "How can you be good?"

"You never *seen* me play, fool," Fat Mancho said. "I was your age, I was all-spic. Played the best. Beat the best."

I looked over his shoulder and saw Carol walking toward us, a cup of coffee in one hand and a cold beer in the other.

"Good news," I said. "It's halftime."

WE SAT AGAINST THE handball wall, sitting on top of three copies of the Sunday *Daily News*, Carol and I sharing the coffee, Fat Mancho slurping gulps of Rheingold.

"How's Irish holdin' up?" Fat Mancho asked about Michael.

"I only know what I see in court," I said. "That end seems good. His side of the table's finished."

"He did good," Fat Mancho said. "I seen lawyers *weren't* tossin' the case look more fucked up. You *didn't* know, you *won't* know. That kid's colder than a hit man."

"John and Tommy are starting to smell something," I said. "They just don't know what."

"A spic be livin' in the White House time it reaches their fuckin' brain," Fat Mancho said.

"O'Connor's come through big," Carol said. "He looks like F. Lee Bailey's twin brother out there."

"He *was* a good one," Fat Mancho said. "Then he lost a few and he found the bottle. Been chasin' nothin' but skid cases since."

"He sobered up for this," I said. "He's got a shot at a win. Even without a witness."

"He's a drunk, but he ain't a fool," Fat Mancho said, putting the can of beer on the ground next to him. "He wins this, every killer both sides of the river have his card in their pocket."

"Is that true?" Carol asked, lifting one of the scarves up to where it covered everything but her eyes.

"Is what true?" I said.

"Can we win the case without a witness?"

"You already won," Fat Mancho said. "You got the taste. Now you're just lookin' to get away with it."

"They've got to walk, Fat Man," I said. "We win only when John and Tommy walk."

"Then you gotta get 'em outta the shootin' hole," Fat Mancho said. "Put 'em someplace else. Only your witness does that. And he's doin' a Claude Rains so far. Nobody's seen the fucker."

"What if he doesn't show?" Carol said. "What if we go in the way we are?"

"You *got* street justice," Fat Mancho said. "That's the real. You come up with empty hands on court justice, that's the bullshit."

"They both take your life away, Fat Man," I said. "The street just does it faster."

"Street's only one matters," Fat Mancho said. "Court's for uptown, people with suits, money, lawyers with three names. You got cash, you can *buy* court justice. On the street, justice got no price. She's blind where the judge sits. But she ain't blind out here. Out here, the bitch got eyes."

"We need both," I said.

"Then you *need* a witness," Fat Mancho said, standing up, taking the pink rubber ball out of his pants pocket. "And I *need* to finish beatin' your ass. Let's go, loser. You down to me by four."

"Can we finish this later?" I asked, too numb from the cold to stand.

"When later?" Fat Mancho asked, looking down at me.

"The middle of July," I said.

17

DANNY O'CONNOR PIECED TOGETHER A CREDIBLE DEFENSE
for the jury to ponder during the course of his first three days
on the attack. He called to the stand a limited range of John's
and Tommy's friends and family, most of them middle-aged to
elderly men and women with sweet eyes and trusting faces. All
of them testifying that while both boys were sometimes wild,
they were not killers.

None of them had ever seen John Reilly or Tommy Marcano hold a gun.

The two waitresses on duty the night of the shooting testified that they knew both defendants and found them to be
pleasant whenever they entered the pub. Neither remembered
seeing John Reilly or Tommy Marcano the night Sean Nokes
was killed. The women said they were in the kitchen at the time
of the shooting and did not come out until the police arrived.

"Were the two shooters in the pub when the police got
there?" O'Connor asked one of the waitresses.

"No," she said. "I guess they already left."

"Why do you guess that?"

"Killers don't wait for cops," she said. "In the neighborhood,
nobody waits for cops."

"You're from the neighborhood," O'Connor said. "And you
waited."

"I was getting *paid* to wait," she said.

Jerry the bartender testified he served the defendants two drinks and two beers on the afternoon of Nokes's death. They sat quietly and were gone in less than an hour. They paid the tab and tip with a twenty left on the bar. He was in the back picking up his dinner when the shooting occurred and therefore did not see anyone pump shots into Sean Nokes. Jerry also phoned the police as soon as the gunfire died down.

Through it all, Michael kept his cross-examinations simple, never venturing beyond where the witnesses wanted to go, never calling into dispute any parts of their accounts. He was always polite, cordial, and relaxed, easily buying into the professed innocence of those called to the stand.

O'Connor's intent was to continue to mine the doubts planted in the jury's mind, doubts that had first taken root with the testimony of the prosecutor's key eyewitness, Helen Salinas.

To that end, Dr. George Paltrone, a Bronx general practitioner who also ran a detox clinic, was called to the stand as an expert witness. In Dr. Paltrone's opinion, if Mrs. Salinas drank as much alcohol as she claimed in the amount of time that she stated, her testimony had to be deemed less than credible.

"Are you saying Mrs. Salinas was drunk?" O'Connor asked Dr. Paltrone.

"Not quite drunk," Dr. Paltrone said. "But she had more than enough drink in her to impair judgment."

"Wouldn't witnessing a shooting sober her up?"

"Not necessarily," Dr. Paltrone said. "The fear she felt may have made a rational judgment even more difficult."

"In other words, doctor, drink and fear don't always lead to truth?"

"That's right," Dr. Paltrone said. "More often than not they don't."

I sat through the three days of O'Connor's defense in my

usual third-row seat, barely listening, unable to focus on the action before me. My mind was on Father Bobby and what he had decided to do. I knew without him that our best chance was a hung jury, which meant nothing more than another trial and an almost certain conviction.

I had not seen Father Bobby since the night I asked him to take the stand. I thought it too risky to approach O'Connor and find out what he knew, and Michael was beyond my reach. Everyone in the neighborhood seemed aware that we had a witness stashed.

But no one, not even King Benny, had the word on who the witness was and when he would show.

"If he's not here tomorrow, then forget it," I said to Carol as the third day ground to an end. "It's over."

"We could try to find somebody else," Carol said. "We still have some time."

"Who?" I said. "The Pope's in Rome and I don't know any rabbis."

"We can go and talk to him again," Carol said. "Or maybe have somebody else talk to him."

"He's not afraid of King Benny," I said, walking with Carol down the courthouse corridors. "And Fat Mancho won't even go *near* a priest."

"Then we can force him to do it," Carol said with a shrug and a half-smile. "Put a gun on him."

"You want your witness to have one hand raised in court," I said. "Not two."

WE STOPPED BY THE elevator bank and waited, Carol pushed closer to me by the surrounding cluster of court officers, reporters, lawyers, defendants, and their families. The down arrow rang and lit, and the double doors to the elevator creaked open. We squeezed in with the pack, pushed to the back of the car.

We both managed to turn and face forward, my eyes looking at the scarred neck of a husky Hispanic wearing an imitation leather jacket with a fake fur hood. He was breathing through his open mouth and his dank breath further fouled the musty air.

As we rode down the nine floors, the elevator stopping at each one, I looked over to my far left and saw Danny O'Connor standing there. He had his back against the elevator buttons, a Tudor hat on top of his head and his eyes on me. He was chewing a thick piece of gum and had an unlit cigarette in his mouth.

If he knew anything, his face wasn't showing it.

The doors finally opened onto the main floor and the passengers stormed out of the car. I grabbed Carol by the arm and made my way closer to O'Connor, who was content to let the rush of people pass him by before he stepped off. The three of us came out of the elevator at the same time, my elbow brushing against O'Connor's side.

"I'm sorry," I said.

"Not a problem," he said, looking at me and Carol. "Riding these elevators is like riding the IRT. Only not as safe."

"Lucky it's cold," I said. "I'd hate to see what it's like in there during a heat wave."

"It was nice bumping into you," O'Connor said with a smile, moving toward the revolving exit doors.

"Why the rush?" I asked, watching him leave.

"Gotta go," he said over his shoulder. "I'm late."

"Late for what?"

"Mass," O'Connor said.

18

"CALL YOUR NEXT WITNESS," JUDGE WEISMAN SAID TO Danny O'Connor.

"Your honor, the defense calls to the stand Father Robert Carillo."

Father Bobby walked through the courtroom with the confidence of a fighter heading into a main event. His thick hair was brushed back, his eyes were clear, and his careworn face shone under the glare of the overhead lights.

"Raise your right hand," the bailiff said. "And place your left hand on the Bible."

"Do you swear that what you say shall be the truth, the whole truth, and nothing but the truth?"

"I do," Father Bobby said.

"Take the stand," the bailiff said.

"Father Carillo, to which parish do you belong?" Danny O'Connor asked.

"The Sacred Heart of Jesus on West Fiftieth Street."

"And how long have you been there?"

"It will be twenty years this spring."

"And what is your position there?"

"I'm a priest," Father Carillo said, smiling.

O'Connor, the spectators, and the jury all joined in the laugh; even Judge Weisman cracked a smile, but John and

Tommy sat in stone silence, hands cupped to their faces, while Michael chewed on the end of a blue Bic pen.

"I'm sorry, Father," O'Connor said. "I meant, what do you *do* there?"

"I'm the school principal," Father Bobby said. "I teach seventh grade and coach most of the sports teams. I'm also acting monsignor, serve mass daily, listen to confessions, and try to repair whatever needs fixing."

"They keep you busy," O'Connor said.

"It's a poor parish," Father Bobby said. "Low on funds and short on staff."

"Do you know most of the people in your parish?"

"No," Father Bobby said. "I know *all* the people in my parish."

"Do you know the two defendants, John Reilly and Thomas Marcano?"

"Yes, I do," Father Bobby said.

"How long have you known them?"

"Since they were boys," Father Bobby said. "They were students of mine."

"How would you describe your relationship with them today?"

"We try to stay in touch," Father Bobby said. "I try to do that with all my boys."

"And how do you do that?"

"Through sports, mostly," Father Bobby said. "We either organize a game or go to one. It's a common ground. Makes it easier to get together."

"Father, do you recall where you were on the night of November sixth of this past year?"

"Yes, I do," Father Bobby said.

"And where was that?"

"I was at a basketball game," Father Bobby said. "At the Garden. The Knicks against the Hawks."

"What time does a Knicks game begin?"

"They usually start at about seven-thirty," Father Bobby said.

"And at what time do they end?"

"Between nine-thirty and ten," Father Bobby said. "Providing there's no overtime."

"Was there any that night?"

"No, there wasn't," Father Bobby said.

"And who won the game, Father?"

"Sad to say, it was the Hawks," Father Bobby said. "They were a little too much for our guys that night."

"Were you at the game alone?"

"No," Father Bobby said. "I went there with two friends."

"And who were those two friends, Father?"

"John Reilly and Thomas Marcano," Father Bobby said.

"The two defendants?"

"Yes," Father Bobby said, gesturing toward John and Tommy. "The two defendants."

The spectators sitting behind the wooden barrier gave a collective cry. Carol put her head down, her hands covering her mouth, her shoulders shaking. Michael took a deep breath and looked toward the ceiling.

John and Tommy turned around, scanning the spectators, their bodies relaxing. As they turned to face the bench, they looked over at me. I smiled as they looked down at the cover of the book in my hands.

John had tears in his eyes.

I was holding a copy of *The Count of Monte Cristo*.

"WHAT TIME DID YOU meet with Mr. Reilly and Mr. Marcano?" O'Connor asked soon after Judge Weisman hammered a call to order.

"They picked me up outside the school playground," Father Bobby said. "It must have been six-thirty or thereabouts."

"How did you get to the Garden, Father?"

"We walked," Father Bobby said. "It's less than twenty blocks."

"And Mr. Reilly and Mr. Marcano walked with you the whole time?"

"Yes," Father Bobby said. "We walked together."

"And at eight twenty-five P.M., the time police say the victim, Sean Nokes, was murdered, were you still with Mr. Reilly and Mr. Marcano at the basketball game?"

"Yes, I was," Father Bobby said. "If they were out of my sight at all during the game, it was either to go to the bathroom or to get something to drink."

"What did you three do after the game?"

"We walked back to the parish," Father Bobby said.

"Was it a cold night?"

"Windy, as I recall," Father Bobby said.

"Did you stop anywhere?"

"At a newsstand on Eighth Avenue," Father Bobby said. "I bought an early edition of the *Daily News.*"

"And at what time did you, Mr. Reilly, and Mr. Marcano part company?"

"About ten-thirty, maybe a few minutes later," Father Bobby said. "They left me in front of the rectory, near where they picked me up."

"Did the two defendants tell you where they were going after they left you?"

"No," Father Bobby said. "But I would imagine after a night spent with a priest, they went looking for the first open bar they could find."

O'Connor waited for the snickers to subside.

"So then, Father, if the two defendants were with you on

the night of the murder, they couldn't have shot and killed Sean Nokes, as the prosecution claims. Isn't that correct?"

"Unless they shot him from the blue seats at the Garden," Father Bobby said.

"No, Father," O'Connor said with a smile. "He wasn't shot from there."

"Then he wasn't shot by those boys," Father Bobby said.

"I have no further questions," O'Connor said. "Thank you, Father."

"It was my pleasure," Father Bobby said.

"Your witness, Mr. Sullivan," Judge Weisman said.

"Thank you, your honor," Michael said, standing up and walking over to Father Bobby.

"Did you buy the tickets for the game, Father?" Michael asked. "Or were they given to you?"

"No, I bought them," Father Bobby said.

"On the day of the game?"

"No," Father Bobby said. "I went to the box office about a week before."

"How did you pay for the tickets?"

"With cash," Father Bobby said. "I pay for everything with cash."

"Did you get a receipt?"

"No," Father Bobby said. "I didn't."

"Did anyone know you were going to the game," Michael asked, "other than the two defendants?"

"I don't think so," Father Bobby said.

"When did you ask the defendants to go to the game with you?"

"The Sunday before," Father Bobby said.

"Was anyone else present?"

"No," Father Bobby said.

"So, no one saw you buy the tickets," Michael said. "There's no record of any purchase. And no one else knew you were going with the defendants. Is that right?"

"That's right," Father Bobby said.

"So how do we know you were there?" Michael asked. "How do we *really* know you and the two defendants were at the game on the night of the murder?"

"I'm telling you both as a witness *and* as a priest," Father Bobby said. "We *were* at that game."

"And a priest wouldn't lie," Michael said. "Isn't that right?"

"A priest with ticket stubs wouldn't *need* to lie," Father Bobby said, putting a hand into his jacket pocket and pulling out three torn tickets. "And I always keep the stubs."

"Why's that, Father?" Michael asked, standing next to him. "Why do you keep them?"

"Because you never know," Father Bobby said, looking straight at Michael, "when someone will want more than your word."

"Has anyone questioned your word before today?"

"No," Father Bobby said. "No one *ever* has. But there's a first time for most things in this world."

"Yes, Father," Michael Sullivan said. "I guess there is."

Michael turned from Father Bobby and looked up at Judge Weisman.

"I have no further questions at this time," Michael said. "Witness is free to go."

The spectators applauded as Father Robert Carillo, a Catholic priest from Hell's Kitchen, stepped down from the stand.

19

I PUT ONE FOOT ON A RUSTY MOORING, MY HANDS IN MY pockets as I looked out at the Hudson River. The skies were overcast and the winter air felt heavy with impending snow. Carol had her back to me, staring past the iron legs of the West Side Highway toward the streets of Hell's Kitchen. It was early evening, six hours removed from Father Bobby's testimony.

I still hadn't recovered from seeing him take the stand and lie for us. He didn't just testify for John and Tommy, he testified against Wilkinson and the evil that had lived there for too long. Still, I was sorry he had to do it, to tell the lie that I know must have cost him dearly, just to help us get our ounce of revenge.

I was sorry any of us had to go through this trial. I wondered about Carol, and how these days would affect her. She was smart and attractive, and should have been spending her time meeting men who did more than simply combat the ghosts of their pasts. I prayed that the trial would free Michael of his demons and allow him to go on with his life. As for John and Tommy, I hoped the best for them, but feared only the worst.

It just seemed that no matter how hard we tried, no matter how many of them we got, we could never rid ourselves of the

Wilkinson Home for Boys. My friends and I *had* to live with it. Now Carol and Father Bobby had to live with it as well.

Carol turned toward me and, sensing my unease, leaned over and hugged me.

"That place is a part of me and a part of Father Bobby too," Carol said. "In different ways, maybe. But it's in our lives. And it's going to stay in our lives. No matter what we do now."

"None of it helps make it even," I said. "We've got a long way to go till we get to even."

"But you've got to admit," Carol said, "you're off to a helluva nice start."

"I was real proud of him up there," I said, wiping tears I couldn't control.

"We were all proud of him," Carol said. "And Father Bobby did it not because we asked him to. But because it was the *only* thing he *could* do. He had no choice either, Shakes."

"He looked like Cagney up there," I said. "Looked everybody square in the eye. Didn't back off for a second."

"More like Bogart, you mean," Carol said, smiling, putting an arm around my waist.

"I'll never understand how you could have grown up around here and still think Bogart's better than Cagney," I said.

"I suppose you think the Three Stooges are better than the Marx Brothers too."

"Hands down, porcupine-head."

"And you probably like John Wayne westerns too," she said.

"There's where you're wrong," I said. "I *love* John Wayne westerns."

"You're hopeless." And then Carol Martinez laughed out loud. It was the first time I'd heard real laughter in a very long time.

"We're all hopeless," I said, walking with her alongside the dock, up toward Pier 82, her arm under my elbow. "That's why we're still together."

"But I swear, if you tell me you still think Soupy Sales is funnier than Woody Allen, it's gonna be all over," Carol said. "I mean it."

"Can Woody Allen do White Fang?" I asked her.

"Probably not," she said.

"That's right," I said. "*Nobody* does what Soupy does, because *nobody* can."

"No, Shakes," Carol said. "It's because nobody *wants* to."

The sound of our laughter echoed off the empty steel piers and out into the rough waters of the Hudson.

20

AT NINE-TEN A.M., ON A RAINY THURSDAY MORNING in January 1980, Michael Sullivan stood in the well of a courtroom and addressed a jury for the last time in his career.

That morning, he had carefully chosen his dark gray suit, blue tie, and black loafers. Two thin specks of dried blood clung to his right cheek, thanks to a close shave with an old razor. He had a Superman wristwatch on his left hand, an egg-shaped college graduation ring on his right, and a cherry Life Saver in his mouth.

"Is counsel ready?" Judge Weisman asked.

"Yes, your honor," Michael said. "I'm ready."

"Please proceed," Judge Weisman said.

Michael pushed his chair back and walked toward the jury box, twelve faces studying his every move. He put one hand in his pants pocket, caught the eye of the eldest member of the panel, and smiled.

"You have to admit, it's been an interesting couple of weeks," Michael began, his free hand rubbing the rail of the jury bench. "And it sure beats deciding a civil court case."

He waited with his head down for the scattered laughter to fade.

"But now you have a decision to make. A very difficult decision. A decision whose weight will determine the fate of two young men.

"You've heard the arguments from both sides. My side tells you the defendants, John Reilly and Thomas Marcano, shot and killed the victim, Sean Nokes. The other side tells you they didn't. In fact, if you *really* want to know the truth, they weren't even *there* to kill him.

"So, who to believe? *That's* what you must now decide."

Michael moved slowly down the jury box, taking care to look at every member of the panel, looking beyond their faces, beyond their eyes.

"So how do you reach a decision? You start by going over what you know based on the evidence that was presented. You *know* that Sean Nokes was murdered on November 6, 1979, at eight twenty-five in the evening. You *know* he was shot to death while sitting in the back booth of the Shamrock Pub. And you *know* he was gunned down by two men in black jackets. But which two men? That's where things start getting a little fuzzy."

Michael had both hands in his pockets now as he walked past the court stenographer, his head raised, his back to the jury. The spectators in the crowded courtroom were, with a handful of exceptions, all from Hell's Kitchen.

"You heard testimony that painted the two defendants as less than ideal citizens. *Does that make them killers?* Then you heard testimony that described Sean Nokes as a man with an ugly past. *Does that make it less than a crime to kill him?* You heard from an eyewitness who saw the two defendants walk out of the Shamrock Pub moments after shooting Sean Nokes dead. Then you heard from a priest who said the two defendants were with *him* at a Knicks game, eating hot dogs and drinking beer at the same time Sean Nokes was sitting up dead in a back booth. So, who do you believe? Who's lying? Who's telling the truth?"

Michael ambled past the defense table, inches away from John and Tommy, hands still in his pockets, his eyes back on the jury.

"It's not going to be easy for you to decide," Michael said. "It's not supposed to be. Decisions where people's lives are at stake *should* be hard. They should take time. They should take a great deal of search and thought. You have to look at the facts, and then beyond them. You have to listen to the testimony, and then read through it. You have to weigh the witnesses and then go past their words and search out *their motives*. You have to go beyond the one victim and the two defendants. You must look to the lines that connect them."

Michael stopped at his desk and sipped from a cup of cold coffee. He put the cup down, unbuttoned his jacket, and moved back toward the jury box.

"With this case, I'm asking you to do what few juries are asked to do," Michael said. "I'm asking you to look at the facts and *then* look at the reasons for those facts. I'm asking you to find the truth in what you've heard, in what you've seen and in what you *believe*. It might be the only way for you to come up with a decision you can live with. A decision that will not cause you doubt. A decision that you will *know* is the right one."

Michael had both hands spread across the jury rail, his body leaning against it, his eyes focused on the men and women before him.

"You have to make your decision based on the guilt of two men and the innocence of one, and you have to *believe* it. You have to go *beyond a* reasonable doubt; you have to go to where there is *no* doubt. You take everything you know to be true and then you take all the time you need to move past the truth and past the doubt and come out with a decision we can all live with. A decision that many may question, but *you* know to be the *right* one. Because now *you* are the only judges. In your hands will rest the evidence and the testimony. In your hands will rest the facts. In your hands will rest the fate of two men and the memory of a third. In your hands will rest the truth.

"I have confidence in those hands. I *believe* in those hands. And I believe those hands will find a verdict that will be filled with truth. And filled with justice. An honest truth and an honorable justice."

Michael Sullivan then thanked a jury for the last time, walked back to his seat, and put his legal pads into his black briefcase.

"Do you have anything to add, counselor?" Judge Weisman asked.

"No, your honor," Michael Sullivan said. "There's nothing else. I've said it all."

21

"LET ME HAVE A HOT DOG WITH MUSTARD, SAUERKRAUT, and onions," Michael told a chubby vendor in a leather flap cap, standing on the sidewalk outside the courthouse. "And let me have a Coke too."

"No ketchup?" I asked.

"I'm on a diet," he said without turning around.

It was a snowy, windy Monday afternoon and the jury had been in deliberation since the previous Thursday night. The courthouse rumor mill was working on overdrive, with most of the gossip predicting a verdict of guilty.

"You got a place to eat that?" I asked Michael, pointing to his hot dog.

"Behind you," Michael said, lifting the bun toward a park bench over my shoulder.

"Okay if I join you?"

"What can they do?" Michael asked. "Arrest us?"

"You did good in there, counselor," I said to Michael, sitting on the bench, taking a bite out of a pretzel.

"How I did won't matter until they come back in and hand me a win," Michael said.

"Will you settle for a loss?" I asked, smiling over at him.

"I can live with it," Michael said, finishing his hot dog and snapping open his soda can.

"What happens to you now?" I asked. "After this ends?"

"I walk away," Michael said. "Wait a few weeks and then hand in my notice. After the way I handled this case, there won't be a rush to keep me from the door."

"You can switch to the other side," I said. "Work as a defense lawyer. More money in it, probably, and you'll never be short on clients. There are always going to be more bad guys than good. The work from John and Tommy's crew alone will get you a house with a pool."

"Not for me," Michael said. "I've seen all the law I want to see. It's time for something else."

"Like what?"

"I'll let you know when I know," Michael said.

"You're too old to play for the Yankees," I said. "And you're too young to take up golf."

"You're shooting holes all through my plans," Michael said, smiling. "I'm starting to panic."

"You'll work things out," I said, finishing the last of my soda. "You always have."

"It's time for quiet, Shakes," Michael said, staring down at the ground. "That I do know. Give things a rest. Find a spot where I can shut my eyes and not have to see the places I've been. Maybe I'll even get lucky and forget I was ever there."

"It took pieces out of us, where we were," I said. "What we had to do to get out. Big pieces we didn't even know we had. Pieces we gotta learn to do without or find again. All that takes time. Lots of time."

"I can wait," Michael said.

"You always seemed to know how," I said. "The rest of us didn't have the patience."

"I've got to get back in there," Michael said, standing up and moving toward the courthouse. "The jury may be coming in."

"Don't disappear on me, counselor," I said, my eyes meeting his. "I may need a good lawyer someday."

"You can't afford a good lawyer," Michael said. "Not on your salary."

"I may need a good friend," I said.

"I'll find you when you do," Michael said. "Count on it."

"I always have," I said, watching Michael walk through the revolving doors of the courthouse to the elevators and up nine floors to face a jury's verdict.

22

THE AREA OUTSIDE PART 47 WAS CROWDED WITH THE familiar faces of Hell's Kitchen. They stood against stained walls, smoking cigarettes and drinking coffee, or sat on long wooden benches, reading the *Daily News* and *Post*. Others jammed the phone banks, calling in their bets and checking in on either an angry parole officer or an impatient loan shark.

They were waiting for the verdict.

Walking past them, I shook a few hands and nodded to a few faces before finding an empty spot in a corner near the black double doors.

After fifteen minutes the doors swung open. A court officer, tall and muscular, his gun buckle hanging at an angle, held the knob in one hand, his body halfway in the hall.

"They're coming in," he said in a listless voice. "In about five minutes. You wanna hear, better come in now."

I stood to the side and watched as the crowd slowly trooped in. Then I moved away, and walked over to a bench and sat down. I leaned over, my head in my hands, eyes closed, sweating, shaking, praying that we could finish this the way we planned. I went over everything we did and tried to think of things we should have done. The plan had only one flaw. Its success or failure hinged on the whims of twelve strangers.

"You're not going in?" Carol asked, standing above me.

"I don't want to go in alone," I said, taking my hands from my face.

"You're not alone," she said.

"I don't want to lose either," I said.

"You're not going to lose."

"It sounds like you've got all the answers," I said, standing up and taking her by the arm.

"Maybe I do," Carol said. "Maybe I do."

* * *

"HAS THE JURY REACHED ITS VERDICT?" JUDGE WEISMAN asked, sitting impassively behind his bench.

"We have, your honor," answered the jury foreman, a stocky bald man in a plaid shirt.

The bailiff took the folded piece of paper from the foreman and walked it over to Judge Weisman. The judge opened the paper and looked down, his face betraying nothing.

I looked past the wall of heads and shoulders surrounding me and glanced over at John and Tommy, sitting up close to their table, their hands bunched in fists. Danny O'Connor sat next to them, rubbing a hand against the back of his neck, beneath the frayed collar of his shirt. Across from them, Michael sat and stared at the empty witness box. He was taking deep breaths, his fingers twirling a felt-tip pen over his knuckles.

Judge Weisman nodded to the foreman, who stood in front of his seat.

"On the count of murder in the second degree, how do you find the defendant, John Reilly?" Judge Weisman asked.

The foreman bit his lips and looked around the courtroom with nervous eyes.

"Not guilty," the foreman said.

"On the count of murder in the second degree, how do you find the defendant, Thomas Marcano?"

"Not guilty," the foreman said.

The courtroom erupted in a thunder of applause, screams, shouts, and whistles, few hearing the judge's call to order and dismissal of charges against the defendants.

I stood up and hugged Carol.

"You did it, Shakes," she whispered in my ear.

"*We* did it," I said, holding her tight. "We *all* did it."

I looked over and saw Michael pick up his briefcase, shake hands with Danny O'Connor, and walk into the crowd, where he was swallowed up by the mass of bodies. I saw John and Tommy smiling and laughing, reaching out for as many hands as they could, cries of not guilty filling the air around us. I saw Judge Weisman walk down from his place behind the bench.

Flashbulbs popped.

A pair of women in the middle of the room began to cry hysterically.

Four young men in the back, heading out of the room, sang the words to "Danny Boy."

An old lady behind me stayed seated and fingered the beads of her rosary, her lips moving to a series of silent prayers.

The jury members filed out of the box, some with their heads bowed, a few waving to people in the crowd.

Danny O'Connor, all smiles and sweat, walked out of the courtroom to a chorus of men and women chanting his name.

John and Tommy stood by their places, arms in the air, basking in the glory of their moment.

Michael Sullivan was already in the elevator, heading down to the lobby, his mission completed, his career over.

I took Carol by the hand and led her out of the courtroom, the loud, happy sound of the crowd following us down the corridor.

It was the sound of justice.

23

SPRING 1980

THE LONG TABLE AND CHAIRS RAN NEARLY THE LENGTH of the restaurant's back room, just off the main dining hall. Pitchers of beer and bottles of Dewar's and Johnnie Walker Red dotted the cloth, along with candles flickering inside hurricane shells. Two large floral arrangements, resting in the middle of a pair of wicker baskets with half-moon handles, anchored the ends.

A full month had passed since the acquittal. In those few weeks, our lives had reverted back to what they had been prior to the murder of Sean Nokes.

Carol returned to her stack of social service files, helping troubled teens and single mothers fight a system that had neither time enough nor funds enough to care.

John and Tommy went back to the streets, running the West Side Boys, drinking heavily, and once again breaking laws with abandon. No one had expected them to change. It was too late.

King Benny went back to his club and Fat Mancho returned to his bodega.

I was promoted from clerk to reporter trainee, covering the entertainment beat. It meant I got to go to the movies for free, just like I used to do when I was a kid. Except now I didn't have to sneak my way in.

Michael was the only one of us who had made any significant change in his life. As he had promised, he had resigned from his job, three weeks after working the losing end of a can't-miss case.

* * *

I WAS THE FIRST TO ARRIVE AND CHOSE A SEAT AT THE center of the table, my back to the wall. A young waiter in white shirt and black bow tie came into the room and asked if I wanted anything. I looked at the line of beer and whiskey and smiled.

"This is an Irish table," I said. "And I'm Italian."

"What's missing?" the waiter asked.

"Wine."

"Red or white?"

"Both," I said.

The waiter bumped into John and Tommy on his way out of the room. I stood up and we stared at each other for a few minutes. Then they both came around the table and squeezed me in a long, silent hug.

"I don't even know *how* to fuckin' thank you," Johnny said, holding me even tighter.

"I can't believe what you did," Tommy said. "And I can't believe you got away with it."

"What do you mean?" I said. "Don't tell me you *really* killed him?"

They both laughed, and loosening their hold, pulled back chairs on both sides of me.

"Besides, I had nothin' to do with it," I said, sitting down as well. "It was all Mikey. It was his plan."

"I gotta tell you," John said, pouring himself a glass of beer.

"When I first heard he took the case, I was gonna have him burned."

"What stopped you?"

"He was a friend," John said. "And if you're gonna go away on a murder rap, who better to send you?"

"Then, the way he was handlin' his end of the case, I thought he just sucked as a lawyer," Tommy said. "I started feelin' sorry for the bastard."

"Never feel sorry for a lawyer," Michael said, standing in front of us, a wide smile on his face.

"Get over here, counselor," John said, grabbing Michael's arm and dragging him around the table.

Tommy rushed in from the other side and squeezed me against them as they hugged. We were nothing more than a small circle of arms and crunched faces.

"You're the real count!" John shouted. "Alive and well and working in downtown New York City!"

"Not after this week," Michael said. "This count's on the dole now."

"What'd you do with all that buried treasure?" Tommy asked. "Gamble it away?"

"How do you think we paid off King Benny?" Michael said.

Carol stood in the entryway, her arms folded, laughing and shaking her head.

"What is this?" she asked. "A gay bar?"

We turned when we heard her voice. Her hair was freshly cut and styled, and she wore a short, tight black dress, a black purse hanging off her shoulder on a long strap.

"It *was*," John said. "Till you walked in."

"You want us to hug you too?" Tommy asked.

"How about just a hello," Carol said.

"How about a kiss to go with the hello?" John asked.

"Deal," Carol said, coming around to our end.

"Hurry up," I said. "Before the waiter comes in."

"Yeah," Tommy said. "Then we're gonna have to kiss him too."

"I saw him on my way in," Carol said. "He's cute. I'd throw him a kiss."

"That's funny," John said. "That's what Shakes said."

We sat around the table, ordered our dinners, poured our drinks, and talked until night turned to morning.

We talked about everything we could think of, five friends with so many shared moments, afraid to let our time together come to an end. We talked about everything but the trial. And the months we had sworn never to resurrect with speech.

Carol let loose her frustration with city bureaucracy and the battles she lost each day.

John and Tommy talked about their lives of crime. They knew it was a fast lane that could end only with a bullet or iron bars. But it was the only way they knew to feel in control, to push away the demons that gnawed at them during their rare sober moments.

Michael was at peace with his decision and curious about where it would take him. He had saved enough money to live for a year without working and had already invested in a one-way ticket on a plane leaving for London the following week-end. He had made no plans beyond that.

I half joked that my career choices were narrowed down to two. I was either going to be a reporter or an usher at one of the theaters whose running times I knew so well.

Eventually, the beer, wine, and liquor took hold and we switched gears, laughing over simpler times, in the years before Wilkinson starved us of laughter. Over and over we recalled our many pranks, relishing the freedom and foolishness a Hell's Kitchen childhood allowed.

"You guys remember when you formed that stupid singing group?" Carol asked, pouring water into a glass.

"The Four Gladiators," Michael said, smiling. "Best quartet to ever hold a Hell's Kitchen corner."

"Remember what Shakes wanted to call the group?" Johnny said, lighting a cigarette.

"The Count and His Cristos," Tommy said. "Man, that woulda sent albums flyin' outta the stores."

"We weren't *that* bad," I said. "Some people *wanted* to hear us sing."

"That group from the deaf school don't count," John said.

"Why not?" I said. "They applauded."

"You guys were *awful*," Carol said, laughing. "Kids cried when they heard you sing."

"They were sad songs," I said.

"Fat Mancho was gonna be our manager," Tommy said. "And King Benny was gonna be the bankroll. You know, get us suits and travel money, shit like that."

"What happened to *that* plan?" Carol asked.

"They heard us sing," I said.

"Fat Mancho said he'd eat flesh before he put his name next to ours," John said.

"What'd King Benny say?" Carol asked.

"He didn't say anything," I said. "He walked back into his club and closed the door."

"We stole from everybody we liked," Tommy said, finishing a mug of beer.

"So what's changed?" Carol asked, watching me pour her a fresh glass of wine.

"We had enough cuts to make an album," I said. "We ripped off Frankie Valli, Dion, Bobby Darin."

"The cream," Carol said.

"Only with us it was sour cream," Tommy said.

"Let's do a song from our album," Michael said, leaning across the table, smiling. "For Carol."

"Don't you guys have to go out and shoot somebody?" Carol said, hiding her face in her hands.

"We *always* got time for a song," John said, standing and leaning against the wall.

"You pick it, Mikey," Tommy said, standing next to Johnny. "Nothin' too slow. We wanna keep Carol on her toes."

"Let's do 'Walk Like a Man,'" Michael said. "Shakes does a good Valli on that one."

"Back us up," I said to Carol, handing her two soupspoons. "Hit these against some glasses when I point."

"Not too loud," Carol said, looking through the doorway behind her. "Some people might be eating."

"We sing better in men's rooms," Tommy said. "The walls there hold the sound."

"There's one downstairs," Carol said. "I'll wait here."

"This is like the Beatles getting together again," I said.

Carol just snorted.

The four of us huddled in a corner of the room, me in front. Michael, Tommy, and John each kept one hand on my shoulder, snapping their fingers to an imaginary beat. Carol sat back in her chair, looked at the four of us, and smiled.

She clapped her hands as we started to sing "Walk Like a Man" in our best Frankie Valli and the Four Seasons voices.

Then we all cupped a hand to an ear, fingers still snapping, and hit all the right a cappella notes.

Carol stood on her chair and slapped the spoons against the side of her leg, mixing in with the beat.

Three waiters stood in the doorway and joined in.

Two diners standing behind them whistled their approval.

The bartender drummed his hands against the counter and handed out free drinks to all.

An elderly couple, in for a late-night espresso, wrapped their arms around each other and danced.

It was our special night and we held it for as long as we could. It was something that belonged to us. A night that would be added to our long list of memories.

It was our happy ending.

And it was the last time we would ever be together again.

24

EARLY ON THE MORNING OF MARCH 16, 1984, JOHN Reilly's bloated body was found faceup in the hallway of a tenement on West 46th Street. His right hand held the neck of the bottle of lethal boiler-room gin that killed him. He had six dollars in the front pocket of his black leather coat and a ten-dollar bill in the flap of his hunter's shirt. A .44-caliber bulldog nestled at the base of his spine and a stiletto switchblade was jammed inside his jeans.

At the time of his death, he was a suspect in five unsolved homicides.

He was two weeks past his thirty-second birthday.

THOMAS "BUTTER" MARCANO DIED on July 26, 1985. His body was found in an empty cabin in upstate New York, five bullets shot into his head at close range. The body lay undiscovered for more than a week, the heat of summer and the gnashing of animals rushing its decay. There was little in the cabin beyond a dozen empty beer cans, two bottles of Dewar's, and three fully loaded semiautomatics. There was a crucifix and a picture of St. Jude in the pocket of Butter's crew-neck shirt.

Thomas Marcano was thirty-three years old.

―――

MICHAEL SULLIVAN LIVES IN a small town in the English countryside, where he works part-time as a carpenter. On his infrequent visits to New York he has never returned to Hell's Kitchen. He no longer practices law and has never married. He lives quietly and alone.

He is forty-four years old.

CAROL MARTINEZ STILL WORKS for a social service agency and still lives in Hell's Kitchen. She too has never married, but is a single mother supporting a growing twelve-year-old son. The boy, John Thomas Michael Martinez, loves to read and is called Shakes by his mother.

Neighbors all say he has his mother's smile and her dark olive eyes.

The rest of his features come from his father, John Reilly.

Carol Martinez is forty-three years old.

FATHER ROBERT CARILLO IS the monsignor of an upstate New York parish, where he still plays basketball every day. He keeps in touch with all his boys and is always there when needed.

He prays every day for the boys he lost.

Father Bobby is sixty years old.

KING BENNY LIVES IN a home for the elderly in Westchester County, miles from his Hell's Kitchen kingdom. He still drinks strong coffee, hiding his stash from the duty nurses charged to his care. He still hates to talk and suffers from Italian Alzheimer's. "I forget everything these days," he says. "Everything except my enemies."

King Benny is seventy-eight years old.

FAT MANCHO SUFFERED A mild stroke in the middle of August 1992. It left his right hand numb and blinded him in his right eye. He passed the bodega on to a nephew, but still takes half the profits. He divides his time between his three Hell's Kitchen apartments and a new house in Queens.

He still bets on stickball games.

Fat Mancho is seventy-two years old.

SEAN NOKES WAS SHOT to death in a back booth in the Shamrock Pub on November 6, 1979. His killers have yet to be apprehended.

Sean Nokes was thirty-seven years old at the time of his death.

ADAM STYLER WAS FIRED from the New York Police Department on February 22, 1982, brought up on corruption and murder charges. He pleaded guilty and was sentenced to a twelve-year prison term as part of a plea-bargain agreement. He served eight of those years in a maximum security prison. He was transferred to a minimum security facility only after a fourth attempt on his life left him paralyzed from the waist down. He was paroled in the spring of 1991 and now lives in a New Jersey suburb in a home for the disabled.

Adam Styler is fifty years old.

HENRY ADDISON RESIGNED FROM his job as community outreach director working for the mayor of the City of New

York in the spring of 1980. He found work in a downtown investment banking firm. After six months of impressive earnings, he was in line for a promotion. On New Year's Day, 1982, his body was found in a marsh off a La Guardia Airport runway. Autopsy reports indicated he was beaten and tortured to death.

His killer or killers have never been found.

Henry Addison was thirty-six years old.

RALPH FERGUSON'S WIFE FILED for divorce soon after he testified at John and Tommy's trial, gaining custody of their only child. He quit his job and fled the state, fearful of being brought up on multiple charges of child endangerment and rape. He eventually settled in California and, under another name, opened a hardware business. A second marriage ended when his wife was informed of her husband's true identity and hidden past. The business closed after a fire gutted it in 1989. He now works as a shoe salesman in the San Francisco area. He lives alone, is heavily in debt, and has trouble sleeping at night.

He was the man brought to me by King Benny in 1993 to beg my forgiveness. I lived for nearly a year afraid of his every move. He will live the rest of his days equally afraid of mine.

Ralph Ferguson is forty-nine years old.

IN THE FALL OF 1982, a board of inquiry impaneled by the New York State Department of Juvenile Justice looked into allegations of abuse at the Wilkinson Home for Boys. They were confronted by a list of forty-seven witnesses, including the parents of three boys who died under the care of the institution and a dozen guards who were witness to a variety of assaults. In a report condemning all past and present directors of the Wilkinson Home for Boys, the board of inquiry called for a complete and total overhaul of the system and method of operations at the juvenile facility. A new warden was appointed and video cameras were installed on every block. Inmate privileges were extended and the hole was eliminated. Even the cells were freshly painted.

EDWARD GOLDENBERG "LITTLE CAESAR" ROBINSON is serving a life sentence in a maximum security prison in upstate New York, convicted on charges of drug trafficking and murder in 1990. He will be eligible for parole in twenty-one years. He was never questioned in the murder of Henry Addison.

Edward Goldenberg "Little Caesar" Robinson is fifty-one years old.

GREGORY "MARLBORO" WILSON RETIRED on a full pension and lives on a Pennsylvania farm. He spends his days reading books, writing letters to his children, and playing cards with friends. Every Christmas he gets two cartons of Marlboro cigarettes from a Sleeper who remembers.

Gregory "Marlboro" Wilson is sixty-three years old.

I AM NOW FORTY YEARS OLD, with a wife and two children. I love my wife and adore my son and daughter. My family has helped me escape from many of the pains of my past. But the haunting memories of childhood are always close at hand. My body is older than its years, and my mind is filled more with horror than with the pleasures of life. The dreams I have are still vivid, the nightmares painful, the fears steady. The night-time hours always carry a sense of dread.

I sometimes feel that the lucky Sleepers are the ones who died.

They no longer have to live with the memories.

They are free of the dreams.

"Many's the road I have walked upon
Many's the hour between dusk and dawn
Many's the time
Many's the mile
I see it all now
Through the eyes of a child."

—VAN MORRISON, "TAKE IT WHERE YOU FIND IT"

Epilogue

SUMMER 1966

REUBEN, A PUERTO RICAN KID WITH DARK, CURLY HAIR and tight gray slacks, the crease sharp enough to cut skin, was the favorite to win the contest and the $50 first prize. He stood in a corner of the gym, his back to the three-piece band, chewing gum, sneaking puffs on a Viceroy, waiting for the disc jockey onstage to signal a start to the school-sponsored Chubby Checker King Twister competition.

"He looks good," I said, staring over at Reuben. "He looks ready to win."

"He looks like he seen *West Side Story* a couple of times too many," Johnny said.

"He won't figure you to be any good, Shakes," Michael said. "Since he don't know you."

"I don't figure you to be any good neither," Tommy said, putting an arm around my shoulder. "And *I* know you."

"He's got you beat on the shoes," John said. "He's wearing those roach stompers. They're good twist shoes. They got a light look, but good soles."

"Who are you, Thom McAn?" I asked. "The shoes I got are okay."

"Who else is in this?" Michael asked. "Outside of him."

"Three Irish guys from Forty-sixth Street," Tommy said.

"They any good?" I asked.

"I hear they're pretty stupid," Tommy said.

"Now you need to go to college to do the twist?" Michael asked.

"They just signed on as a goof," Tommy said. "Make each other laugh. These guys couldn't get laid in a women's prison."

"There's that goofy kid from the pizza place," I said. "I hear he signed up."

"I know him," John said. "He's got all those zits and that black shit on his teeth. I make sure he *never* touches any of my slices."

"Anybody else?" Michael asked.

"That black kid who spits when he talks," Tommy said. "The one whose father just got shot."

"They might give it to him just for that," I said. "Start feelin' sorry for him."

"Don't worry, Shakes," Michael said. "We see the vote goin' that way, we'll have somebody stab you."

"Not too deep," I said. "I need this shirt for school."

"Just deep enough to win," Michael said.

THE GYM'S OVERHEAD LIGHTS were turned off, the spotlights shining on the center of the floor. Eighty or more kids surrounded the circle, many of the boys and girls holding hands, some sneaking soft kisses in the dark.

"Will the twist contestants please enter the circle," the disc jockey ordered from the stage, his jacket tight around his shoulders, his pants cuffed, white socks sagging below the ankles.

"Go get 'em, Shakes," Tommy said, patting me on the back.

"Anybody gets close to us, we push," John said. "Knock 'em off balance."

"We'll be here waitin' for you, Shakes," Michael said. "Win or lose."

"We can't let you go out there without a good-luck kiss," Carol Martinez said, easing her way through the crowd to join our group. She was wearing a white dress with black shoes and white lace stockings. Her long, dark hair was done up in a ponytail.

"You give it to him," Michael said. "We already kissed him once today."

Carol put her arms around my neck and kissed me firmly on the lips.

"Kiss or no kiss," Tommy said, "we ain't cuttin' her in on the prize money."

"You're nothin' but heart," John said.

EACH CONTESTANT WAS PLACED under one of the six spotlights, the circle large enough to give us all room to dance. I was sandwiched between the kid from the pizza parlor and one of the Irish guys from 46th, still in his St. Agnes school uniform. Reuben was across from me, a relaxed look on his face, a toothpick hanging from the side of his mouth. The tall black kid, the best-dressed of the group, was the only one who looked nervous.

"C'mon, everybody!" the disc jockey shouted in a poor Chubby Checker imitation. "Clap your hands, we're gonna do the twist and it goes like this."

Chubby Checker's joyful voice boomed out of the faulty sound system and we began to twist, cheered on by the screams and cries of our friends in the crowd. We all kept it simple at the start, except for the three Irish guys, who tossed in spins and whirls to impress the audience.

It was an easy contest to lose. If you fell, missed your motion, or stopped twisting, you were automatically bounced.

Barring that, the disc jockey, the designated twist judge, walked among the dancers and tapped out those he felt were not up to the demands of the dance.

It would take less than twenty minutes to declare a winner.

The Irish kid in the St. Agnes uniform was the first out, losing his balance on a one-knee twist. One of his friends followed soon after, trying to do a foot and hand move that backfired.

"They're Irish," Tommy said, laughing and nudging Michael. "Just like you."

"They're stupid too," Michael said. "Just like you."

By the third go-around I was getting winded, sweat coming off my face and back, the heat of the spotlights and the constant movement causing the faces around me to blur. Reuben kept his pace steady, his eyes on me, every so often flashing a smile to show he was in the game and breathing easy.

By the end of "Twistin' U.S.A." the kid from the pizza parlor grabbed his side, stopped dancing, and walked out of the circle. A short girl reached toward him, put her arms around his waist, and kissed his cheek.

"You see that?" John asked with a look of disgust. "She kissed him on the zits."

"A connect-the-dot face has a girlfriend and I go to movies alone," Tommy said, shaking his head. "Is that fair?"

"Yes," Michael said.

Reuben was moving faster now, shaking down lower, twisting his body till his knees seemed to be waxing the floor. The toothpick was still in his mouth and a sneer had replaced the smile, his confidence building with every beat.

The black kid was all sweat and little style, his legs starting to cramp, the overhead lights bothering him more with each move. He was favoring his right knee, wincing whenever he went down on it.

The disc jockey, hands folded behind his back, walked over

and whispered something in his ear. The black kid looked at him and nodded. He stopped dancing and limped off the floor.

"Poor guy," Carol said. "His knee must be really bad."

"His father takin' a bullet meant nothin'," Tommy said.

"You gotta have somebody *die* to catch a break in this contest," John said.

It was now down to three dancers.

I figured I had enough left in me for five more good minutes. Any more, and they could use the fifty dollars to bury me. Reuben looked like he could twist all night, with or without the music.

"Let's hear it for these guys that are left," the disc jockey shouted. "The twisting kings of New York City."

The Irish kid stopped dancing to applaud along with the crowd and was forced to leave the contest.

"That guy's dumber than a plant," Johnny said.

"The deejay?" Tommy asked. "Or the Irish kid?"

"Both," Michael said.

"All right, boys, let's see what you got," the disc jockey said to me and Reuben. "You're the only ones left."

I was soaked through with sweat, my shirt sticking to my chest and back, my hair matted to my face. My jeans were loose and the sweat around my waist made them looser. Even my shoes were starting to slip on the gym floor.

I had a few moves left and started to use them, twisting down on one knee, leaving the free leg up. Through the darkness, my end of the crowd reacted with applause and whistles.

I moved as low to the ground as I could, still twisting, then planted my hands between my legs, did a split, and brought them back up to twist position.

"That's it," Tommy said. "That's what you gotta show 'em. They eat that Fred Astaire shit up."

"The Puerto Rican has to make his move now," Michael said. "Or take the loss."

"What happens if he swallows that toothpick?" John asked.

"We win," Michael said.

Reuben made his move, but it was the wrong one.

With his end of the crowd clapping and cheering behind him, Reuben went down to a low position, laid his hands flat on the ground, and tried a head-over flip. He made the flip, an impressive head-past-shoulder acrobatic move, but the soles of his shoes slipped when he landed back on his feet. He slid to the ground and fell onto his rear, toothpick still in his mouth.

I stopped dancing, walked over to Reuben, reached out my hand, and helped him to his feet.

"Great move," I said.

"I'll get you next summer," he said.

"You almost got me *this* summer," I said, shaking his hand.

The crowd closed in on us, applauding, whistling, and shouting. Their screams and chants grew even louder when the disc jockey slapped a $50 bill in my palm and raised my hand in victory.

"We're rich!" Tommy shouted, rushing toward me with John, Michael, and Carol fast behind. "We're rich!"

"We can live for a month," John said. "Pizza. Comic books. Italian ices. The town's ours."

"You were lucky," Michael said to me with a smile. "It's always better to be lucky."

"Don't expect another kiss," Carol said.

"I'm too tired to kiss anybody," I said. "I'm too tired to even walk."

"You don't have to walk," Tommy said. "You're the champ. We'll drive you."

He grabbed one of my legs, and John and Michael grabbed the other, hoisting me on their shoulders, the crowd behind me still chanting their support.

They carried me through the gym, carefully lowering me past the black exit doors and out onto the street.

"Where we goin'?" I asked, tilting my head back, letting the warm evening breeze cool my face.

"Anyplace," Michael said. "Do anything we want."

"We got the time," John said. "And we finally got the money."

"We can go anywhere," Tommy said. "There's nothin' can stop us."

WE WERE UNDER A streetlight on the corner of West 50th Street and Tenth Avenue. John, Tommy, and Michael holding me on their shoulders. Carol next to them, a smile on her face, slowly dancing around a garbage can.

THE NIGHT AND THE streets were ours and the future lay sparkling ahead.

AND WE THOUGHT WE would know each other forever.

ACKNOWLEDGMENTS

THIS BOOK WOULD NOT HAVE BEEN POSSIBLE WITHOUT the support of the silent citizens of Hell's Kitchen. I will honor their requests to remain anonymous voices and never forget their contributions.

Through the years, I've been fortunate to have worked with many editors who have helped me in various stages of my career. None has had more confidence in my abilities than Peter Gethers. With this book, he made a leap of faith few editors are willing to risk. Then, he guided the work and shaped it and edited it as few can. He also supplied an endless stream of jokes that helped ease me through the rough spots. No writer could have a better partner.

Any writer would love to have a great agent. I have three. Loretta Fidel was *always* there, *always* listened, and *always* cared. Amy Schiffman and Adam Berkowitz believed in me as much as they did in the book. Together, they kept the wolves from the door and the book on everyone's front burner.

Clare Ferraro found a place in her heart and on her Ballantine shelf for my first book. Then, over a terrific lunch, she fell in love with my second. Then, she waited and she waited and she waited. Through it all, she supplied patience, friendship, and encouragement. I would also like to thank Steve Golin and the people at Propaganda Films for their passionate belief in *Sleepers,* and Barry Levinson, Peter Giuliano, and the cast and crew of the movie for bringing that passion to life, and Dr. Paul Chrzanowski, Dr. Nancy Nealon, and my main man David Malamut at the Rusk Institute for their help.

Then there are the cops—Steve Collura for the kind words; Joe Lisi for the laughter and concern; and, above all, Sonny Grosso, for everything he has meant to me throughout a friendship that now numbers in the decades.

To my phone buddies—Hank Gallo, Carlo Cutolo, Mr. G., Marc Lichter, Leah Rozen, and Keith Johnson—for being there and for listening. To Liz Wagner for the laughs. And to Bill Diehl for the wisdom and the care.

To my wife, Susan Toepfer, I owe everything. She has always had my respect, will always have my love, and will always be my friend.

To my son, Nick, thank you for the smiles and the chance to forget my work for a period of time. To my daughter, Kate, thank you for showing me what a warm heart can beat beneath such a pretty face.

And thanks to my crew of suspects—the Fat Man, Bobby C. Bam-Bam, Carmine, Doc, Big D., Mike Seven, and Sammy Weights. You were always where you were supposed to be. I never expected any less.

IF YOU ENJOYED

SLEEPERS,

READ ON FOR A PREVIEW OF

TIN BADGES

AVAILABLE FROM

BALLANTINE BOOKS

1

MANHATTAN

AUGUST 2015

I HATE LAST DAYS OF PRETTY MUCH ANYTHING YOU CAN think of—from vacations to the end of baseball season to the final time I'll be able to share a laugh with someone I love. Some last days you can prepare for, knowing there will be the start of another cycle waiting with the flicker of a few months off the calendar. And then there are those days that hit hard enough to send the strongest of us cowering for cover.

That's what my last working day as a New York City Police Department first-grade detective was like for me. Going in, it never entered my mind my career would end before my shift was through. But I imagine no one ever knows when it's their last day of doing anything. Especially not in my line of work.

The day began with my usual routine—a two-hour workout, a cold shower, and two double espressos sipped slowly while I scanned the morning tabloids and overnight police reports. By and large I am a creature of my habits, good ones for the most part, though now and then I'll slip and spend more than I should on a great bottle of wine or play a few more hands of poker despite knowing the cold streak I had been running all night was never destined to warm up.

By 8:00 A.M., I sat on the front steps of my Greenwich Village brownstone, waiting for my partner, Frank "Pearl" Monroe, to drive up. The early-morning sun warmed my face, and it was already starting to feel like one of those New York City August days when the heat-and-humidity combo clouded your vision and made you long for a bitter blast of winter.

By the way, in the event you're wondering how a gold-shield NYPD salary is enough to land a guy a Greenwich Village brownstone, let me set you straight—it isn't. Not even close to it. My cop salary wouldn't cover the monthly expenses. In my case, you can chalk it up to a little bit of luck and a father with a nose for real estate.

"When you go looking for a house," my dad would tell anyone within earshot, "always move toward the cheapest home in the best neighborhood. That's how you end up with a winner."

My father worked as a lugger down at the old 14th Street meat market. He had been a boxer in his younger days, rising up as far as the number-three contender for the middleweight title. A broken right hand and a damaged left eardrum forced him to give up any dreams of being a champion. So, instead, he got up each morning at 2:00 A.M., regardless of weather, put on his white butcher's smock, and walked to the meat market, which by 3:00 A.M. was lit by floodlights, truck headlights, and wood-burning fires from rusty iron barrels as workers from more than two dozen companies loaded up freezer shipments to be delivered to restaurants throughout the city. This was decades before the area became the super-chic neighborhood it is today, filled with high-end boutiques, expensive restaurants, and monthly rents that make your legs buckle.

My father made good workingman's money, some weeks clearing as much as five hundred dollars when overtime was heavy, and my mom was even better at socking it away. Back then, in the early 1980s, people like my folks could afford to buy themselves a brownstone in the Village, if they played it right, which my parents did and then some.

The brownstone is a four-story walk-up, and for twenty years my aunt Nancy and uncle Aldo rented the top two floors while me, my brother, Jack, and my folks lived in the bottom two. The mortgage got knocked off years ago, and today I still live in those same bottom two floors and rent out the top ones to a retired shoemaker and his wife, still working part-time at a local bakery. I charge them what they can afford. I'd much rather have quiet and steady neighbors than ones with deeper pockets and friends always in need of a place to crash.

The brownstone has been my home for as long as I can remember, and I imagine it will be until my final days.

MY PARTNER, PEARL, PULLED up to the curb, his late-model fire-red Mustang as shiny as his shaved head. He had a wide smile on his handsome face, Sam Cooke's smooth, sweet voice belting out through the four speakers. I moved from the stoop and slid into the front seat, and before I had my seatbelt latched Pearl had the Mustang gliding halfway down the street. "We still a go?" I asked.

"Checked in with my guy before the sun came up," Pearl said. "If there's a deal going down, then today's the day for it."

"I'd still feel a lot better if we had one of our sources vouch for the guy," I said.

"You worried about him because he's a user?" Pearl asked.

"There's that," I said, nodding. "Plus, he's looking to slice considerable time off a jolt that's sure to land him a serious upstate stretch. Under those conditions, a guy like him will say and do anything to get that sentence reduced."

"I ran his priors," Pearl said, swinging the Mustang toward Sixth Avenue, heading uptown. "Every stretch he did, he did for a job on behalf of Rico's crew."

"Still doesn't make him an inside guy, Pearl," I said. "He's never been in the room when the plans go down. He's a runner. Ready to move when told to move."

Sixth Avenue was its usual early-morning slow traffic crawl, and Pearl turned to look at me.

"This ain't the first time you and me made a move off the word of a stoolie we barely knew," he said. "Hell, not even the twenty-first time. So, what makes this particular guy an itch you can't seem to scratch?"

"It's nothing solid," I said. "Just a feeling. A bad vibe. Nothing more."

"Let's work off of what we know," Pearl said. "The source broke it down from first step to last. He gave us the delivery time, the number of the building and the apartment. He told us who would be in there and how much cocaine they would be cutting up. Minus us having a wire dropped behind their television, we're not going to get a better picture of what to expect than what he gave us."

"I'm not saying you're wrong, Pearl. Truth is, you're more than likely on the mark."

"If you're feeling shaky about it, we can hold off. We can take a step back and come at Rico from another direction another time."

I stared out at the now-congested streets crammed with people rushing to work. Most of them walked with earbuds solidly in place, either listening to music or getting a morning fix of gossip. "Let's stick to the plan," I said without turning to look away. "No better way to start a morning than to cause Rico and his boys their share of grief."

ONE HOUR LATER, I was crouched down, my back against a splintered and grimy cement wall, hidden by a stairwell lodged between the third and fourth floors of a dilapidated tenement.

My black short-sleeve T-shirt was soaked through, the sweat a cocktail of adrenaline mixed with a dose of fear.

My eyes were slow to adjust to the shadows. I could make out a series of overhead bulbs long since burned out. Blasts of television sound echoed from all sides, a strange brew of Kelly Ripa, ESPN, and Univision. The high volume easily pierced the thin wooden doors that posed as sentries to the neglected railroad apartments.

Pearl was hunched down to my right, his shaved head and base of his neck dripping wet. "Second door on your left," he whispered, gesturing with the gun he held in his right hand. "They should be in the room just past the kitchen."

"How many you figure are in there?"

"Eight at the minimum," Pearl said. "That's a best guess. I could be off by one, maybe two."

I rested the back of my damp head against the cold wall and closed my eyes. I took in a few deep breaths, looking to control my breathing and slow down my heart rate. For any cop, the precious minutes before an anticipated shoot-out or takedown are both exhilarating and frightening. It is during that brief interlude when thoughts of life and death mingle with images of the unknown that awaits.

Those are the moments a cop is at his most vulnerable.

"I always forget how hot it gets in these hallways," I said, opening my eyes. "It's like they save the heat they need in winter for the summer months."

Pearl smiled. "You should have worn shorts. Maybe even a cutoff T to match and a pair of flip-flops. They would have never fingered you for a cop, decked out like that."

I glanced at Pearl and returned his smile. It was a smile I had known since my first week at the police academy, the two of us sitting next to each other, doing our best to listen to a too-eager instructor alerting us to the fact that "there is a ninety-five percent chance the majority of the recruits in this room will go their entire careers without once firing their weapon." Pearl had turned to me and flashed his megawatt smile and whispered, "I guess that means we're all going to be working out of a Staten Island precinct."

"No fun in that," I said. "Might as well put in our papers now, save everybody the trouble."

The friendship started that very minute and has never wavered, the Italian kid from Greenwich Village and the African American from Harlem doing the job we had dreamed of since we were old enough to distinguish good from bad. We were both parochial-school boys, from grammar straight through high school; he was happily married and I was even happier being single. We were instant friends and, over time, proved to be the best of partners. Pearl and I worked as one. I trusted him with my life and he put his in my hands every day. And never once did we let the other down.

We were an effective team from the start, and it didn't take long for the brass to notice. We were assigned to foot patrol, first out of the 10th Precinct in Chelsea and then up to Harlem. From there, we quickly graduated to the night watch dispatched out of a squad car. We worked our sector hard, were on a first-name basis with the area merchants, and began to build a solid network of trusted informants, from the hookers on the Eighth Avenue line to the dealers who claimed the after-hours clubs on Eleventh and Twelfth Avenues as their private terrain.

Those connections led to busts, and those busts led to a rapid succession of promotions—a boost to second grade and slots in a plainclothes unit out of Washington Heights. From there we were assigned as detectives in the South Bronx, where we bumped heads with Luther Wiley and his "Pain Train" crew of drug dealers, up to today, where we were both gold-shield first-graders in an elite narcotics unit going up against the top-tier Colombian drug outfits working Manhattan's upper rings.

During those years and through all those busted-down doors and volleys of bullets aimed our way, Pearl and I grew to be more than partners, more than mere friends with a badge and a gun dependent on one another to survive.

We were family. As close as any two brothers could ever hope to be.

Off the job, we had much in common. We loved sports, jazz, Sam Cooke, Leonard Cohen, and museums—though I preferred the literary bent of the Morgan Library, while he liked the exhibits at the Museum of Natural History. We liked wine and we loved to read—he tilted toward John Grisham legal thrillers intercut with an occasional attempt at a Charles Dickens novel; I read any biography I could get my hands on, tossing in a Linda Fairstein mystery to the mix.

Pearl was married to a terrific young woman in her first year as a resident at Roosevelt Hospital. Her hours were about as long as ours, and while their time together was limited, Pearl made the moments count.

I was just starting to keep company with a lady who co-owned and managed a restaurant a short walk from my brownstone. We cared for one another and gave each other the space required to keep our relationship on solid ground.

Pearl and I complemented each other. Our humor blended with our street savvy, our instincts with our skills, and we each maintained a keen understanding of what day-to-day life was like inside neighborhoods where the criminals often made the call as to who lived and who died on any particular day.

I FLINCHED WHEN I heard a loud bang coming out of the apartment just beyond the stairwell to our left. It was followed quickly by the foul smell of burning drugs. Three rats the size of kittens scurried past us, running in formation down the stairs, frightened more by the smoke than by the noise. "We better get our asses in there before the dumb bastards blow up the entire building," Pearl told me.

I stared at the rats as they stopped, turned, and jammed themselves up against a corner. "You see that?" I said. "They stopped. They always stop when I'm around. It's as if they know how scared shitless I am of them."

Pearl Monroe eased up against the wall and nudged me forward. "How about we get away from the big, bad nasty rats and break through that door and bust us some dealers? Would that help ease your mind?"

"Big time," I said, getting to my feet and checking the clips in both my guns. "But if they follow us up, I'm shooting them first."

I took a final look at the rats and then ran up the half-flight of steps, taking a hard turn around the corner.

Pearl Monroe was right behind me.

2

MANHATTAN

MOMENTS LATER

A THIN TEENAGER IN A MIAMI HEAT CAP AND A STEPH Curry jersey walked down the center of a long hallway heading in our direction. Rays of thick sunlight coming through the large window behind him cast him in a warm glow. He was bouncing a basketball.

Pearl held a finger to his lips, signaling for the boy to stay quiet. The kid slowed his pace and kept bouncing the ball, a smile slicing across his face. I was several feet from the apartment door, my eyes on the teenager. "He's not here looking for a pickup game," I said to Pearl. "He's already playing his game."

The teen rammed the basketball under the crook of his right arm, stopped in the center of the hallway, and let out a shout loud enough to be heard for several stories. "Five-O," he screamed. "Five-O on the floor."

The next five minutes forever changed two lives and ended several others.

Bullets ripped through the ramshackle wooden door to our left, sending both me and Pearl hurtling face-down on the concrete floor. The stink of stale urine and ammonia burned our eyes and stung our nostrils. We crawled forward for a few inches and then Pearl rose slowly to his knees. I flipped onto my back, both my guns poised toward the now-shattered door, thin lines of smoke snaking through the slanted openings. Pearl now aimed his weapon at the teenager down the hall. The kid had the basketball resting by his right foot, and his hands gripped a nine-millimeter.

The tight smile was still on his face.

"Whoever steered you into this hall wanted to see you put down," the teen said. "You walked into it, no doubt."

"Maybe so," I said. "But it would be rude to leave now."

"Besides," Pearl said, "we couldn't leave without checking in on our friend Rico."

"Now, let me guess," I said. "Would he be behind door number one or door number two?"

"You need to make the move to find out," the teen told us. "But there ain't no prize waiting no matter which door you pick. There's eight in there and I only see two of you out here. If you're smart, you bolt while you can."

"And it would be wiser for you to be on a court playing a three-on-three," Pearl said. "That'll keep you in the game. Not banging for these losers."

I glanced at Pearl and nodded.

HE HAD HIS EYE on the teen, who'd lost the smile and tightened his grip on the gun. Bracing my legs, I rushed toward the door to my left, ramming my right shoulder full force against the thin wood. The door easily gave way and I half-fell, half-stomped, into the foul-smelling foyer of the railroad apartment.

The apartment was lined with low-hanging clouds of smoke and reeked of stale beer and fresh-cooked coke. The hall was narrow, a small bathroom to my right, a brown ragdoll cat coiled next to a cracked and stained toilet bowl. I heard the pump of a shotgun before I saw it, a hot blast coming at me from the first bedroom. Two men, both in their twenties, each with a Rikers cut, walked toward me. They were wearing black sweatpants topped with White Cuban shirts, spraying bullets in my direction as they moved. I crawled into the bathroom, the ragdoll watching me with glazed eyes, and aimed my weapons at the two approaching men. Every shot—theirs and mine—missed their mark.

Forget what you see on movies and TV cop shows. That agile gunman who never misses is myth, not reality. Fact is, the accuracy rate of the best-trained cop in the country is 16 percent. And for drug dealers strung out on their own product, the rate is even lower. It takes as much luck as it does skill to walk away from a firefight, especially one in close quarters. I was banking on a high dose of both as I sprawled down in that filthy bathroom, an indifferent cat my only company.

I poked my head into the foyer and caught a glimpse of Pearl, his hulking body half in the apartment and half out. It was, at best, an untenable situation, and we knew we had to move fast if we were going to step out of the mess we had walked into.

The two shooters closest to me were wedged behind a tipped-over torn leather red couch. The duo closing in on Pearl were stopping to do a fast reload of clips. I could hear sirens wailing in the distance. But they weren't close enough to do us any good.

Three gunmen emerged from a second apartment and were now positioned in the hallway.

"There's too many," I shouted out to Pearl. "Let's pick one end of the hall and shoot our way out."

"I got three fresh ones coming at me from my left," Pearl yelled back. I turned to look at him and saw he had taken a hit, a thick line of blood oozing out of his right leg.

"What about the kid?"

"He's down," Pearl said. "I nicked him in the shoulder."

Everyone held fire, waiting for someone on either side to make the next move.

"How bad you hit?" I asked Pearl.

"I can move."

The two shooters who had been using the flipped-over couch as cover were reloaded and standing now. They were heading toward me, firing rapid shots as they moved, their bullets sending shards of wood flying in all directions. The gunmen behind Pearl stood dead center in the middle of the hallway, lined up three across and firing point-blank into the apartment.

We were flat in the middle of a cross fire.

And it was the first piece of good luck we had caught all morning.

Pearl and I made our move.

I came running out of the bathroom, fired off two quick rounds at the shooters at my back, and moved for the smashed-in front door. Pearl was on his feet, bouncing bullets at the three in the hall. We each hit one of our targets, judging by the loud groans behind me and the sight of a fallen gunman in my path.

We were less than fifteen feet from the open window leading to the fire escape.

I was low on bullets and figured Pearl was as well. The blood from his wound covered his entire leg and dripped to the floor. I had taken a hit just below my right rib cage. From the quick flow of blood, I knew it went a lot deeper than a flesh wound.

The teenager was lying in the center of the hallway, a circle of blood forming a dark pool around his shoulder, his nine-millimeter resting beyond the fingers of his right hand. The basketball was near the side of his head. I jammed a gun into my waistband, bent down, and picked up the nine. "Take deep breaths," I said to the teen. "You caught luck today. Pearl wanted to end you, he would have. Something for you to remember." I turned, steadied my feet, and emptied the nine in the direction of the shooters closing in. Pearl did the same with his weapon, until we were both holding empty guns.

I tossed aside the nine and checked out the damage we had inflicted—two shooters lay dead; two more were wounded enough not to be a problem. The four others were stretched out in the hallway, expecting more firepower to come their way. I nodded to Pearl and we bolted for the open window and the rusty railings of the fire escape.

I got there first and dove through the window, a sliver of sharp wood slicing across the back of my neck. Pearl was fast on my heels.

Below us, blue-and-white patrol cars were screeching to a halt, close to a dozen uniform cops jumping out and running toward the building from every possible angle.

"Looks like the cavalry's finally here," I wheezed to Pearl. "Little late, but at least they showed."

The fire escape was old—half the railings were missing, the metal steps were cracked, and most of them were broken. We raced down them fast as we could, working off pure adrenaline, hearts pumping, senses alert, bodies numb to the pain. I turned a tight corner around a landing between the third and second floors and looked up at Pearl. He was resting his back against an outside railing. "We ducked ourselves another one, Tank," he said, wide smile on his face, blood flowing as if from an open faucet.

I never got a chance to respond.

The third-floor railing Pearl leaned on wobbled, then he began his fall, moving as if in slow motion. I lunged and tried to make a grab for him. I held tight to a rusty bar, and the fingers of my right hand gently brushed against his. Pearl fell three floors and landed with a loud thud against the sharpest edges of an empty old dumpster. I could hear bones break from where I stood. Our eyes met and I looked at his lower body dangling off the side of the dumpster, his strong legs limp and lifeless. Blood dripped out the sides of his mouth and his breathing appeared to be shallow, yet he still managed to give me a reassuring nod.

I couldn't move and didn't want to. There wasn't anything left for me to do now other than to stare at the ruined body of my partner and best friend.

At that moment, I knew neither of our lives would ever be the same again.

And I also knew that for me and for Pearl, this hot August day would be our last as New York City detectives.

LORENZO CARCATERRA is the #1 *New York Times* bestselling author of *A Safe Place, Sleepers, Apaches, Gangster, Street Boys, Paradise City, Chasers, Midnight Angels, The Wolf,* and *Tin Badges.* He is a former writer/producer for *Law & Order* and has written for *National Geographic Traveler, The New York Times Magazine,* and *Maxim.* He lives in New York City and is at work on his next novel.

lorenzocarcaterra.com